Just Call Me Moose!

Just Call Me Moose!

Growing Up Italian in America

Karl R. Bossi

Gondola Press
Venice, Florida

Published by
Gondola Press
1435 E. Venice Ave. #109
Venice, Florida 34292 USA
http://www.gondolapress.com

Library of Congress Control Number: 2004115698

ISBN 0-9759811-0-2 (hardcover)
ISBN 0-9759811-1-0 (trade paper)

Cover photo of author: 1946–Dorchester, Massachusetts

Cover design by Sherry Erb of Sketches, etc.

Manufactured in the United States of America

10 9 8 7 6 5 4 3 2 1

Publisher's Note: This memoir is not a work of fiction. It
contains no composite characters, no contrived scenes.

This book is printed on acid-free paper.

For mother Pia and father Romeo

While reading in the den, he heard the front door chimes. Later when he came downstairs and met his mother in the kitchen, she had a contented look on her round, cherubic face.

"Mum, who rang the bell?"

She spit out the words. "Some scrawny floozy with no brains. She said she met you at the beach and was lookin' for Moose.

"I told her no animals live here."

"IT WAS AN OVERCAST APRIL DAY, a day that only years keep at bay. It was spring break and I was sitting alone after lunch in the den upstairs. On the lamp table beside me, a radio blared Elvis Presley's first big hit, 'Heartbreak Hotel.' Not yet a man, no longer a child, I thought about the high school Senior Prom, a few days away, and dancing with my date.

"My peaceful reverie came unwound as I heard my mother howling in the distance like a rabid wolf in the final throes of agony, a hysterical plea that tore at my soul and shook it. Peering over the balcony I saw her motion for me to follow. As we ran outside to the garage, she mumbled, 'Something happened,' then beat me to the side door and pushed it open."

–from *Just Call Me Moose!*

There is a land of the living and a land of the dead and the bridge is love, the only survival, the only meaning.

Thornton Wilder, *The Bridge of San Luis Rey*

I

___

ON A SOUTHWEST AIRLINES FLIGHT back to Boston from my home in New Mexico, I started to reminisce about my last assignment in the Air Force. In my airbase office, over the taupe leather couch, a picture of a grizzled prospector faced the desk. The old man had stubble on his face, the look of a newly cut wheat field. A large safety pin in the crumpled, dirty Stetson kept the brim up. I had bought the poster at a local flea market; it appealed to me, especially the phrase in bold at the bottom: "In Youth, We Learn; With Age, We Understand."

During all the years I served in the realm where bombs and bullets ruled and headed a bomb disposal team in Vietnam, I had never taken the time to confront my father's tragic death. Only the years kept that day at bay. Just as the fallout from a nuclear weapon often takes decades to wreak havoc, my father's suicide two days before my Senior Prom gnawed silently inside me.

When I returned to see my mother I could see she was in decline and had only a few years left to live. The robust woman with boundless energy who had raised me, the last of three sons, resembled a brittle ceramic doll. Pop made Mum a widow when I was in high school. Since then, loneliness haunted her.

My mother always put on a good front and rarely complained, even though most of her friends had passed on. She rarely went outside the flat other than go to the beauty parlor or attend Mass.

When I was growing up, the Catholic Church played no role in my mother's personal routine. But as the years slipped away, she began to pray again and reach out to God for solace. A telephone mounted on the kitchen wall served as her primary link to the outside world. Now my mother resided a few miles from the old neighborhood, inside a kaleidoscope of vivid memories of the past. The auburn hair of her youth was white and thin like a dusting of new fallen snow. A rinse applied during frequent trips to the beauty parlor gave it a bluish tint. The first time she proudly flaunted the new look, I teased her.

"Mum, have you joined the ranks of the blue-hairs?"

"Oh, keep quiet, I like it."

Sliding past me to her bedroom she returned with a wrinkled brown paper bag and said, "I've got something to show you."

She slowly pulled a large clump of bright auburn hair out of the bag. The hair was thick and braided and appeared as soft as the day it was cut. When I reached to touch it, she said, "Be careful. That's how my hair looked when I was a girl."

AFTER I LEFT HOME TO GO INTO THE AIR FORCE, real estate taxes and utility expenses kept spiraling higher. Many properties in my Dorchester neighborhood had deteriorated and the crime rate spiked. Most of the people Mum knew had already left for the suburbs. She had become a prisoner in her own house, afraid to venture out on the streets to go grocery shopping. My mother's meager Social Security stipend and a small nest egg could no longer cover her mounting expenses. With some trepidation and sadness, yet with strong resolve, she left the homestead where my father died, in the only neighborhood my parents ever knew.

Just Call Me Moose!

Now she lived in nearby Roslindale in a rented first-floor flat with two bedrooms on a street dotted with two-story, two-family wooden houses—a residence far less imposing than the old neighborhood icon, the place she had called home. My mother felt that her life would be safer in the new neighborhood, but she was wrong. On the phone shortly after the attack, she recounted the event that troubled me deeply.

"I was walking down to the square to have my hair done. It started raining so my umbrella was open. Next thing I know, I'm flat on my *keister* on the sidewalk."

"What happened?"

"A guy across the street saw a kid smack me in the head with a brick and grab my shopping bag. He chased him but the kid got away. I had to go to the hospital for a few stitches. Someone found my purse later and called me. The money was gone; the police thought whoever did it was a druggie."

"Mum, you were lucky. You need to be more careful."

"I'm fine, I'm fine now. Next time I'll take a cab."

The story made me furious. *What kind of people attack defenseless old ladies? Scumbags*, I thought. My mother's world was much different than the one she knew as a youth.

On that trip home, she took me aside and gave me a family heirloom; a treasure I never expected. In the Boston accent that colored her speech, she said, "Kahl, your father always wanted you to have the family coat of arms."

"I thought it would go to the oldest son?"

"No, Pop wanted you to have it."

I leaned over to hug her. "Thank you, Mum. It's always been special to me."

I thought about my brothers. *What would they say?*

My father had spent the entire summer in Italy between his sophomore and junior years at MIT as the guest of an affluent brother-in-law, a widower, who had paid his way. Pop visited Turin, Milan, Venice, Florence, and Rome. Walking through exquisite art museums and ancient buildings in the land of his ancestors had to be an unforgettable adventure for a student of architecture. My father never returned to the Old Country nor ever shared with me all the wonders of that special summer vacation.

In Milan, he visited the *Archivio Araldico,* the heraldry archives. An artist there had created a hand-painted replica of the family coat of arms. The earliest documents place our family name in the province of Varese during the 12th Century. The parchment coat of arms depicts a silver ox moving across a red shield, topped off with a knight's black helmet adorned with ostrich plumes. The ox in the Italian narrative is a symbol of patience, sustained effort and perseverance. These are traits I never subscribed to as a child. I remember thinking, *if Pop had royal Italian blood surging in his veins, how come we ate SPAM so often?*

The family coat of arms always hung in our living room inside a simple mahogany frame. As a chubby preteen kid, when I looked at it, I'd think about the wise guys in my class calling me "Bossy Cow." I hated that name. Only as a teenager after I had shed those extra pounds and learned to defend myself did my tormentors stop heckling me.

Over the years my brothers and I had pleaded with our mother to fly back to Switzerland to visit her hometown and see the few relatives still alive. We promised to make all the travel arrangements—a free trip—but no matter how hard we tried the answer stayed the same.

"My traveling days are over. That's it! End of story."

Her inflexibility made me appreciate Pop's frustration in trying to get my mother to go places with him.

Mum felt safe at home and rarely threw anything away. Collecting knick-knacks and other bric-a-brac had been a life-long quest. But when she moved to Roslindale most of my childhood treasures ended up in the trash. My high-school championship track jacket, a wooden lamp I'd made in a high school shop, the Knights of Columbus jacket, model planes, my collection of baseball cards including the ticket stub from the 1948 World Series disappeared forever.

"Don't complain now. I had no time to go through everything; I only kept a few things like your bedroom doorknocker, an old photo album, stuff like that."

"It must have been hard to leave those memories."

But Mum chose to save my childhood stamp collection. The stamps came from all over the world; profiles of Hitler and Franco adorned several of them. As a kid pasting them on the pages, I never dreamed that one day the Air Force would send me to places like Germany, Spain, Italy, and Japan.

After my father brought home our first television set, Mum had to be dragged into the parlor to watch it. Now she spent most of her days with a TV remote clutched in one hand, sitting glued to the tube watching soaps.

"Mum, what else do you do to make the days go by?"

"My journals. Every day I write about what happened. I've saved a stack of them through the years and someday you'll get to read them."

I picked one of them up and slowly turned the pages. In her perfect handwriting that I always envied, she wrote about who had called, the jokes she heard, and feelings she held close. About the time I noticed my name she pulled it away.

"I said, 'after I'm gone.' There's some things in there people won't like."

Mum's sizeable two-bedroom apartment had six rooms. In recent years my brothers and I began sending her extra money to help pay the rent. Her little bathroom looked tacky to me; several rolls of toilet paper sat on a shelf hidden under bright-pink and faded-green covers made of woolen yarn that Mum had knit. A long rubber tube connected the showerhead to the bathtub faucet. But I never got used to the squishy foam vinyl toilet seat. She loved it.

My mother brought most of the furniture to the flat from the old house, including an emerald-green Naugahyde vinyl bench Pop had custom-made and a chrome-plated pedestal table. They graced a small alcove in her new kitchen. Seeing them brought back memories of our old kitchen in the big house.

My mother made sure the movers took her huge dining room set, all the china dishes, silverware, a Queen Ann sofa where Pop napped, overstuffed chairs, and the small piano. A cherry wood secretary bookcase with a few of my father's college textbooks stood next to the brick fireplace. Hummel figurines, porcelain objects, and Delft pottery huddled together on the shelves of a matching bookcase.

One bottom drawer of the bookcase contained a number of old snapshots with scenes and people from a bygone era. I lifted a photo of my father taken in his youth on the Gloucester shoreline. He looked lean and muscular and wore a black woolen tank-top bathing suit and grinned for the camera. Then I spotted a faded photo of my mother, a young coquette wearing a dark, tight-fitting, one-piece bathing suit, probably taken on the same day. Another showed Mum and Pop sitting together, smiling on the wide running board of my father's 1926 Nash coupe; her beau is gently holding her hand.

Amidst the pile of old snapshots, one caught my eye.

I turned to my mother sitting in the sunroom, raised it for her to see and said, "Mum, how old am I?"

"Oh, about six."

"And Pop?"

"He must have been about thirty-six?"

"Why is his head cut off?"

"The war was on and your father had a lot on his mind. He didn't like the dark circles under his eyes, so he took a scissors to the picture."

"Isn't this the only snapshot of us together?"

"Yes, I think so."

"Why didn't our family ever take a picture together?

1944—Author and his father on Easter Sunday.

"Your father was a busy man and I hated to look at pictures of myself."

"Mum, you always turned your back to me whenever I pointed my Brownie Hawkeye at you."

She just shook her head and looked down. The room became still.

Suddenly her expression turned serious.

"It's hard to believe your father's been gone for thirty years."

She stopped talking and stared silently at the wall, then began to tap her index finger, gnarled from arthritis, on the arm of the chair. I had to change the subject and get her thinking about happier times. Little time remained to reminisce with her about the past.

"Mum, remember the night when you and Pop celebrated your 25th wedding anniversary?"

"Yes, what a night. We had the food catered and all your aunts and uncles came, along with Pop's key men. Your father surprised me with a gorgeous diamond ring from DeScenza

Jewelers in Boston. See, I still wear it, but I'm careful. Can't take any more bricks."

That Saturday night so many years ago, the delightful aromas of roasted meats, paper-thin prosciutto, salami, hors d'oeuvres and flaky desserts filled the air. The double front gate to the wide, gravel driveway lay open, and cars pulled in or parked on the street. Arriving guests flooded through the front door and moved into the parlor. People could dance downstairs on the linoleum and get a drink at the bar Pop had set up for the occasion. Steep stairs led down to our cellar where red wine, beer, and hard liquor flowed. Bottles of Asti Spumante, kept hidden, awaited the final toast to health and happiness. In the festive atmosphere of the party-decorated cellar, our small record player with 78- and 45-rpm records stacked alongside pumped out music over the din.

A building contractor with a heavy schedule had to deal with stress every day. So, whenever Pop wanted to unwind, alcoholic drinks made the difference. He could relax, open up, and listen to me after a few Canadian Club highballs or glasses of Pickwick Ale, a wicked brew in a tall, green quart bottle. Every day after work, Pop enjoyed a few belts, but I never saw him falling-down drunk. My mother enjoyed a Southern Comfort highball or a glass of sherry, but never enough to lose control.

As I was too young to date, no girls my age were invited, but I couldn't let that stand in my way. Eager to make a good impression, I put on my blue-suede shoes, pegged light-blue pinstriped pants and a thin, rust-colored suede belt. A plain, white long-sleeved shirt, open at the collar, topped it off. As I looked in the bathroom mirror, I slapped some Brylcreem on my dark-brown wavy hair, and my mouth formed the words, "A Little Dab'll Do Ya."

At first the music from my parents' era floated throughout the cellar. After a few drinks some of the guests started to dance, and in the commotion the selection of tunes changed. Rock and roll music made me feel alive and my collection of 45-

records had begun to swell. While no one noticed, I emboldened myself with a few weak drinks and then spotted someone familiar in the crowd. Mike Fucci, Pop's laborer foreman, a short bull of a man, was talking to another guest. Mike's shapely young wife stood next to him wearing a tight, sexy dress. After a quick hello, I found the courage to quietly ask, "Mrs. Fucci, would ya like ta dance?"

With a wide smirk, she replied, "Sure."

As "Rock Around the Clock," cut loose, we boogied on the freshly waxed linoleum floor. But, after trying to fake a jitterbug, I changed the record to "Mr. Sandman," a slow tune by the Chordettes. As we danced cheek to cheek, her luscious perfume brought impure thoughts that only a priest should hear. Luckily for me, her husband, Mike, paid no attention to a kid in hormone heaven, still wet behind the ears.

Everyone in our family knew that Pop's favorite song was "Begin the Beguine," a romantic tune from the 1930s. Cole Porter wrote the song and Mum loved it too. At their party, they laughed and smiled and mixed with the guests. And I snapped the last picture of the two together. The lyrics of their song drifted softly from the speakers in the dim light of the cellar. I had heard the words many times before. The song's lovely phrases spoke of enduring love and a promise never to part. Less than two years later, only my mother shared my life.

"Mum, did you notice anything wrong with Pop before he died?"

"No, he never told me anything. He always kept problems to himself. I always assumed he didn't want to get me upset."

What she did tell me about my father's last few days added little to what I already knew. Then my mother mentioned the name of one of Pop's close associates; she thought he was still alive. When I had some time I needed to contact him and seek the answers to all my questions.

Just Call Me Moose!

1954—Romeo and Pia at their 25th Anniversary Party.

EVERY TIME I CAME BACK TO BOSTON, my mother pressed me to take her to the New Calvary Cemetery. She wore a tailored dress, and her father, an irascible fellow, often chose to come along. I called him *Nonno,* the Italian word for grandfather. Nonno lived with Mum; they shared the rent and he always dressed up in a suit and tie for the occasion.

After stopping at the shop near the cemetery in Mattapan to pick up cut flowers for the graves, I drove through the cemetery gate and parked next to my father's plot. Pop shares an impressive granite monument with his parents, his older brother and wife, a sister and her husband. My mother knew that someday she'd be here, too.

Before we left the grave, Mum stooped over and left a small bouquet in a plastic container by the stone marker. Nearby, a white headstone stood out from the rest. In the shape of a tree trunk, it protrudes through the grass where my mother's sister, Auralia, is buried. A slim, self-assured young lady stares evocatively out from an oval faded photo mounted in the cold simulated bark. Even Nonno, a man who hid feelings from others, seemed to be touched; his eyes were wet. Aurelia had lost her long battle with consumption, a disease known today as tuberculosis, on her 17th birthday. My mother told me that when Aurelia died, the pain drove her parents to silent despair and Mum and her three siblings grieved over their sister's loss.

Further along we approached the grave of Nonno's wife, the grandmother I never met. My mother always kept a portrait of her mother Marta in the parlor. When I was a kid my parents used to take me to the cemetery on Easter Sunday or Memorial Day. Some of the headstones loomed over me; others were so small I had to crouch to read the inscription. Walking amongst the graves of my family meant little to me then, but years later I felt sad never to have known them.

As a child on the way home from those family visits to the graveyard, we drove by an insane asylum. Pop would slow down and with the car windows open he'd yell over the wind, "Can you hear that? It's the nuts in the crazy house." Their plaintive moans always gave me the creeps.

I wish we could have heard my father's silent scream.

IN A FEW DAYS I HAD TO CATCH my return flight to Albuquerque to attend an important meeting at Sandia National Laboratories. My mother seemed pleased that I came home to visit her, but I felt she wanted to tell me something before I left in the rental car for Logan Airport. My intuition proved to be true.

"I've never told this to anyone. You need to know. I have to let it out."

"What do you mean?"

"I've been carrying this around for years and now you have to keep it to yourself. Don't think badly of your father; many men did the same and still do, but it hurt back then. I've always wondered why it had to happen to me.

"You were a baby and I took the subway into Boston to go department-store shopping. I stopped to pick up new nylons.

The salesgirl recognized me right away. As she handed me my package, she smiled and said, 'How did you like the black Teddy? Did it fit?'

"I felt a little queasy and my cheeks flushed but I managed to say, 'Thank you,' and tried to melt into the crowd.

"When I confronted your father that night let's just say he didn't make any excuses. He tried to explain. A fling with a younger woman and said he was sorry."

That's about all that Mum shared with me. She seemed relieved to have told me, but I never understood why she chose to tell me then.

The next morning we hugged and kissed each other on the cheek. "You take care, Mum. I'll keep in touch. Don't wear out any more television remotes. You go through them like candy."

She threw her head back and laughed hard. In the morning light the skin on her slender arms and face looked opaque, albino-like; only her deep brown eyes, blue hair and purple veins in the back of her hands made a difference. She looked frail and vulnerable wearing slippers and a print housedress with nylons up to her knees. The tide of time had slowly eroded the shoreline of her body. Mum seemed to have lost interest in eating properly. But inside she was the same strong-willed woman I'd always known. Above all her sense of humor and elephant-like memory remained intact.

As I started to leave, her last words to me were, "Don't ever forget that I never want to be a burden to my sons," a mantra she had recited as far back as I could remember.

After I descended the steep wooden stairs from her flat, opened the trunk of the curbside car and stowed my suitcase, I looked up. She pulled the sheer curtains back and stood looking out the window. She waved and blew me a kiss and I choked back the tears, got in the car and drove away. Only later did I understand that Mum had never found Pop's channel, the one he transmitted on, but not until I realized that Mum never could tune into her last son any better.

II

ROMEO AND PIA, MY FATHER AND MOTHER, grew up next door to each other in the Dorchester section of Boston, a place the locals call "Dawchesta." I used to hear Pop's friends and associates call him Romey, a nickname less ethnic sounding. But having to listen to Mum kidding Pop made me cringe.

"Oh Romeo, Romeo, wherefore art thou?" He always took her playful teasing gracefully.

I'll be forever grateful that my parents chose a different name for me. Being razzed by other kids for being fat was bad enough. Naming me after my father would have been a prescription for ongoing fistfights. I would have preferred a manlier sounding moniker, something like Clint or Vince.

A man with fine features, dark, soulful eyes, and a deep mellifluous voice, Romey was the baby of his family, something we had in common. I remember Pop's broad shoulders and the confident way he carried himself, but his hands and feet looked small for his size. Only children's stores stocked the small-size shoes Pop slipped on every morning. Those brown chunky-looking Buster Browns never looked cool to me. He was only five feet, five inches tall; by high school our eyes were on the same level. Shorter than my brothers, I would realize later in life that tall people seem to command more respect. Yet, in spite of a short stature, Romey exhibited an air of hard-charging confidence.

A reserved man, an entrepreneur, a perfectionist in every way, my father had honed his keen intellect and analytical mind in college. On a shoestring budget, 18 years after graduating from MIT as an architectural engineer, Pop launched the construction company that bore his name and began to bid on building projects for federal, state, and municipal entities. He got financial help for the fledgling business from his sisters and Nonno, I was told. The only vehicle in the company's inventory was a 1946 International dump truck. One summer vacation, Donald painted No. 47 on the truck's door to give the company a little more status. Pop often hired my brothers after school let out to work as timekeepers, laborers, or drivers. I was too young for those types of jobs.

Nonno worked many years as the Chief Stonemason on many of my father's construction projects and according to Donald, a typical 30-minute lunch for Nonno was a "boilermaker," a shot of whisky followed by a mug of beer. Whenever I observed my grandfather working around our house, I sometimes asked, "Nonno, why are you doing it that way?"

His answer never changed. "Fifty years in the business!"

After 50 years in the same bricklayer's union, Nonno took great pride in joining the ranks of the gold-card members.

MY FATHER'S PARENTS, Romeo Natale and Rosa Maria, came from a small town in Italy near the city of Milan. Samarate is in the region of Lombardy, an area named after the *Lombards*, a barbarian tribe from what is now Germany.

I'll always remember my Swiss mother snapping in her Italian dialect, "You're a *tudesch*," when I chose to balk at her authority. *Tedesco,* the root of tudesch, is the word for a German man; it implies someone who just doesn't get it, a stubborn or hardheaded type. There is no doubt in my mind that Mum was right.

After my mother died, I took a trip to Italy and Switzerland, to my grandparents' towns. The fall day in Samarate was cool and drizzly. Gray clouds hung close to the antiquated squat structures that lined the vintage sidewalks. A few people holding black umbrellas, dressed in clothes of the same muted color, scurried by with eyes averted. Knowing that my grandparents meandered along these same pathways saddened me, for I never heard their stories about life in the Old Country.

In the cemetery, as I kneeled to brush away a few dead leaves from a worn gravestone half-buried in the wet grass, I barely made out the name Antonio and slowly my last name appeared. *Could this be the grave of my great grandfather?* On that drizzly day, I found several other graves with my family name carved in the native stone. And I wondered if these likely ancestors once had the same blood as mine flowing through their veins. Chalk-white marble monuments dotted the ordered landscape and many of them held photographs of the deceased, sealed in glass, staring at me from another time. The pride that these *paesanos*—fellow countrymen—displayed for their departed loved ones inspired me to keep chasing my faded heritage.

IT WAS AN ERA OF PEACE when the Italian Army drafted the twenty-year-old Romeo and assigned him to an infantry regiment. The family saved his army *Libretto Personale*. The cracked cowhide bound Personal Booklet records target practice scores that Grandpa Romeo made on the rifle range. Since a photo for identification wasn't common, physical attributes were listed. I noted that Grandpa measured and weighed about the same as I did at his age. His nose "curled;" it turned downward, the way my nose does. The booklet describes rosy skin and healthy *dentatura*—teeth—and his forehead, mouth and chin are giusto—righteous, or sound. As I read on, I thought Grandpa must have looked a lot like me.

His soldier duties allowed him to stay close to home, but a story passed down in the family relates a trip to Sicily. "It was a very dangerous place. Two of us always went out on patrol."

"When my time was up the army wanted me to stay in as a captain," he later told his family. "But I wanted to go to America."

Soon after Romeo left the army, he proposed marriage to a pretty, local girl. His fiancée was a close friend of Rosa Maria Colombo who was also from Samarate. Rosa knew all about young Romeo from her friend and had secretly loved him from afar. So, when his fiancée died of a virulent infectious disease, Romeo's mother asked, "Why don't you marry Rosa?" Romeo took his mother's advice and in the winter of 1885, Romeo and the slightly older Rosa exchanged Catholic vows.

Rosa often told her offspring about growing up near Milan and all the hardships the family faced. By the end of the first millennium, Milan was already famous for silk. Until her father started drinking heavily and frittered away their savings, the family had managed to get by. Now, to make ends meet, Grandma's mother had to cultivate silk worms at home. The common practice sustained the local textile trade. Grandma told her children, "I stopped going to school when I was nine to help my mother with the worms." Grandma learned to read from the Bible and never returned to school.

At night, Rosa's mother put the silk worms in a box and covered them. Then she tucked them under Rosa's bed away from cold drafts to keep them warm. The voracious silk-producing larvae, fattened with mulberry leaves, secrete a clear, viscous fluid through their mouths that hardens in the air to make silk thread. These worms incessantly spin a cocoon from a single continuous strand. At bedtime when Rosa closed her eyes to sleep, she could hear the hard shells of the cocoons clicking quietly together in the dark. During the day Rosa carefully unwound the spider web-like thread from zillions of cocoons for others to spin them together to weave silk thread.

Before my grandparents left to come to America Grandpa Romeo was already a skilled finish carpenter. The youngest child in his family (as was my father, then me), he had two older brothers. The oldest, Gaetano chose to stay in Italy and the other brother, Giovanni, anglicized to John, left earlier to come to Boston. And like Grandpa, John made his living as a carpenter so Grandpa Romeo wanted to join his brother in America.

A few months after their wedding, with only enough money for Grandpa to make the journey, Romeo hugged and kissed Rosa good-bye. After arriving in America, Grandpa took a train to Boston, then rode a horse drawn street trolley only a few miles to Dorchester, a place the Puritans settled in 1635. Compared to Samarate, Boston was a modern, vibrant place. Grandpa rejoined his brother John and sister-in-law, Maria, and moved in with them for short time.

It took Grandpa over a year to save enough money for Grandma to join him. On the voyage he witnessed that women who traveled alone could be at the mercy of aggressive, unsavory men, especially the sailors on board. So he hired a trusted male escort to accompany Grandma on the trip over.

Around the turn of the century someone took a photograph of Grandma Rosa standing alongside her sister-in-law, Louisina Colombo, and a few neighborhood friends.

Over the next eighteen years, Rosa had three girls and two boys. The first son, Eugene, named after Grandma's only sibling, arrived before the century ended. The family called him Gene and the four females of the house pampered him from the beginning. In a studio photo, my four-year-old uncle reminds me of a fop or a dandy, a far cry from the man that I knew

Just Call Me Moose!

1902 – Eugene, the first son.

Circa 1900 – Norfolk Avenue Neighbors.

Front (left to right): Mmes. Varnerin, Miniutti et al. Back row: Grandma Rosa (3rd from left) and Zia Louisina (Bossi) Colombo (far right)

Just Call Me Moose!

1910–Rear: Eugene (Gene), Palmira (Cecilia), Mary, Maurina
Front: Grandma Rosa, Romeo (Pop), Grandpa Romeo.

My father was born in 1906, eight years after Gene. It must have been difficult for my father living with a strong-willed mother, three teenage sisters, and a much older brother. For me, having two older brothers who were rolling on different tracks was bad enough.

Rosa treated the children much differently. When the boys started to work, she collected money for room and board and opened secret separate accounts in their names. When they married, Rosa produced the bankbooks. Yet, when her girls wed, each husband had to pay all the bills.

Italian immigrants had to join together to advance; the government provided little, if any, help. The Italians in my neighborhood formed a mutual aid society. My grandparents passed down to the family a small booklet labeled the *Statuto Regolamento*—Regulatory Statutes—for the *Societa' Operaia di Mutuo Soccorso di Dorchester, Mass.*—Workers Mutual Benefit

Just Call Me Moose!

Society of Dorchester, Massachusetts. Grandpa Romeo along with more than 100 other northern-Italian immigrants was listed in the booklet as an original founder. Members of the society shared a dialect and cultural bond that brought them together to fight adversity.

***

WHEN I CLOSE MY EYES TO REMEMBER NONNO, a mixture of stale cigar smoke and vintage wine that stalked his clothes comes to mind. The pungent scent told me he was near. His stinky knobby "stogies" and the mellow, dry red wine fermented in a row of oak barrels down in the cool cellar had been life-long friends, always within reach. Yet, other than giving him a ruddy complexion and a twinkle in his eyes, these pleasures affected him little.

Before he bought a wine press, Nonno made his kids stomp the grapes in large vats until their feet and ankles turned purple and the grape juice flowed. The slimy clumps of grapes had to be strained through cheesecloth and poured into barrels to ferment. To sustain this ritual, every year in the fall, Nonno ordered about 50 flimsy crates of overripe Zinfandel grapes that arrived by rail from California.

Nonno, my mother's father, Cesare, grew up in Switzerland in the town of Morbio Inferiore in the Italian-speaking canton of Ticino. The natives of the region call their country *Svizzera*. An area with a climate so mild even palm trees line the shores of its famous Lake Lugano, it's much different from the raw seaside city of Boston.

In his youth Nonno apprenticed as a *muratore*—a mason, or bricklayer—and on the job, tough, seasoned men drove him hard. He carried a crude hod, a wooden trough loaded with bricks or mortar on his shoulders, balanced on a long pole. The mortar looked and felt like warm oatmeal. When an apprentice failed to keep the bricks and mortar moving, the overlords hurled curses or yelled, "*Va presto!*" "*Va presto,*" to make

Nonno move faster. From first-hand experience, I knew that my grandfather never showed any patience for shirkers.

After hitting his mid-twenties, this ornery, wiry fellow decided to marry a girl from the nearby town of Vacallo. He chose the buxom Marta Martinelli, one of four sisters and the only one to move abroad. As a young woman, she had worked long days as a *sigaraia*, rolling cigars from imported tobacco leaves. Knowing my grandfather, I'll bet that he never had to buy a cigar while courting Marta.

In 1908, my grandparents received the sacrament of matrimony inside Santa Maria di Miracoli. Eighty-three years later, on my trip to Europe, I visited the old stone church that sits on a hill. An aunt had told me that from the top of her auburn hair to her shoes Marta wore black, the custom in those times. I imagine that Nonno wore a baggy suit, the only one in his wardrobe. After the ceremony, the couple meandered down the wide, sloped gravel steps to greet family members and friends. Marta held a black parasol in her hand to shield her fair complexion from the bright sun. Every Sunday in this church, Marta's lovely voice blended with others in the choir.

The newlyweds set up housekeeping in a nearby small stucco house bordered by high walls. I snapped a photo of the old place and tried to imagine their life together. Within a year Marta produced a healthy daughter and named her Pia Marta. The local priest christened the baby in the timeworn gray marble baptismal font. During my visit to the town, I ran my fingers over the same marble font, touched the cool holy water and thought about my mother and what she meant to me.

When local building projects slowed, Nonno was forced to take a job as a clerk—*impiegato*—at the sprawling railroad complex in Chiasso. When the promotion the railroad company promised didn't come through, my grandfather felt betrayed. Economic times in the country had to be bleak for people to move abroad. But the letters from his older brother in America offered my Swiss grandparents new hope.

Two years after the wedding, Nonno arranged to go alone to America. His wife and baby would follow after he saved some money. Before the ship sailed from France, Nonno tucked a small, neatly folded Swiss flag into his bulging, banged-up suitcase. For centuries, Swiss fighting men wore into battle the square red flag with a white cross on their tunic or armor. This cherished piece of wool was a replica of the flag once held high on the dusty parade fields where he marched as a soldier. As a child walking over to visit Nonno in his dimly lit, musty Dorchester parlor, I paid little attention to the worn furnishings around me.

But I still remember the neatly framed, sepia-tone photograph that stood on a small lamp table. One day I bent down to see it better. A distinguished-looking military man dressed in a distinct khaki uniform adorned with a thin leather belt across his chest and pillbox cap stared back at me.

"Nonno, who's this?"

"He was-a my general." Nonno's bright, olive eyes had a faraway look as he spoke.

Maybe something out there is bigger than us, I thought. I would come to understand that Nonno still revered the man of honor in the picture, and his pride of military service never flagged. That day Nonno told me a story about the Swiss army and how they trained to blow up strategic mountain passes on the Italian border to slow a German invasion. *An exciting job,* I thought. Nonno seemed to hold a simple view of the world, showing disdain for regional strife and armed hostilities in the news. Whenever we cousins played at being soldiers, shooting toy guns to mimic World War II newsreels, he looked away, a touch of sadness in his eyes. Nonno never approved of us even playing at war.

Five months after Nonno came to America, his wife landed at Ellis Island, traveling without escort. She was pregnant and suffering from nausea. Women in steerage with small babies sought out a lower bunk; it meant less distance to fall on a pitching ship. As Marta moved slowly down the ramp, she clutched baby Pia tightly in her arms. But, unfortunately, according to my mother, a schedule mix-up had delayed her husband. Marta panicked and told the family later how she had felt abandoned. Without a sponsor, she thought they'd be sent back. When Nonno arrived in the reception hall a day late, her paralyzing fear vanished.

At home in Boston many years later, whenever Italian-speaking friends came over to see her they asked, "Marta, when are you going back to Switzerland?"

"When they build a bridge made out of *salamits!*" Only a bridge made of sausages would convince her to return.

After arriving in Dorchester, my Swiss grandparents rented their first flat, a few houses away from my father's family. Close by, Nonno's bricklayer brothers, Guiseppe, the oldest, and Innocenti, younger and milder tempered, resided with their families. Zio Innocenti, known as Eno in America, died when I was a baby, leaving his gentle wife and five children on their own.

Both brothers helped ease Nonno and his wife into the American way. Guiseppe, the uncle I knew as Zio Joe, rarely talked to me even though he lived around the corner. I had heard as a child that the patriarch of eight children and Nonno had a major quarrel many years before and they kept the reason private. I remember Nonno crossing the street whenever Zio Joe approached him on the sidewalk. These headstrong men never made peace, too stubborn to swallow their pride, typical behavior for rough men with their heritage.

A few months after arriving in Boston, Nonno registered at Local 3 of the Bricklayer's Union. When he rode the trolley to job sites in the area and beyond, he carried a scratched leather satchel and a long level. The bag held the special tools of the trade: a trowel, a brick hammer, joiners, a brush, a steel square, a ruler, a roll of line and pins. After years on the job, the prized implements of Nonno's trade looked worn and smooth. As a stonemason toiling many years in all kinds of weather, he made his mark on stone and brick buildings in the region and as far away as New York. And he laughed when he talked about a project to expand the U.S. Army Military Academy.

"I went-a Westa Point-a!"

At home on Norfolk Avenue in Dorchester, Marta gave birth to four more children, three girls and one son, Guilelmo, whom everyone called Willie. The baby of the family, Auntie Marie, and Uncle Willie had been products of the rowdy Twenties and Marie displayed the same rebellious streak as her brother. They all lived in a small, second-floor flat set back from the street, a place with no central heat, no bathtub. It rented for twelve dollars a month.

1922—Front (left to right): Guilelmo (Willie), Cesare (Nonno), Maria (Marie), Marta (Nonna), Ines. Rear (left to right): Aurelia, Pia (Mum).

Whenever my mother mentioned spending frigid winter nights in the three-room flat it made her teeth chatter and I felt cold.

"Even the pee in our chamber pots, the *urinarios*, under our beds froze."

As the oldest, my mother helped care for her siblings. And whenever she spoke about a youthful passion, a dream never fulfilled, Mum got angry.

"I wanted to be a nurse and help people. But your Nonno wouldn't let me.

"He got mad when I asked for permission and said, 'No daughter of mine's gonna work in a hospital. A woman's place is here at home.'"

My mother never forgave her father; she told me the same story many times.

"I felt cheated," she used to say.

Instead of nurses training, my mother enrolled in the Practical Arts High School where the curriculum revolved around sewing and cooking, skills that she used every day as a wife and a mother.

After completing the two-year program and now resigned to her fate, my mother landed a job making dresses on Newbury Street, still the fashion row of Boston. Yet, all her life, she kept a medical dictionary within reach to help diagnose the ills of her friends, neighbors and their children. Just as her mother had, she was ready to help others whenever they reached out.

MY ITALIAN AND MY SWISS GRANDPARENTS arrived in Boston 25 years apart to work alongside other immigrant tradesmen helping to shape their adopted country. They lived next door to each other on Norfolk Avenue and so my parents grew up together, their families bonded in a common struggle.

When I was a child, many of the families in my vibrant, mixed blue-collar and middle-class neighborhood, about five miles south of the heart of Boston, had achieved a comfortable standard of living. After supper, men in white sleeveless undershirts and their wives, wearing cotton frocks, sat on the front stoops to escape the muggy, summer heat. With their kids playing in front, they laughed and greeted friends. Many of them came from Italy or Switzerland. Now they lived on an island in a sea of mostly Irish descendants alongside a smattering of families with French-Canadian, Swedish, and English names, but they still felt at ease conversing in their native dialects. Grateful to be Americans, all shared an intense pride in their new country. Almost every day women swept the sidewalks and stoops; their front brass door handles and doorbells gleamed from frequent polishing.

This part of Dorchester, near Edward Everett Square and Upham's Corner, boasted a rich history dating to colonial times. Hard-working Italian-speaking people with homes on Norfolk Avenue were my neighbors. Rows of flat-roofed, shingle-clad, mostly two-and three-decker houses hugged the old cobblestone street. Nearby in Upham's Corner everything needed to run a household could be purchased. The area had its share of dingy, smoke-filled barrooms to serve its thirsty denizens after a hard day on the job.

Wood-framed, single-family homes with neat yards or shingle-sided, flat-roofed houses lined East Cottage, my street. Since the turn of the century a tall, black wrought-iron fence bounded the Boston Edison Company enclave. The guard in the shack, next to the iron gate that hung from large stone pillars, controlled access to the facility that was tasked to lay underground electric cables throughout Boston. Growing up across from its sprawling grasslands gave me a feeling of living on the edge of the Great Plains.

Before World War I, Grandpa Romeo built a rambling three-decker with a small grocery store. Six families occupied the flats. The landmark flowed along the curved sidewalk; each of its windows had shutters then. Housewives hung their wet laundry on the back porches–*piazzas*–on the south side. The author lived in a second floor flat in his early years.

As automobiles became more affordable in the 1920s, Grandpa erected a series of garages for car owners in the area. With the help of stonemasons, he built a concrete-block garage complex, next to the corner three-decker. People flocked to rent individual garages for only a few dollars a month to keep their cars off the street. In the winter before anti-freeze came into use, Pop had to stoke the boiler to keep car radiators from freezing.

Just Call Me Moose!

Circa 1910 — Grandpa Romeo built this residence and grocery store near Edward Everett Square in Dorchester.

The residential area had been developed between 1820 and 1920. Within twenty years after arriving in Boston my grandparents owned their single family home and two three-deckers on Norfolk Avenue. Grandma handled the family's finances; she made it a point to personally collect the rents. People who remember said that Grandpa rarely questioned his strong-willed wife's authority. My father told me whenever his parents met anybody for the first time, Grandma liked to say, "I'm the boss!"

Grandpa Romeo remained a member-in-good-standing of Carpenters Union Number 67 in nearby Roxbury; he paid forty cents a month, a fee similar to his hourly wage. A homebuilder now, dressed in denim coveralls, ankle-high shoes and a bowler hat, he trod along the muddy, slick cobblestone streets toting a leather bag. A bag filled with wooden planes, augers, a hammer, a level, a square, and a tape measure, similar to basic, present-day tools. On workdays he caught the nearby electric street trolley to West Roxbury or as far as Norwood, estimating the cost of small jobs in his head.

Just Call Me Moose!

```
This Card Expires Sept. 30, 1923          No......................
UNITED BROTHERHOOD OF CARPENTERS AND JOINERS

CARPENTER'S DISTRICT COUNCIL
           OF BOSTON AND VICINITY

Brother  Romeo Bossi
              IS A MEMBER OF

     CARPENTERS UNION No.  67

JU..
AUG.
SE..     TEL. ROX. 1123-W     E. L. JONES, Fin. Sec'y

HOLIDAY: July 4th and Sept. 3rd                    100
```

Grandpa Romeo's Last Union Card.

After my father began the junior year of Mechanic Arts High School, his father died a few days before his sixty-first birthday. He had broken his leg helping workmen move a massive, pre-cast concrete lintel at a church job site and at home while recovering in bed, a blood clot developed in his lung and killed him. So my father became the man of the house, the only child at home, just as I would be one day.

Grandma sold the house where they lived to her neighbors, my mother's parents. My father and his widowed mother moved to a nearby house, my home one-day. Long before my grandfather died, the charming tranquil Yankee town of Norwell on the way to Cape Cod had been a getaway for the family. My father's parents had a vacation cabin "down the country," and the quiet country life appealed to the family. To get there they would take a train to Hingham, then a horse and buggy, long before early automobiles rambled along the dirt roads. As a child, I came to love my day trips there.

One of Grandpa's favorite pastimes was to pick mushrooms in the damp ground, only selecting the ones safe to eat. At home he spread them outside to dry for *Risotto alla Milanese*, a favorite dish from the Old Country, well known in the north.

Just Call Me Moose!

A teenage Romey and his dog, Vic, in Norwell.

Large wood-frame houses on ample tracts of land were scattered throughout the area. Since my father's childhood, his sisters Cecilia and Maurina and their families owned property in this North River Valley community. As a youth, my father enjoyed hunting small game in Norwell, mostly rabbits and squirrels with Vic, the family's beagle, by his side.

In his senior year of high school, my father was accepted to enter the prestigious Massachusetts Institute of Technology across the Charles River in Cambridge. His annual tuition and books cost about $500, nearly a year's wages for a professional person. Paul, a brother-in-law, supplied most of the funds to cover the college expenses. Without Zio Paul, my father couldn't have done it. Pop told me about having to attend classes on Saturday; he had little free time for outside activities other than the Architectural Society. Less than three percent of his class of 500 came from Italian-American families.

Just Call Me Moose!

The Commonwealth of Massachusetts electrocuted Nicola Sacco and Bartolomeo Vanzetti when Pop was a sophomore. These Italian immigrants and radical anarchists died for their alleged role in a robbery and murder, a conviction that remains in question today. Their executions may have resulted more from an Italian heritage and unorthodox political views than actual proof of guilt. Anyone with an Italian heritage felt the sting of prejudice back then; I have to assume that my father endured his share.

On graduation day in 1928, Romey crossed the stage of Symphony Hall wearing a long black academic robe and mortarboard with tassel, and reached for his degree. When describing that day, Pop always said that when the rolled-up piece of parchment touched his fingers, Grandma cried out, "That-sa my boy."

III

———

WITH A COLLEGE DEGREE and a new job in the construction industry, Romey looked forward to settling down with Pia, the love of his life. *Is it just a coincidence that he was also the baby of his family? And he also lived with a domineering widowed mother similar to mine in the house where I grew up, the place where he died? And did marriage provide an escape and independence?* It took years for me to realize that Pop's life and mine ran parallel.

On Columbus Day in 1929, Romey and Pia exchanged Catholic wedding vows in the nearby St. Margaret's Church, a towering, Romanesque-style structure of red bricks completed 25 years before. It is one of several churches in Dorchester the archdiocese had built to serve the burgeoning, immigrant Catholic population. As a child I knelt alone in the shadows and prayed in the clouds of mystical incense on many holy days and Sundays during the Latin Masses. Oddly, my parents rarely kneeled alongside me. Only the death of a friend and the church funeral would bring them there.

Just Call Me Moose!

1929–My parents' wedding party

Left to right: Ines (Mum's sister), Pop's cousin Louisa (Louise) Mazzuchelli, Romeo, Pia, Gene (Pop's brother), Pop's cousin Paolina (Pauline) Mazzuchelli, Pop's cousin Virginia Mazzucchelli.

On their wedding day, the dimple-faced, auburn-haired Pia wore a lovely, hand-embroidered ivory lace dress with a short train. The delicate lace headpiece resembled the traditional costume of Switzerland, the land of her birth. Romey cut an urbane figure in his tuxedo and slick, raven-black hair. A reception for the newlyweds with a sit-down dinner took place on Virginia Street, off Upham's Corner, in the Eastern Star Temple, a large Masonic hall. A lively band played dance music for more than a hundred relatives and neighbors. Early in his career my father considered joining the brotherhood of Masons, perhaps to enhance business opportunities. My mother is said to have strongly objected due to the Masons' longstanding objection to the Catholic Church. So Pop ditched the thought.

Just Call Me Moose!

As the wedding reception wound down, Romey and Pia departed for a hotel in Boston and spent the following night in the western part of the state on the way to Canada. Romey sat behind the wheel of the blue, two-door 1926 Nash coupe his brother-in-law Paul had bought him. They enjoyed a weeklong honeymoon in Quebec City at the opulent Le Chateau Frontenac, a palatial hotel on the Rue des Carrieres. This landmark, built like a castle, still looms over the old city next to the St. Lawrence River. With more than 600 guest rooms, it opened only a few years before the wedding. Quebec was about 500 miles from Boston over primitive roads, with gas stations few and far between. Canada would be the only country they ever visited together; Mum always had an excuse for not traveling, and Pop never took a vacation.

Within weeks of the wedding, the stock market began to unravel, and in late October a national crisis quickly spread from Wall Street to Main Street. My parents grew up during the hollow prosperity of the Roaring Twenties. And unbeknownst to them, the neighborhood children of the Depression would soon be pitted against the youth of Hitler's Germany.

In normal economic times, any architectural engineer could expect to succeed. But now the nation and the region were in a financial Depression and the construction industry lagged as a result. For Romey, the stress of getting through college, starting a new family and making ends meet weighed heavily. Within months of their wedding it became clear that his $35 a week white-collar job was in jeopardy. Overwhelmed with worries, this self-assured man, always proud of being in control, started to come undone. Unable to cope, he stayed home for a few months. Mum never offered any details; she didn't want to talk about it. I always heard the same words.

"Your father had a nervous breakdown."

And I recall Pop describing to me men leaping out of tall buildings. Successful men, now destroyed, after seeing their nest eggs disappear in the failed stock market. As a witness to the loss of fortunes and personal pride, those horrific events must have festered inside him for decades.

WHEN I WAS BORN IN THE FALL OF 1938, long before hurricanes had names, an angry monster stomped through New England creating mayhem in its path. The Great Depression had almost run its course, but the specter of imperialism loomed in Europe and Asia. Not for noble acts, *Time* magazine selected Adolf Hitler as Man of the Year. Before the year had ended, this twisted tyrant showed his true intentions, and my world would never be the same.

In September of that year, with practically no warning, a hurricane struck Boston; its whirling-dervish winds spread 200 miles wide across the landscape. Up from Long Island, it churned through western Massachusetts into Vermont and then finally died in Canada. A storm of this magnitude had never struck New England, especially so far inland, but this beast had long legs.

My mother told me about how she feared this storm as my birth approached. Late in the day, tall poplar trees next to our big, brown three-decker bent over to rattle the second-floor windows of the flat that faced the ocean. When it was over, property damage added up to nearly $400 million; and worse, the storm killed more than 600 people. Fortunately for the neighborhood, no serious damage occurred.

Her mother had died from a chronic kidney illness a few months earlier. If I had known her, Nonno's wife would have been my Nonna. Growing up, all my aunts and uncles on my father's side were zio or zia to me, with the exception of Pop's mother, my Grandma. Mum's siblings went by aunt or uncle, but I had to call my grandfather, Nonno. I never questioned the goofy family rule. Was I confused? Not really, at the time it seemed perfectly natural.

My mother often told me that Nonna liked being a midwife, helping neighborhood woman deliver their babies. A self-taught seamstress, she knitted sweaters for those in need. Neighbors up and down the street came to her, an early "Dear Abby" persona, to share their troubles. After a month in a South End hospital, Nonna came home, further treatment deemed pointless. She died in the cramped upstairs bedroom in the house where my father was born; the same room where his father had died. Besides Snappy, the small, brown and white family dog, only Mum and one of Marta's closest friends stood by the bed to witness her passing. The summer afternoon that his wife passed away Nonno had to be at work laying bricks. Beside, Nonno never went to the hospital; hospitals, churches, and Nonno didn't mix; religion had no role in his life. A hospital stay often led to death and Nonno held his grief inside.

Nonno had always railed against his wife's acts of kindness. He believed that neighbors should keep their problems to themselves. I often witnessed my mother perform acts of kindness for friends, offering advice to new mothers and even bathing premature babies. But when my mother's mother died it was my loss, too; I would never feel the warm touch of this caring, kind woman and hear her stories from the Old Country.

The night I was born my mother made supper and then ate a large helping of her homemade chocolate pudding. When the labor pains began, Pop called Dr. Gillespie and drove Mum over to the St. Margaret's Hospital, about a mile away. Nurses and staff of this Catholic obstetric hospital came from the Daughters of Charity of St. Vincent de Paul, a French order founded to serve the sick and poor in the 17th century. The sisters wore a distinctive white, heavily starched, gull-winged hat.

Dr. Gillespie, a middle-aged physician, and a suave, formal man, stayed busy delivering neighborhood babies including my two older brothers. Donald was born seven years earlier, a brooding boy with a fuzzy, dime-sized birthmark on his cheek. Roger came along a year later. This thin, reticent brother was never known for long conversations. Our names disguised our roots quite well; the choices were deliberate. They had no ties to any relative, living or dead, so we could begin our lives with a clean slate with no connection to the past.

In labor my mother began to feel queasy. Up on the delivery table the race between the dessert and the slippery newborn had a clear winner, the chocolate pudding. And although Mum often made the creamy rich dessert for the family, she never touched it again. My mother often laughed when she told me the story about the night I was born.

"Late that night at the hospital, a nurse walked into my room and said, 'Sorry, I know you wanted a girl, but this baby has a tassel!' "

At 29 with three boys, the "rhythm method" hadn't worked.

"I wanted a girl so badly," Mum used to say. "You were supposed to be Patricia. But don't forget, I still love you."

Her incessant lament always made me grin; a less stalwart boy might have chosen a life as a cross-dresser. My mother's squat stature drew attention to her ample bosom, a reservoir of milk for me. So, as a newborn baby at her breasts, my lifelong appeal for good food began. Of all her boys, when the time came to eat I never was late. Mother doted over me yet sought to exert control in the years to come and around her neck she always wore a gold locket with two tiny photos—one of my father and one of me. With three boys in a row, Pop had beaten the odds. He was the envy of other fathers in the neighborhood that had sired only girls.

My parents brought me home to their comfortable second-floor flat with three bedrooms and most floors made of hard wood or covered with rugs. It had a large central foyer, a big kitchen with a soapstone sink. My mother cooked meals on the black coal-fired cast-iron stove; the flat's hot water came from a small copper water heater she polished every week. By the time I came along, a small General Electric refrigerator, a real luxury item, squatted on the kitchen's linoleum floor. On top, a big round condenser kept everything cold inside. In the morning, a uniformed milkman from the H.P. Hood Company would come up the back stairs carrying his metal carrier with bottles of milk topped with gobs of cream. The squat glass bottles rattled alongside the containers of butter.

When my mother needed something in the flat sharpened, she sought out the little guy in the frayed clothes carrying a big stone wheel who mysteriously appeared on the sidewalk. Sharpening scissors and knives by hand was his specialty, and all the neighborhood wives depended on him to make their lives easier. He never lacked for work, and women up and down the street carried blades of all kinds for him to hone.

Our small bathroom had a commode flushed by pulling on a chain and a bathtub big enough to float a battleship. Wallpaper covered most of the rooms. Our parlor faced the street; my parents' wedding invitation, mounted in an ornate silver frame, hung on a wall by the door.

Donald and Roger shared a bedroom furnished with heavy oak twin beds and separate bureaus just inside the front door. One of Pop's watercolors in their room depicted Walt Disney's seven dwarfs. I had my own bedroom, off the kitchen, next to my parents. I remember the brightly colored wallpaper with sailboats and the framed pictures of Mickey Mouse and Pinocchio that hung over the bed. Pop had painted them in the days he still had time for his kids.

Roger, the baby until I showed up and usurped the right, rebelled over the new littermate and stopped eating and drinking. It took a few days in the hospital for him to recover and to grasp that I wasn't going away. Roger always kept a close grip on expressing feelings, a quality our father bestowed on all of us.

Like other kids, when I started walking, I'd reach for and grab things around me. Even then, my mother loved her knick-knacks, including an early collection of delicate Hummel figurines of children.

In her native dialect, she'd caution, *"La sali sta!"* Those words—"Don't touch it!"—had been burned into my mind.

And when her words failed to get my attention, she'd say, "I'm gonna give you a *cutsote!*"

Just Call Me Moose!

Over the years, my habit of biting my nails evoked the same response and although she rarely unleashed a threatened slap, I behaved.

When the weather cooperated, Mum would jam me in my heavy, wooden high chair and air me out on the piazza. Sitting next to the ocean made our weather fickle; the dreary, gray, overcast skies of Boston could easily bring on the blues for anyone past childhood. In wintertime the damp, cold air wrapped tightly around us; a tall steam radiator in my room clanged and sputtered but kept me warm. Flats like ours stayed hot and muggy during the short, rainy summers, and nights without breezes were typical. With no fan in my room it could be hard to sleep between sheets damp with humidity. Yet, one sunny, bright day made up for all the bad ones. When the season mellowed, my mother or her pretty, high-strung sister, Auntie Ines, still at home with Nonno, took me for a stroll in a brown, tank-like, wicker pram. On cold days, Mum dressed me in a navy blue, wool Eton coat and matching cap. Always concerned about the neighbors, my mother made sure her last child looked good.

Before live panda bears became all the rage, I owned a stuffed one to take to bed. And my mother made sure I said my prayers every night. Sometimes she'd say, "If you're bad, the boogey man is gonna get you." I didn't want to take any chances and on most days before I went to sleep, I got down on my hands and knees and peeked under my bed. Every night I knelt down with Mum at the side of my bed and said a prayer.

"Now I lay me down to sleep, I pray the Lord my soul to keep. If I should die before I wake, I pray the Lord my soul to take."

After tucking me in and kissing me goodnight, she quietly whispered, "*Va fa nana nin.*" Telling me to sleep well as she melted into the shadows. Lying there in the semi-darkness, all outside light was muted by a window roller shade that touched the sill. Before I drifted off to sleep, my eyes followed the beams of headlights darting from wall to wall from cars on the street below.

SHORTLY AFTER MY THIRD BIRTHDAY, Japanese carrier aircraft attacked our ships at Pearl Harbor; the dastardly event roused the nation from its isolationist slumber. Hitler joined Japan against us. Support for fascist dictator Mussolini faded early and during the war more than 500,000 Italian-Americans signed up for military service. Often, fit men who failed to don a uniform were perceived as shirking responsibility and vilified by neighbors and co-workers. All through the war, President Roosevelt made radio broadcasts, famous fireside chats, which brought comfort to the nation. In the twilight of her life, Mum would reflect upon these messages that kept her and the country calm during those years of turmoil and uncertainty.

I would learn afterward that many of my male cousins served the country during the war. Zio Joe had a son, Joe, who became a Navy pilot and flew submarine patrols in Grumman Avenger torpedo bombers off aircraft carriers in the Pacific. Victor, his brother, and Zio Eno's boys, John and Henry, also joined the Navy. Silvio, Zio Joe's oldest son who had a family, became a machinist in the Charlestown Navy Yard. In 1944, the army drafted Zio Gene's only son, Genie, a student at Dartmouth. During the Battle of the Bulge the Germans captured him; luckily, he was liberated a few months later. Although I knew virtually nothing of their military exploits, I was proud of their service and wondered how I'd look in a uniform.

AFTER MY MOTHER DIED, Auntie Ines let slip that the family nickname for Pia was *La Lumaca*—The Snail. A slowpoke around the house as a child, she enjoyed sleeping late, a trait she passed on to me.

But the mother I knew seemed never to rest in her castle; in the kitchen she cooked tasty meals that stuck to my ribs, and kept the house clean. Even though Gerber baby foods had lined grocery store shelves for years, my mother wanted a homemade product for her babies. So, all the vegetables and fruits my brothers and I consumed, she peeled, steamed, strained and then processed in a food mill. She even cooked and shredded the meat we ate; a time-consuming labor of love, but she felt obliged to do it.

But when meat became scarce during the war, we ate slices of SPAM with an egg on top. Yet, on Sundays around two o'clock, we enjoyed an elaborate meal of antipasto, minestrone soup, and a small roast.

Most immigrants who come to a new country continue to cook their Old Country favorites so my parents grew up on *risotto* and *polenta*.

Once a week, Pop looked forward to Mum making *Risotto alla Milanese,* a dish that became a favorite of mine. Risotto was served before the main course or by itself. My mother cooked it in a heavy, cast-iron skillet on top of the stove, adding dry white wine, chicken stock, onion, mushrooms and the most important ingredient of all, a pinch of saffron. Saffron gives the yellow color to Milan's famous treat. This expensive spice is made from the dried stigmas of the autumn-flowering crocus. A legend says the recipe originated during a medieval Italian festive wedding dinner for the daughter of a Flemish glass artisan. Saffron gave stained glass its yellow color and since the banquet took place in a hall off the *Duomo*, the magnificent Gothic cathedral in Milan, a small bag of saffron accidentally fell into the rice during cooking. All the guests loved the elegant taste and that's why this dish is yellow.

When she served us risotto, a mist of heat rose above each generous bowl. We waited for it to cool or risked searing the roofs of our mouths.

Mum always warned, "Start from the outside edge where it's cool." When I failed to heed the advice I wound up with a blistered mouth.

Polenta, another staple of northern Italy and southern Switzerland, was usually reserved for special occasions since it took much longer to prepare. Polenta is a simple dish made from coarse yellow cornmeal that goes back to the Roman Legions. To prepare a stiff polenta it took a lot of hard stirring, so Nonno often came over on holidays to make it. As a child, when he came over, I'd watch him boil water in a large, heavy pot, then slowly add the cornmeal, stirring until it thickened using a worn, stout, wooden stick called a *cannelo*. When it was cooked, he plopped the steaming, moist golden cake onto a smooth cutting board covered with a clean dishtowel. Everyone got a thick slice and I liked to daub my piece with some cold cream cheese. Mum would cook a rich stew made with red wine, chicken, wild rabbit or squirrel and *luganega*, a mild, pork and garlic sausage. She ladled it over the polenta and I couldn't wait to eat. After a meal like that it was difficult to move around. *How did the Romans manage to conquer their enemies after eating polenta?*

One afternoon after supper the grownups were laughing about an old family story. It seemed a little far-fetched to me but they swore it happened. During the Depression Nonno was out of work and couldn't put food on the table. So a few times he trapped a stray alley cat to go with the polenta. The story goes on that my grandparents invited the Brebbias, neighbors from downstairs for dinner and the main course was *polenta e gat*—polenta with a stew made of cat meat. No one mentioned the meat and the guests never questioned the free meal. When hard times hit, people sometimes take extreme measures.

Before I started school my father still had a little time to spend with his sons. The pressing responsibilities that came with owning a business came years later; then he became a shadowy figure in my life with different priorities.

Just Call Me Moose!

In our parlor, Pop brought Mother Goose Nursery Rhymes and Grimm's Fairy Tales to life from hardcover books too heavy for me to carry. He sat next to me on the green Queen Anne sofa and began to read. His was a strong, mellow voice that took me on a journey to faraway places. A blend of Old Spice after-shave lotion and Kreml hair tonic hung in the air as he shared the classic stories with me. I laughed when he grinned and wiggled his ears for me. He taught me how to perform the trick; it made me proud to emulate him. Just before bedtime, with his fist casting a shadow from the tall upright lamp, Pop flashed outlines of rabbits and geese on the wall. The simple scenes, some with barnyard sounds, made me giggle.

On our sofa, Pop taught me the ancient lessons of Aesop's Fables. They showed me right and wrong, and that every action has a consequence. And when I could read, these short fables held me spellbound–the importance of integrity and being truthful. The stories and their distilled lessons of life made a lasting impression on me. "Self-help is the best help," "It is too late to prepare for danger when our enemies are upon us," "Live and let live," "It is not always wise to take people at their word," and "People are judged by the company they keep," remain timeless teachings. Those few short interludes on the couch lit a small flame within me. Although those stories are just a faded memory, the values my father instilled in me as a child served me well.

IV

DURING WORLD WAR II, families across the country would display a small red and white banner with a blue star in the front window. One blue star represented each child in the war. When a service member died the family exchanged it for a gold one. Fortunately, the stars in my relatives' windows never had to be replaced.

Blackout shades shielded the street below from the light behind the windows. The measure made it harder for Nazi submarines—U-boats—lurking off shore to find their targets. They sought to torpedo merchant ships silhouetted against the coastline. Uncle Willie wanted to wear a military uniform but couldn't pass the physical. A childhood bout with rheumatic fever had damaged his heart. So, he volunteered to be an Air Raid Warden, carried a gas mask, and wore a white, dome-like helmet and an armband with a Civil Defense emblem. Uncle Willie used to patrol neighborhoods and blew his whistle and rang the doorbell whenever he caught a glimmer of light.

As a child and surrounded by females, Willie always seemed to be at odds with his father. Perhaps Nonno resented the attention his wife gave their only son? I had heard that Willie, a skinny kid, often felt the wrath of his father. It began with a childhood prank when Uncle Willie and a neighbor pal sneaked into the chilly, musty cellar where his father kept a row of weathered, wooden barrels full of homemade wine. Willie turned the wooden spigot of one barrel until the blood-red wine slowly dribbled onto the uneven stone floor. As the boys took turns gulping at the steady trickle, they tried but couldn't stop it. The cool brew kept flowing, and soon they began to feel its effects. Their tiny stomachs rebelled and they threw up. When Marta told Nonno that night, Willie got spanked. From that day on, wine never again touched Uncle Willie's lips, but apparently whiskey and beer didn't count.

I remember my mother holding my hand as we climbed the flights of stairs to our flat. One day she paused and slid her hand over the smooth varnished oak banister.

"Your Grandpa built all this when I was a little girl."

Years later, I learned that Grandpa Romeo had erected the three-decker before World War I began. Six families lived there. He built it for his daughter Maurina and her husband, Balthasar Cugnasca, a man everyone called Billie. She ran the small Italian grocery store when Billie was at work. Their only child, Richard, joined the army during the war. Later he became a veterinarian in rural Norwell where he married and raised a family.

Sometimes my mother let me go over to visit my aunt and uncle. Maurina was a no-nonsense woman who was hard of hearing and Zio Billie, her "servant for life," worked as a waiter in Boston. They lived in a flat next to ours; their store had changed hands long ago. Zia Maurina often handed me a piece of candy and made me feel special. But I kept my chubby hands in my pockets since Rex, their bug-eyed, bad-tempered Boston terrier, loved getting a piece of me whenever I tried to pat his little round head.

As the war intensified, my father worked as an estimator, an "inside man" at the John A. Volpe Construction Company. Volpe was an old friend, another son of an Italian immigrant. The low bidder got the jobs; many of those projects involved defense contracts. Pop's age, breadwinner status, and a job involving important defense contracts shielded him from military service. Since people had no respect for men who didn't join the military maybe it bothered him. I recall him telling me, "I had flat feet; that's why I didn't go in."

Gasoline, meat, butter, bacon, cheese, sugar, and other commodities became scarce. The government imposed price controls and people used ration books with coupons to buy certain items, even ice cream. Silk became scarce because it was used to make parachutes, so some young women painted their legs using a sponge dipped in pancake makeup to simulate the stockings no longer available on store shelves. A girlfriend used an eyebrow pencil to make the seam.

Like other mothers, mine touted the benefits of cod liver oil; every morning at breakfast I got a heaping dose.

"Open your mouth....Now!"

I'd hold my nose and close my eyes as the huge tablespoon loomed before me. I wanted to believe it when Mum said, "It's good for you. Make your bones strong," as I gulped the slippery elixir down.

And she'd smile knowingly as she screwed the cap back on the bottle. Children in those days faced German measles, scarlet fever, chicken pox, mumps, whooping cough and infantile paralysis, a disease called polio that paralyzed many people. Fortunately, sickness rarely came my way.

Medical remedies were limited. Doctors couldn't prescribe antibiotics; they didn't exist. After I suffered from a series of persistent sore throats, my mother decided to act.

"Get ready, we're goin' shopping," she said.

Mum clasped my little hand in hers and I tried hard to keep up as we walked briskly to Windemere Road, close to Upham's Corner. We moved quickly up the steep, white stairs to the Harley Hospital, once a grand, summer estate. Even to a little kid, it didn't resemble a store. All at once two guys in hospital garb lurking in the hallway grabbed me and slammed a mesh mask covered with gauze over my face, then applied chloroform to knock me out.

Just Call Me Moose!

The author about the time his tonsils went missing.

In the operating room a doctor removed my inflamed tonsils and after a short nap, I awoke with a queasy stomach, a headache, and a sore throat. Confused and upset, I was still too young to understand what took place. But after I ate a small dish of vanilla ice cream, Mum smiled and stroked my forehead. Her soothing words made a difference, *she thought*.

"I'm sorry, but I didn't want you to make a scene."

My mother's promise had been a cruel hoax; someone who controlled my life had lied about taking me shopping and it hurt. An innocent decision with little regard for the consequences may have introduced my sprouting psyche to the concept of cynicism.

Just Call Me Moose!

THE LIBERTY MARKET, MY MOTHER'S FAVORITE butcher shop, was a short walk from our flat. Locals called the food store the "Black Market" because the Italian owners always had marbled steaks, roasts, veal and cold cuts on hand. All of these were scarce commodities during the war. Mum would drag me to this shop, where damp sawdust littered the wooden floor, and foreign smells tweaked my nostrils. Odors from Gorgonzola, a mold-ripened, blue-veined cheese smelling like sweaty socks; *pancetta*—Italian bacon made from pig bellies; Genoa salami made with spiced pork; *mortadella*—an Italian bologna from the Middle Ages; *capocolla*—cured Italian sweet ham; fresh chickens; and hanging slabs of bloody beef.

The two Old Country butchers in their blood-spattered white aprons always smiled and greeted my mother in Italian. One butcher was rotund, the other lean, and together they reminded me of an Old Country parody of Laurel and Hardy. Mum wasted little time and pelted one with orders for the meats. The butcher quickly sliced everything while she watched. She kept a close eye on the scale as he weighed everything and carefully wrapped them in heavy paper.

Outside the store Mum lectured me, "You have to make sure they don't weigh their thumb."

At home she'd sauté the thinly sliced veal cutlets, floured and breaded, in white wine and sliced mushrooms, accented with lemon juice. *Costelletti di Vitello alla Milanese* still makes my mouth water.

Whenever my mother took me into Boston we took the electric-powered, wooden MTA orange "cattle cars." These behemoths used to lumber along on steel tracks down the cobblestone streets. The commuters sat on hard wooden benches or stood and clutched overhead leather straps. When I slid into a seat before a lady did, Mum dug an elbow into my ribs. "Be a gentleman, get up." Most men felt compelled to give a woman their seat.

As my streetcar lurched along, daring kids hung on the back until the conductor spotted them. Before they darted off, the kids often yanked the pulley off the overhead line to keep the streetcar from moving. Later the Kingston Trio made "Charley on the MTA" famous as he rode on the same subway cars that snaked through tunnels to Boston from Andrew Square or Dudley Station. Words close to my heart, "He may ride forever 'neath the streets of Boston. He's the man who never returned."

Other than going shopping, my mother liked to stay home and disliked traveling, but in 1944 Pop drove her to South Station to board a train bound for California. Traveling alone, she wanted to attend her sister Marie's wedding. Marie, a bubbly, petite brunette, with big brown eyes, lived in Los Angeles. As the oldest child, my mother felt obligated to represent the family; Nonno and Pop had to work. Marie was a product of the rowdy Twenties and displayed the same rebellious streak as her brother, Willie.

Several years before, Marie left Boston in a huff after years of battles with her widowed father. She wanted a life of her own; Nonno didn't condone this daughter's habit of staying out late and smoking cigarettes. Neighbors might gossip. Marie had stayed in touch with old neighbor friends, the Brebbias, who had moved to California. They offered to help her now. The laid-back ways of warm Southern California fit the baby of the family's liberated lifestyle to a tee; Los Angeles wasn't stodgy and cold, like Boston. And the faraway city provided an opening to flee from under the thumb of her domineering father. In California, Marie took a new surname, Berné; I have to assume Nonno never found out. For the perky Marie, an ethnic-sounding name like Bernasconi, especially in a time of war, may have cramped her employment opportunities.

Around the supper table, Auntie Marie used to tell us funny stories about working in defense factories. Marie's bosses kept moving her from job to job because she often screwed up even the simplest task. Being pretty and chirpy, I imagine, must have played a major role in staying hired. One night after work, she met Bill Schmidt, a tall, handsome young man, a California native and an army officer. Bill's earthy, infectious grin and his distinctive laugh set him apart from others on the prowl. Uncle Bill had to be the best thing that ever happened to Marie, a girl close to 30 and primed for marriage.

An Army Air Corps pilot, Bill flew the P-38 Lightning and the P-61 Black Widow, but the war ended before he could be deployed to fight. Long after the war ended, my Uncle Bill, a man with a military mind who wore his uniform with pride, loved to regale me with glowing verbal snapshots of living overseas in Germany and France. The fascinating pictures he painted of life in the military made an enormous impression on me.

While my mother was out West Pop shuttled me between relatives and friends. My older brothers could fend for themselves; I still needed to be watched. Mum's exciting, solo train trip through barren lands and bustling cities had to be the best trip of her long life. She was alone, yet surrounded by soldiers and sailors in uniform on furlough. When the train chugged through the Santa Fe depot in New Mexico she got to see sweaty, real cowboys on horseback herding cattle. Although only a few weeks had passed, it seemed forever before she came home. Pop picked her up at South Station. That night she told me about a present for me and I couldn't wait for her to unpack.

"Close your eyes. And put your hand out."

I felt something small and cold in my palm.

"Open your eyes. I met the Lone Ranger out there. He gave me this for you."

I looked down and saw a shiny silver bullet on a tiny chain.

When I showed the bullet to my friends and told them what my mother had said, they didn't believe the story. But I was convinced even though she'd lied before about my tonsils. I treasured my present for years. I had grown up listening to the Lone Ranger and his sidekick Tonto on the radio, then watching them on television. Out West they led the fight for law and order; I could relate to their quest for justice from paying attention to Pop. That night in bed I closed my eyes and could visualize the Lone Ranger as he rode off into the night on his white stallion.

"Hi-Yo Silver, Awaaaay!"

One day my silver bullet fell out of my pocket, never to be seen again. Whenever the William Tell Overture is playing in the background, I think of the man with the mask who conquered evil for all of us and then the shiny silver bullet my mother gave me comes to mind.

When peace came, the radio blared "Happy Days Are Here Again," a feel-good popular song. Shortly thereafter, my father launched his own construction company. He leased office space on Leon Street, off Huntington Avenue and hired a few key players to head up primary functions. But, as president and treasurer of the company, all the responsibility for success rested on his shoulders. Pop kept so busy on the job there was less and less time for me. My brothers didn't notice; they had already moved on past the stage where a father's attention is important.

On the day a few neighborhood ruffians kidnapped me I was grateful that Pop wasn't at work. My cousin, Joey, and I were walking up the street on the way to the movie. As we passed a three-decker where several Irish families lived, some of the kids we knew darted from the house, surrounded us, and blocked our path. They linked hands and started to call us names.

"Look who's here? Two Ginneys. What're you doing in front of our house?"

"None of your business," I yelled back.

Joey broke loose and took-off running.

"Tell my father," I called after him, as they grabbed me.

One of the kids, a boy named Dennis Murphy, had a father who was a Boston cop. I'd seen the big brute coming and going from the house. Mrs. Murphy used to mop the front porch as sailors at sea do on the deck. She never smiled or said hello like other mothers did; it made me wonder about her.

A few days before, a few of us had serenaded her as we walked by.

"Who threw the overalls in Mrs. Murphy's chowder?"

The gangly woman with stringy black hair reached for the bucket and hurled dirty water our way. Just a little splashed us as we ran away laughing.

After Joey got away, my captors led me inside the hallway and down the creaky wooden stairs into their gloomy cellar. Someone tied my hands behind my back and blindfolded me.

Dennis started, "How do like that? Nobody's gonna know your down here. I heard about what you did. My Ma didn't appreciate that song.

Then I heard footsteps on the stairs and my father yelled, "Karl!...Karl!....Are you down there?"

The kids had nowhere to run and stood frozen in their tracks. Dennis untied the rope and pulled off the blindfold.

"I'm here, Pop, here I am."

Like the masked man of my radio fantasies, my father had ridden to my rescue and he became my defender of freedom.

Pop stood there defiantly and said, "You kids better stay away from my boy or there'll be big trouble."

My tormentors stood transfixed and silent as my father slowly eyed each of them up and down. Then Pop reached for my hand and pulled me toward him. The bright sun hurt my eyes as we stepped out onto the porch.

"Next time you better be more careful. I don't trust those kids."

LOOKING BACK, IT SEEMED to be a much simpler world, neighbors shared common goals trying to raise large families and still make ends meet. Family life remained intensely personal, but most adults showed concern about how others viewed them. As Mum used to say, "People who live in glass houses shouldn't throw stones." It seems to me that the glue holding my multinational neighborhood together was civility and respect for others.

Just Call Me Moose!

In an era when the proud survivors of the Great Depression shared the same lifeboat, most people pressed forward unselfishly to fight fascism. Neighbors learned to accept the sacrifices made in their daily lives; the concept of a "Me" generation would come much later.

Big, burly Irish cops in their somber uniforms, more black than blue, patrolled our streets swinging long billy clubs. An aura of authority clung to them that roused our respect and made us feel that our protectors genuinely cared about us. Children who dared utter "bad" words had to chew on a bar of soap; I can still remember the sharp bite of lye. Far fewer murderers, rapists and robbers prowled the alleys. When a child walked to school alone, rode the bus or took the subway, parents worried more about them getting lost than falling victim to a pedophile. Most potential offenders feared the wrath of this tested social order.

Schools were like an annex of home. Teachers made us toe the line; drug abuse we see today and school shootings didn't happen. Alcohol was the only drug that seriously affected some neighborhood families. Most men smoked or chewed tobacco, but "decent" women didn't indulge, since it might be a sign of a woman who went "all the way." A reliable reputation could be easily sullied, and once damaged, impossible to repair. Newlyweds stayed around after marriage; grandparents lived close by. When we walked home from school for lunch, our mothers were there. Both parents didn't need to work outside the home to make ends meet.

In most neighborhoods, parents rarely worried about the safety of their kids and little by little, Mum gave me permission to play nearby with my wild-boy cousins. Playing war with toy guns and helmets grew to be one of our favorite pastimes. After the war, all kinds of military stuff, like canvas leggings, gas masks, canteens, and web belts seemed to be everywhere. Dressing and playing the part of a soldier was easy. One day after shooting at each other, hiding under cars and behind fences, one of the kids talked everyone into trying something different. But we needed a victim.

My cousin Frankie, a kid called Kiki, and his older sister, Marilyn, lived with their parents on the corner of Humphreys and Elder streets, across from L.F. Daloz, a dry cleaning company. Kiki never played with his cousins, but one summer afternoon something bad happened to him. Among my skinny cousins was Joey, bird-like compared to me. Joey's diminutive father Silvio, a wiry bald-headed guy known as Sil, owned a small auto repair shop behind his family's flat. My cousin Sil seemed like a regular guy to me after I saw the racy pinups taped on the shop's back block wall. A shot of Betty Grable in a skin-tight bathing suit looking over her shoulder, and other glossy posters of less famous beauties, told me so. Sweet odors of gasoline and oil permeated the dim grotto where he toiled. He could fix anything on wheels, people said. Every time I saw this honest-to-God grease monkey, layers of engine oil covered his hands and arms and axle grease spotted his coveralls. But after watching Sil work miracles deep in the grime, I knew that auto mechanics would never be my strong suit.

Sil loved to irritate his son Joey and called him in a special way when he wanted to talk to him.

"Hey, Joe-Joe...the Dog-Faced Boy, get ovah here."

Joey didn't appreciate the nickname, especially when his friends parroted the words.

The day Kiki came under siege it all started when another cousin exclaimed, "Let's get Kiki!"

Kids have a pack mentality so someone found an old burlap sack in the trash and another filled a sock with sand to make a blackjack, like commandos often used.

"Here he comes," the lookout whispered, and we all hid under his piazza.

My blonde-haired cousin Kiki swung open the wooden gate and walked past, oblivious to us. Joey threw the smelly sack over his head and another cousin rapped Kiki on his head with the heavy sock. He let out a blood-curdling scream and we scattered like a flock of birds. Kiki never knew who hit him until I told him later. Standing under a piazza close to Sil's shop we couldn't stop laughing. But, alone that night in bed, I felt differently. It wasn't funny anymore, and going along blindly with the crowd had been a mistake. I can't remember being punished so maybe Pop never heard what happened.

Not long after the ambush, cousin Kiki and his family moved to Assinippi, near Norwell but far away from Dorchester and his rowdy cousins. I can't imagine that Kiki ever forgot the rumble in his backyard and the sand-filled sock. It stayed with me.

EVERY TIME MY BIRTHDAY came around, my mother brought up this old story. I had to sit still and listen.

"Just before Halloween and I was pregnant with you, your father took me to the Strand Theater to see a movie. Bela Lugosi, bloodsucking, vampire, Count Dracula was playing. After coming home, I started to pull down a shade in the unlit parlor. The outline of my black, upright vacuum cleaner caught my eye. It looked like Dracula and I let out a blood-curdling scream. Your father came running and together we laughed."

I can't remember Mum telling me about any other movie. As she got older, getting out wasn't much fun for her, a trait that frustrated my father in many ways.

My simple birthday parties always included one of my mother's layer cakes and fresh, Neapolitan ice cream. Birthday cards from relatives always bore the salutation "Master," a carryover from colonial times, until I reached the age of puberty. Many aunts and uncles sent cards addressed to "Master Karl" that included a few crisp dollar bills. A cousin or two usually came over to help me celebrate. Using a dishtowel as a blindfold, Pop spun me around and with tail in hand, I'd try to pin it to the donkey tacked to the kitchen door. A rum cake from the Café Roma on Hanover Street in the North End made the day extra special.

Just Call Me Moose!

One birthday, Pop proudly presented me with a large, red, metal steam shovel. I was thrilled. With its movable rubber treads, it resembled the real thing. In my barren, shaded yard, filling the bucket with sand and dumping it in a different spot was a lot of fun. Playing alone and making believe with the toy brought the fantasy to life. Since it was heavy for me to carry, one night I left it under the piazza behind the stairs. The next morning, my steam shovel was gone. After searching everywhere in the yard, I noticed my mother looking down.

"Mum, I can't find my steam shovel."

She stared at me and then slowly shook her head. After Mum helped me search, all she said was, "Son, I think you learned a lesson today." Sobbing quietly, I nodded.

That night, Pop scolded me. "That's the last toy I'll ever buy for you." It hurt to think a stranger, or even one of my friends, took a prized possession. No one at home ever warned me this could happen. The first harsh experience of my short life taught me to always lock up my things. After my wonderful steam shovel disappeared, sharing my "stuff" with others never came easily to me.

Although our Indian summer of fall days was a welcome change from the heat and humidity, every kid's favorite time had to be Christmas. It took on a special aura at home when Mum and Pop decorated the full, fragrant tree with bubble lights, various old ornaments, and individual strands of tinsel. Close to the tree, Mum used to hang five large homemade red stockings with fuzzy white tops for Santa to fill. As Christmas Day approached, she always said, "Be good or there'll be coal in your stocking." But instead of coal, I'd find things for school and tiny cardboard boxes of the traditional Italian candy, *Torrone,* a chewy nougat brick made of honey, citron and toasted almonds and covered in an egg-white wafer.

The long line of Lionel electric trains snaking around the tree was a special treat. Pop's old Kodak Bellows camera from the 1930s used large 620-film. I loved to watch him open the camera and expand the railroad-engine-like bellows to take a picture. Taking photos had been a favorite pastime in his youth. Before my time, Pop made little lead soldiers for my brothers. One time he made me a few. In the cellar, after melting strips of lead, he poured the molten metal into molds. After cooling, each was pried open and another soldier came to life. Pop would place the remaining militia left in the collection in the folds of the white sheet under the tree to guard the train.

Make-believe candles with electric bulbs sat on the parlor windowsills for neighbors to see. All the houses were lit up, and St. Margaret's and St. Kevin's each erected a beautiful outdoor Christmas manger scene. During the festive season, our 78-rpm record player blared forth holiday music and classic Christmas carols. Perry Como sang "Santa Claus is Coming to Town," a tune from the early thirties. "Rudolph the Red-Nosed Reindeer," sung by cowboy movie star and singer Gene Autrey, hit the pop charts in 1949. And when Bing Crosby crooned, "I'm dreaming of a white Christmas," I prayed for snow.

As Christmas approached Pop liked to read to me about Santa.

"He had a broad face and a little round belly that shook when he laughed, like a bowl full of jelly."

Mum used to take me to a Boston department store to wait in line to see Santa, and listen to me reel off my memorized list of toys. On Christmas Eve my mother left a few cookies and a glass of milk on the kitchen table for the man in red. My brothers knew the real story, but I still imagined Santa and his reindeer landing on our roof. On Christmas Day, before light, I would quietly creep past my parents' bedroom. The cookies and milk were gone, a good sign; then, even better, I'd see the neatly stacked presents under the tree.

Soon, both parents in their nightclothes stood grinning broadly in the doorway. Then Donald and Roger darted into the parlor and started to shake boxes addressed to them. Toys had a simple quality. A sled, bow and arrows, a cap gun, or a slingshot sometimes magically appeared under the tree. A Slinky or a gyroscope showed up sometimes. Tearing open the wrapping around a big bulky box uncovered a set of Lincoln Logs. Another contained an Erector Set; maybe Pop was trying to tell me something? And if it looked like a package contained clothes, I saved it for last.

At Christmas and Easter, my mother made *panettone* for dessert. This large, round, sweet yeast bread had originated in Milan during the 15th Century. Its delicious moist texture comes from raisins, citron, pine nuts and anise. It was a real treat for grownups and kids alike.

Years ago the Thomas Groom estate sat on a large tract of land off Humphreys Street. Today, Groom Street covers the former driveway to the long-gone Groom Mansion and its gardens. In winter after snow fell, we would coast down the steep hill on our Flexible Flyers to slide through the street; a lookout had to be posted to watch for cars. At the end of Groom there was a large open area called Gately's Hill. We patrolled the nearby streets after the holiday and collected the dry Christmas trees on the sidewalk and dragged them to the top of the hill. After stacking them as high as possible we lit a roaring bonfire at dusk that turned the black neighborhood sky to shades of red and orange and melted the crusted snow on our winter garments. The smell of burning pine trees permeated our clothes and our cheeks felt flushed from the heat of the fire. It felt good to be alive.

V

"SHUUUSH, DON'T MAKE A SCENE." Whenever my mother took me anywhere, I had to mind my manners. It was an obsession with her. Around friends or strangers there was no excuse for not acting civil and being polite. She had to be in control and became visibly upset if I acted up or raised my voice.

An incident at school best describes Mum's passion for perfect behavior. The first few months of my fifth grade seemed to go well until the day my homeroom teacher retaliated. All the kids recognized Miss Mary O'Leary, a tested, no-nonsense educator, by her flaming red hair. The gaudy color came out of a bottle, we all knew. More at ease with the new teacher as each day passed, my compulsion to captivate other kids at the wrong time or talk out of turn became insatiable. I craved attention and home never fulfilled my need. One day at school, frustrated over my antics, Miss O'Leary ran out of patience.

The skinny girl with mousy-brown hair sitting in front of me never felt it when I dipped her pigtail in my inkwell. It never showed. But a friend squealed on me, she told the teacher. As Miss O'Leary handed out papers I instigated a commotion. She brushed back a lock of her hair and glared hard at me.

"Get up here! Clean out your desk and bring all your books." Pointing to the desk next to hers, she said, "This is yours until you learn to behave."

The class snickered as I lifted slowly out of my chair and started up the aisle. My new desk was close to the blackboard at the front of the class. *This extra attention could be trouble,* I thought.

Soon after Miss O'Leary made me an example, it was time for the first meeting of parents and teachers. A notice went out. When Mum said she'd go, I got a sinking feeling in my stomach. On that infamous day, school let out and most kids came happily home. But I kept thinking the worse.

My mother had grown up in an era when women took pleasure in buying very expensive hats and she felt that a "proper" woman wore nice, soft gloves on her hands and a lovely hat on her head whenever she left the house.

By the time I opened the front door, she had already stepped into a rigid corset and pulled on hose, then carefully applied rouge and lipstick, and finally slipped into a nice dress and stepped into her heels.

Since the beginning of the Edwardian era women squeezed themselves into the ubiquitous, rigid corset; the "S" shape became "the look" in the early part of the century. For women, wearing a corset had serious moral overtones, and should a woman not wear one, it showed "she had let herself go." It often baffled me why my mother would torment herself getting into such a contrivance just to go grocery shopping. Sometimes when Pop wasn't around, Mum would ask me to yank on the strings and tie them in a bow. "Make it tighter," she'd say, as she held a deep breath. On that day I don't remember my mother needing me.

I never understood why Mum spent time looking in a mirror and plucking her eyebrows to make them thin. None of those old Italian women ever plucked their moustaches.

According to Auntie Ines, Mum enjoyed the exotic fragrance of an expensive perfume. Before leaving the house she always daubed a little Nuit de Nöel by Caron on her wrists and behind each ear. Then she looked in the mirror to straighten her hat and pin it. After helping put on her red coat with the mink collar, I opened our heavy front door.

"Goodbye, Mum, hope you like my teacher. She's the one with jack-o-lantern hair."

I crossed my fingers and smiled. Mum walked alone to the school and stood with a group of other mothers. After a few minutes she decided to introduce herself.

"Hello, Miss O'Leary, I'm happy to meet you. I'm Karl's mother."

My mother told me later that she had stepped forward anticipating a warm response, maybe some words commending her boy. Instead, my teacher stared back and my mother reeled back from Miss O'Leary's high-pitched, staccato voice.

"Oh!...*You're* Karl's mother. Do you know that your son's the class clown?"

"The other mothers gasped and I was speechless," Mum told me. "Can't remember anything else your teacher said," she added.

When Mum came home I heard the door slam and she yelled for me.

"Son, come here!"

It sounded like things hadn't gone well. The look on her face, and the high, pink glow on her cheeks didn't look right. Sitting in the parlor, she recounted, in minute detail, the visit to my school.

"I was never so mortified in all my life! How can *I* be the mother of the class clown? Your father won't be pleased."

My mother enjoyed making me feel guilty. Maybe she learned it in church. That night Pop gave me a long lecture about my bad behavior and what he expected. When I brought my report card home and showed it to him, Pop shook his head and said, "Starting today, I want to see all your homework. You'll do a lot better next time."

Just Call Me Moose!

Ironic how a kid who got a D in Conduct, a D in Effort, and a D in Arithmetic ended up disarming bombs and managing stockpiles of nuclear weapons. But after Pop paid special attention to me, I made all A's in those subjects next time. Getting noticed to this degree wasn't my intention.

My formal education began at the old Richard C. Humphreys, a public grammar school behind Columbia Road near Holden Street. Humphreys came from an old Dorchester family that had intermarried with the Upham clan of Upham's Corner.

My mother walked me to kindergarten and waited for me at the corner when school let out. Leaving the comfort of home for a strange place with strange adults and kids didn't sit well with me. For several mornings I rebelled and cried but Mum spoke quietly to me and made things better. One day a vigilant teacher called my mother to pick me up. My ruddy complexion was the color of an overripe apricot. After taking my temperature, the teacher told my mother, "Your son looks sick. He might have scarlet fever. Please come and get him." When Mum arrived at school I told her, "I feel fine." She shook her head, but took me home anyway. The next day, I heard Mum tell my teachers, "My boy's cheeks are always red."

One day in the first grade, I won a green Boston Public Schools lead pencil for showing proficiency in a spelling bee. It was my first school prize and when the final bell rang, I left it in my desk. That night at the supper table, I told my family, "Today I won a pencil for good spelling."

"So?" said Roger.

Donald stared silently at the ceiling. Mum kept me home the next day after I showed signs of the mumps. The next morning she woke me up, "Your school burned down last night." Rubbing the sleep from my eyes I wasn't sure if it was a joke. But the look on her face said it all. *No pencil. No school. Now what?* In a few days all of my classmates and I had to transfer to other area schools.

Just Call Me Moose!

After the fire I was transferred to the venerable brick William E. Russell School on Columbia Road, not far from my house, close to the original town center of Dorchester and its first schoolhouse. My new school was named after William Eustis Russell, the governor of the Commonwealth around the turn of the century, a few years before my parents attended the school.

Kids can be cruel to their peers. Sometimes in the playground when tempers flared a kid would scream, "Hey, fatso, you dumb WOP, gimee da ball." And I'd yell back, "Shut up you little Mick!" My parents always disapproved of any display of prejudice. They taught me the "Golden Rule," and when someone confronted me they expected me to reply, "Sticks and stones may break my bones but names will never hurt me." It sounded good but it never made sense to me.

Edward Everett Square sits between my old house and school, a spot once known as Five Corners because of the intersection of five major roads. The first Dorchester settlers lived here. A tall, weathered bronze statue of a man from another time still stands in the nearby park. I can't recall my teachers ever talking about Everett, but he must have done something special. One day after school I brandished my homemade slingshot to shoot at a pigeon squatting on his head. *Why does this guy deserve a statue?* Many years later, I found out.

History remembers Edward Everett, a statesman and native son of Dorchester, for giving a lengthy and boring prelude to President Lincoln's brief and moving Gettysburg Address. Lincoln's words will be celebrated forever; Everett's speech will not.

Next to the Square, different kinds of stores and shops lined Columbia Road. In the pharmacy I'd order a chocolate frappe or a Coke from the soda jerk and sit at the white marble counter with friends. Tony Giaccobe ran a barbershop nearby with a red and white barber pole out front that twirled round and round. In the summer, the pint-sized Italian barber gave me a "wiffle," a style known as a crew cut in most places today. My mother said Tony came to our flat for my first haircut. Growing up I remember little Tony cutting my hair in his shop. He wrapped a thin piece of tissue around my neck and pinned a sheet around me before trimming my locks. And in the smoke-filled room, I could hear the waiting grownups whispering dirty jokes to one another.

A pleasant married couple owned Stacey Stationery, a store close to the barbershop. During all my years in school, I haunted the place for notebooks, writing paper and other supplies. For small change, the Chinese Laundry next to Walsh's Tavern washed, pressed, and starched our shirts. The family lived in the back, and the smells of Oriental food cooking on the stove continually drifted past the door of the steamy shop.

One day a friend said, "Watch this!"

As he peered at the Chinese man behind the counter, he exposed his gums and rubbed a finger across his front teeth.

"Hey, that makes your eyes slanted like him," I said.

"Yeah. It drives a Chinaman nuts."

The old guy inside the laundry started to yell but I didn't stick around to see what happened.

In the old days, everyone jaywalked; no one cared. I did it all the time, cutting across the byways and main streets with wild abandon. Boston had to be a jaywalker's paradise. And whenever I hit the streets, Mum never failed to caution, "Look both ways for *cahs*."

More than vehicles bore watching. The sharp clippitty-clop echo of hooves from a swayback nag as it ambled along, slobbering wet oats from a canvas bag, is hard to forget. Yelling "rags, old iron," the tired, dirty ragman with a whip in hand plied the neighborhood looking for junk, anything for a few pennies. The rundown wooden wagon loaded down with old newspapers, pieces of metal, and bundles of old rags swayed along. A round scale with a pan hung from little chains hung on the back. Kids brave enough to grab on to the tailgate felt the wrath of the ragman's whip. So, to be safe, I always kept an eye out for the forlorn, plodding steed and the steaming brown muffins it left in its wake.

When I walked to school I couldn't avoid seeing the old, spooky, frame structure that was once home to an early settler, Deacon James Blake. Built about 1648, it is reputed to be the oldest house in Boston. Originally located near present-day Massachusetts Avenue, the historic building was moved to prevent demolition. My teachers never mentioned the dilapidated dwelling; it had been boarded up and forgotten.

After school one day, a pugnacious classmate of Irish heritage challenged me to fight. I can't remember why we chose to do battle on the damp, battered grass next to the Blake House. Surrounded by a circle of jeering boys, after slowly circling one another, our fists flew wildly. Earlier he had mentioned that his father had taught him how to box. I could tell since he quickly broke through my defenses and I backed away to prevent further damage to my self-esteem. Over the years, the lesson on the grass had served me well. In high school, a physical encounter with a high-school loudmouth turned out in my favor.

When a new school year began, the sounds of our leather heels on the hard stone floors echoed as we lined up by the nurse's station for eye and ear exams. She would carefully check our scalps with a comb for cooties. I dreaded getting weighed and measured in front of my classmates. In the third grade, when the school scale read 80 pounds, the other kids laughed. I blushed and seethed inside, but had only Mum and myself to blame. A kid too short for his weight took a lot of abuse, no differently than today.

I was my mother's special pet, so she loved to ply me with groceries and I steadily packed on the beef. Mum hated to put leftovers away, so she'd look at me with pleading eyes.

"It's just a daub."

All those extra helpings made a difference. Quality pants and jackets in my size couldn't be found in any neighborhood stores. Before Easter or when a new school year rolled around, my mother took me downtown on the subway to Kennedy's, a large, upscale department store. The Husky Shop catered to kids with a rotund shape like mine. Mrs. Kramer, a pleasant Jewish saleswoman who excelled at her job, made sure my mother always left the store happy. And for me, "husky" had a better ring to it than just "fat."

Every classroom displayed an American flag and every morning we proudly said the Pledge of Allegiance. The words "under God" were added when Eisenhower was president. Teachers labored daily with few resources to bring fun to school for us. Sometimes music blared from the scratched records played on an old wind-up Victrola, and kids square-danced in the hallway, a short reprieve from the boring grammar and arithmetic classes. And we got to perform on stage in the auditorium.

One day my third grade teacher told me, "You're going to be a tomato in the school play. We'll be making costumes." I wanted my mother to come and see me. She did. Mum sat in the front row and applauded politely over my few stilted sentences. At supper Mum never divulged to the family that the cardboard tomato and her chubby boy on stage had a lot in common. Round and with red cheeks, her baby *looked* like a tomato.

Every year Chief Nee-dah-beh, a Penobscot Indian, came to our auditorium to put on a one-man show. A Native American who lived in Maine, his name means friend. With a face the texture and color of a well-worn cowboy saddle, he covered his shiny, coal-black hair with a war bonnet made from eagle feathers. The chief wore a colorful beaded vest over his wide chest; beaded cuffs and armbands adorned his wrists and exposed biceps. Buckskin leggings and a decorated breechcloth covered his lower body. He wore buckskin moccasins on his bare feet. During the performance the chief enthralled us by throwing a tomahawk into a wooden cutting board that leaned against a chair in the aisle. When this serious warrior reached for his bow and quiver of arrows, the audience gasped. One arrow after another whistled through the air, down the long aisle into the target. The chief never missed.

As a classmate beat on a big, tight leather drum, the warrior from Maine hopped around to its throbbing sound. He danced in the aisle, then jumped to the wooden stage. Often he got another kid to sit cross-legged there and when my hand shot up, he nodded and showed me how and where to sit. As his dark eyes met mine, he touched my shoulder and whispered, "Don't move." Then he started to move around me in a circle and swing a heavy spiked war club wildly above my rigid trunk. His moccasins drove hard into the stage; I could hear the sound of his pounding feet over the shrieks and howls of the kids. Volunteering had offered an opportunity for me to get attention, but never again did I muster the courage to expose myself to a war club at school.

Only a few boys still wore knickers: bulky, loose pants gathered below the knees. Made of coarse corduroy fabric, they made a droning, squeaky sound when my legs rubbed together. Only boys about to reach puberty in my family wore long pants. My long argyle stockings and plain, brown leather shoes complemented them. Boys ordinarily wore shirts with a collar and a necktie, usually loosened. Girl classmates usually wore dresses or a blouse and skirt just above their more-often-than-not scabbed knees. Leather shoes and droopy socks made the outfit complete.

The boys in my class took extreme measures to avoid mingling with the girls and vice-versa. No boy wanted to be tagged a "sissy," someone who cavorted with the opposite sex. But when Valentine's Day came around, any girl I liked received my small card to help engender my genteel reputation amongst the females.

Our teachers stressed good penmanship; they drilled us on the Palmer Method of handwriting to help our little hands write clearly. After all, it was said that legible script revealed character and breeding. Tightly holding my black Public School metal quill pen, I'd dip it into the small, glass inkwell in a cutout in my desk. To ensure our ovals and push-pulls were perfect, Miss Misite, my fourth-grade teacher, strolled up and down the aisles, like a beer-barrel on thick legs. Almost as wide as she was tall, she had a crown of braided, gray hair atop her round, little face. A faint shadow of a moustache touched her upper lip. She wore gray or light blue tailored dresses, girded with a thin belt, and tightly laced, black leather shoes with a short heel.

Reading gave me great pleasure, especially when my teachers called on me to show my stuff out loud to the class. Always being selected to read for the class and reeling off complex sentences made me feel special since many of my classmates tripped over words. Although Pop brought home several Bobbsey Twins and Rover Boys books, I never got hooked on the stories. They bored me. Like most of my generation, I liked to read comic books. The mix of cartoon images and vibrant action-packed situations intrigued me. The first Superman comic book hit the newsstands a few months before I was born and Pop hung a framed picture of my hero "The Man of Steel" on my bedroom wall before I could walk.

In grammar school my pile of other comics like *Batman* and *Captain Marvel*, the boy who cried "Shazam," grew higher. I treasured these comic books. Dick Tracy spoke into a radio wristwatch; today's cell phones do the same for real. Those superheroes in the blurry, colored pages took us to a special world of good versus evil. But for many kids, reading took a back seat when the age of television arrived.

Miss Haney, an elderly woman, taught us general science, a subject she lectured about to my parents. Every morning the wizened science teacher heated a beaker full of water on the Bunsen burner next to the blackboard until it boiled. Then she poured the superheated water into a mug and after a few minutes it was ready to drink. I often wondered if plain hot water had added to her longevity.

At noon we went home for lunch. But after teachers grumbled about the extra time that extended the school day, our lunch period got cut back, so kids and teachers ate at their desks. After the rule changed, Mum made my lunch, adding a few other snacks, and packed it in my little metal lunch box.

"I'm makin' you a cream cheese and jelly *sangwich*. You betta eatit!" She never could say "sandwich."

And every Friday Mum got creative because the Church didn't allow Catholics to eat meat on that day. By now my mother recognized that I was allergic to certain types of seafood and nuts; my lips would swell up and my breathing became labored. So Mum put tuna fish, plain cheese or a fried egg in my sandwich. And when she made brownies those nuts stayed out of the mixture. The rest of the week she made sandwiches with *cacciatore*, a hard, small Italian salami, or *mortadella*. For a small price, the school supplied a cold pint of Hoods whole milk.

For decades, most teachers were woman and they had to remain single. In 1900, the Boston School Committee clarified the early rule: "The marriage of a woman teacher shall operate as a resignation of her position." In 1953 the state legislature finally outlawed the policy. In spite of this obstacle and the low wages paid, my teachers worked hard to prepare us for further studies. My teachers: Misses Misite, O'Leary, McCarthy, Rhilinger, and Roche, had kept the legacy of excellence in the classroom alive.

On Saturdays, I used to walk past the old creepy cemetery at Upham's Corner; the high, cement walls and the padlocked wrought-iron gate kept visitors away. A quick glance inside showed the weathered, lopsided headstones that marked the ancient graves but I never saw anyone come to pay respect. The North Burying Ground dates to 1634 and by the early 1900s, more than eight thousand people lay buried there, many of them important Dorchester citizens.

At night in early times wolves had roamed the thick woods dotting the present-day landscape; nothing stopped them from digging up any fresh remains. So, the Pilgrims laid heavy flat slabs of stone over the graves. And town fathers offered a reward of twenty shillings for any wolf killed.

About 1800, Amos Upham built a full-service store at the intersection of Columbia Road (formerly Boston Street), Stoughton Street and Dudley Street. In 1886, Upham's Corner developed into a center for commerce and services. By the turn of the century Boston knew it as a major shopping area. Two banks served local patrons—the Dorchester Savings and National Shawmut, an old Indian word for present day Boston. Shawmut means "near the neck" after the narrow neck of land that flooded at high tide. It joined the mainland of Roxbury to the Boston peninsula.

Pop didn't make a lot of money in construction, but the family lived quite comfortably. And Mum kept tight control of the household budget and spent family money wisely. I used to save all the pennies that came my way in a piggy bank. My mother taught me to wrap them in brown paper for "real money" at the Shawmut Bank under the watchful gaze of the smooth bronze Indian brave. With the few dollars tucked safely in my pocket I'd walk around the F.W. Woolworth or S.S. Kresge stores looking at toys, or buy candy at Fanny Farmers across the street.

People came from miles around to shop at the gigantic Upham's Corner Market the Cifrino family built in 1920. The streetcar tracks at the entrance across from the early colonial cemetery helped the store grow into an early one-stop supermarket. Customers exchanged pleasantries in English or Italian with one another. Fresh damp sawdust was scattered on the wooden floor; the sights and smells of fresh meats and seafood and neatly stacked fruits and vegetables, made it a special place. In her youth, my mother had been a checkout girl there.

"We didn't have cash registers so all the items had to be added in my head then listed on a long strip of paper."

My mother had worked in the fish market then and had carried the strong odors home. That's where Mum developed a knack for picking out the best produce and leanest cuts of meats. And every time she took me shopping there I heard the old story.

OUR SECOND-FLOOR FLAT HAD NO DINING ROOM, so the family dined in the kitchen. The suppers we ate included mostly meat and potatoes except on Fridays. The five of us sat around a plain wooden kitchen table covered with a bright pattern oilcloth near the big black oil cook stove. Before the meal began no one bowed their head and said grace but when my parents drank wine, Pop would say, "*Salute!*"–"to your health." Only on holidays do I seem to remember Pop offering a prayer of thanks.

My mother scrubbed and mopped the decorative linoleum floor and waxed it to a high shine. I remember Pop, with a small dishtowel draped over his shoulder, helping Mum with the meals. We rarely ate spaghetti, but my mother sometimes made *gnocchi*, which are an Italian version of potato dumplings. She rolled the flour-coated doughy mixture then cut it into pieces before cooking them in boiling water and covering each heaping serving with steaming homemade tomato sauce.

The hair on the skin of whole chickens and chicken feet had to be burned-off before they were roasted or fried. Boiled chicken feet tasted good to me; I loved crunching the bones after I stripped the meat off them. Years later, when I torched-off unserviceable rocket motors in Vietnam, the smell reminded me of those days in our kitchen.

An old remedy for eating spicy food was a product made in Italy. In every Italian-American kitchen a cobalt blue bottle full of small white antacid crystals sat on a cabinet shelf. I can remember Pop using the ubiquitous Brioschi to alleviate indigestion. But I never touched it until alcohol entered my life.

When the cold Boston winters began to bite, Pop stoked the coal fire in our cellar furnace and made sure our coal bin stayed full. Donald helped out after school. The shiny, black chunks of coal that slid down the chute through the cellar window came from a cheerful neighbor and businessman, Emilio Mazzetti, "Mecca" to us. Sometimes I watched him carry heavy blocks of ice using steel tongs. A thick leather pad lay between his back and the frozen cargo. Many families still depended on daily deliveries of ice to keep their food fresh.

As soon as I walked in the front door, my mother fixed something for me to eat—a piece of pie or a brownie or a big helping of chocolate pudding, it didn't matter what. Her baby never washed the dishes; I rarely ever took the garbage out. I'm sure my brothers resented the special treatment, but I had no reason to complain.

My mother loved to bombard her boys with trite sayings like:

"You're full of balloon juice,"

"Beggars can't be choosers,"

"Runaway laffin'!'"

And should we ask, "Ma, what's for supper," she responded without hesitating.

"Don't call me Ma! You're havin' crabs and ice water."

"We had that last night," Roger quipped, but Mum had to reply.

"*Merda de piyon,*" she said. We knew what that meant. *Pigeon shit.* It's what she always said. So we' d shut up.

She was irreverent, but not sacrilegious. Whenever we got out of line she shouted out, "S*ac de frumento,*" literally, 'a bag of wheat,' to avoid the expression *Sacramento*—Sacrament, a term considered blasphemous. She had learned the innocent phrase as a child and used it on her own children to get her message across: Leave me alone! And we did.

Should anyone in the family sneeze around her, Mum always replied, "*Crepa bestia!*"—"Die beast!"

People spoke these words in the Old Country to scare away the devil, but sometimes the tone she used made me wonder if the phrase was directed at the sneezer rather than the devil.

Just Call Me Moose!

If someone in the family disagreed with her on any subject under discussion, she liked to raise her eyebrows, tilt her head and reply, "I beg to differ."

Although painful migraine headaches had plagued her for years, she rarely complained. Yet, her callous sons still dubbed her "The Martyr" or "The Warden," since she always kept close tabs on us.

Our mother laid down the law when it came to the bathroom. Her sons couldn't loiter in there: in and out, no books, no magazines, no reading allowed. Sometimes while sitting on the pot, I used to invent wild characters and make up adventure stories, then retell them out loud.

If Mum happened to hear me, she'd pause outside the door and repeated an old expression she had heard as a child.

"People who talk to themselves must have money in the bank!"

She harangued us to put the toilet seat down and like other wives and mothers, became exasperated with our proclivity for spraying the white ceramic pot and the floor while urinating.

Her axiom, "We aim to please, your aim will help," made the point over and over.

With three boys at the table and a stressful job, Pop had a low threshold for wisecracks. Donald showed a surly side at times; Roger usually played it safe and when I hogged the conversation, my mother called me a *chiacchierone*. She always told me I talked too much and when I tried to leave the spinach on my plate Pop acted like Popeye the Sailor Man. To make me eat, Mum kept repeating, *"Mangia! Mangia, tas."* Eating and being quiet wasn't easy for me, and Mum wanted me to stay fat.

Should a son step over the line, Pop began to move anything in his path—glasses of beer and milk, bottles, or a jar of pickled pigs feet. Then with his arm extended and a face made of stone, he silently began to take practice swings. Rarely did anyone get whacked; this massive show of force got our full attention. Sometimes Pop leaped to his feet without warning and frantically unbuckled his belt, stripping it violently from his pants, like Zorro drawing his sword. Every boy at the table stopped moving and we stared quietly into our plates. On the rare occasion when Pop lashed out with his hand, Mum would scream, "Open hand! Not in the head!"

At mealtimes, when I dawdled over my plate and blabbed about my day, her patience quickly wore thin. And if I didn't clean my plate, I felt pressure radiate from her. It never worked when I tried to hide a crust of bread behind my dish. Then my father made a point to tell me one of Grandma Rosa's old stories.

Pop said, "When I was growing up, my mother pushed me to eat by saying, 'If children didn't clean their plates, after they died, God lit each little finger so they could see the food they left behind.' Is that story scary enough for you?"

This family legend didn't help my expanding waistline. For dessert, my mother often made homemade angel cake, chocolate pudding or tapioca pudding, a dessert I ate to please my mother. Even with vanilla added this fish-egg-looking concoction tasted strange to me. No one ever told me that people used the same ground-up root of a poisonous, tropical plant to make glue.

My parents' families rarely broke bread together; it's impossible to recall these relatives ever being in the same house together. Pop's sisters and brother took cruises to Europe, attended symphony concerts and were interested in art. In contrast, my mother's siblings, for the most part, struggled to make a living.

In my house Pop took on the role of CEO, an overseer from on high, and Mum was in charge of Operations and Logistics, making sure our daily needs were met. My brothers acted like the silent partners, doing their own thing off to the side. Some kids grow up living a sheltered life constantly under their mother's thumb. That's how she made *me* feel.

VI

AFTER BREAKFAST ON SUNDAYS AND ON HOLY days
Mum shooed me out to the door for Catholic Mass. My parents
stayed home, but I didn't have a choice.

"Do as I say, not as I do," justified all things.

Most of my relatives only showed up at church during
weddings and funerals so it didn't seem unusual. St. Kevin's
Church occupied the renovated Telephone Exchange Building
on Columbia Road. Those attending Mass touched the font of
holy water in the foyer without thinking.

When I tapped my forehead to make the sign of the cross, I
remembered my priest's words, *In nomine Patris*—In the name
of the Father, *et Filii*—and of the Son, and *et Spiritus Sancti*—
and of the Holy Ghost. I touched my breastbone and my left
shoulder and my right shoulder; I had learned to end the Sign
by crossing my thumb over the index finger and then kissing my
thumb as a symbolic way of "kissing the Cross."

Women were obliged to cover their heads either with a veil,
scarf or a hat—a rigid practice, a sign of reverence and humility,
no longer required. The interior of St. Kevin's was light and
airy—unlike the somber shadows of St. Margaret's. Its blonde-
oak pews with padded kneelers and the modernistic altar
adorned with bright colors gave new meaning to an ancient
religion.

Just Call Me Moose!

The pageantry of the Latin Mass, the aroma of the incense, the soft tinkle of chimes, the beautiful organ music and the evocative sermons made me feel at peace with my world. The memories of the ephemeral sweet smells and soothing bells still linger in the deepest recesses of my mind. And who in the church could forget the powerful biblical epigraph on the wall next to the altar? It read, *I Am The Vine; You Are The Branches. Without Me You Can Do Nothing.* The words resonated with many parishioners long after Mass was over. And they stayed with me all my days.

Although Bishop Dalton was the pastor, a portly sort who drove around in a big black Chrysler Imperial, everyone seems to remember Father Joe Kierce best. In spite of an ascetic appearance to strangers, the lean, bespectacled priest was, in reality, a good-natured extrovert. All of us in reach of his effortless smile felt the serenity and comfort he bestowed during his long ministry. He touched everyone with a powerful yet gentle demeanor.

During Mass the priest at the altar says, *Dominus vobiscum*; the ancient Latin salutation means, May the Lord be with you. These words are repeated eight times before the collection baskets are passed. As ushers began to move the wicker baskets up and down the aisles, I recall one of my irreverent friends nudging me, grinning and whispering, "Dominec go frisk 'em." Being solemn during Mass was never easy for me.

When I heard the priest sing, *Ite, missa est*—Go, the Mass is ended, followed by *Deo Gratias*—Thanks be to God—the end of the services was imminent. By now the hard wooden bench had stolen all the feeling from my rear and thoughts of playing baseball whirled around in my head. Like a green traffic light, the final Latin phrases made it legal to break for the door, bless myself with holy water, and push through the heaving crowd until next week.

To prepare for the Sacrament of Holy Eucharist, Holy Communion, Catholic kids my age attended Sunday school in the church hall. Uncompromising nuns wielding wooden clappers drilled us from the Catechism in the tenants of Catholicism, the roadmap to our Faith. The walnut clappers they carried signaled us to kneel, be quiet, or line up. But sometimes a cantankerous sister brandished the heavy brick-shaped clappers to rap knuckles or heads should we fail to pay attention.

On the pleasant spring day I made my First Holy Communion at St. Kevin's, all the kids wore white from head to toe to show their innocence and purity before God. Instead of long pants, I wore shorts with knee socks, a long-sleeve shirt and a tie. The day before in the confessional booth I had recited the Act of Contrition that began, Bless me Father for I have sinned. Then I told the shadow behind the screen how many times I had impure thoughts, missed Mass or disobeyed my parents. The faceless priest in the dark booth absolved me and blessed me. My penance was to say 10 "Our Fathers" and 10 "Hail Marys," a fairly standard penance according to the other kids. Confession grants Catholics a way to wipe mortal sins, the worse kind, and the lesser venial sins, off the slate. It's quite a concept to be absolved for misdeeds. Yet, for some, the guilt may be difficult to shake.

On Sunday, after fasting overnight for communion, I approached the altar and knelt down, ready to receive the sacred host. Being an altar boy seemed too much like work, so I never sought that apprenticeship. I could never see myself wearing lace and red capes in front of all those parishioners. One by one each of us clasped our hands together and waited for the priest to glide by and perform the magic the nuns had prepared us to visualize. The priest carefully dipped a translucent wafer into the gold chalice holding consecrated red wine—the blood of Christ and the host was transformed into the body of Christ. I opened my mouth and closed my eyes and savored the delicate taste on my tongue before the wafer vanished in a puddle of saliva and dissolved in my mouth. After making the sign of the cross I rose to my feet feeling content and warm inside, knowing full well that should a car kill me on the way home I'd go straight to Heaven.

On every Ash Wednesday before Easter, the priest used his thumb to imprint Catholic foreheads with a smudge of blessed ashes. Traditionally, the ashes come from burning the palm fronds from the previous year's Palm Sunday celebration. Ashes are a biblical symbol of mourning and penance and death and so remind us of our mortality. Thus the priest says, "Remember, man, that thou art dust and unto dust thou shalt return." Most of my classmates displayed the same black dollop. And on the streets of my neighborhood, young and old alike had one.

But whenever Nonno saw the blotch on my brow, he'd grin and say, "You don't need-a go ta church for ashes. I got some in the cellar."

No one ever spoke or even hinted of child abuse at the hands of a priest in my neighborhood. Every cleric that ever crossed my path treated me with respect. And I looked up to them. Yet, other Boston children, unbeknownst to me and not so fortunate as I, surely suffered in silence for years. Without any doubt, my Faith and the priests of my youth gave me the strength to face my grief and go on after my father died.

BESIDES NOT GOING TO CHURCH, I never saw my parents sit through a movie together. My mother hated to go; I have no idea why. Once, and only once, Pop and I caught an early show at the Upham's Corner Theater on Columbia Road, a short walk from the house. By 1914, the old Winthrop Hall had become a moving picture and vaudeville theater, a place the locals called the Uppies Theater. The main feature that day was *The Man in the Iron Mask*, a black and white film first released in 1939. The male lead played two parts in the movie, King Louis XIV and the man who wore the iron mask. It seemed scary for a little kid, but it was fun to be alone with Pop.

For 11 cents anybody could see the Saturday summer matinee, and once we settled inside the pitch-black chamber, the damp, cool air felt good. Pop loved to eat licorice, Black Crows, little half-domes of candy. He bought a small box of popcorn and a cup of Coca-Cola for me. White-gloved, uniformed ushers carried small flashlights to escort us to our seats. The latest newsreel about the war came on first and then animated cartoons played; a second feature film filled the remaining time. In the early 1950s in the Uppies, my friends and I wore flimsy cardboard glasses with plastic lenses to watch 3-D movies, such as the horror film *The House of Wax* starring Vincent Price.

The more opulent Strand Theater, across the street, had another choice of movies to see. When it opened in 1918, vaudeville shows were in vogue. On many Saturday matinees in either theater, the feature films either frightened us or made us laugh. We related to the slapstick antics of *The Bowery Boys* with Leo Gorcey; every day some of my friends acted like them. And when Boris Karloff as Frankenstein first sat up, our screams drowned out the dialogue. Western movies starring Hopalong Cassidy, Gene Autrey and Roy Rogers thrilled us; they carried us to faraway plains where cowboys and Indians fought. And I tasted my tears watching the sad scenes of Lassie movies. Yet, all those war movies set in the Pacific and Europe had the greatest effect on me. I could never shake the memories of fanatical Japanese snipers hiding in those tall palm trees waiting to kill U.S. marines or deadly Nazi machine guns mowing down American GIs. I imagine that the seeds of my long military career took root as I watched those vivid scenes in the dark.

WE KIDS NEVER LACKED for other forms of entertainment. Situated close to the Atlantic Ocean, Dorchester offered residents a place to swim and lie on the sandy beaches during the warm weather. In the summer Mum enjoyed walking with me and other neighborhood kids in tow for a day at Carson Beach. Long before, Pop had stopped going to the beach; I never saw him in a bathing suit. As we neared Columbia Circle and the shoreline the cool, salty breezes surrounded us. Beneath the misty, seaside overcast my mother unfolded an old blanket and spread it on the brown sand for a place to lie down and soak up the rays of a veiled sun.

"Put your hat on. Let me put some Coppertone on your back. Don't go in the *watah* now. You just ate."

"Geeze, Mum. Can I go play?"

My mother used to recite a litany of do's and don'ts, tightly scripted phrases that I knew by heart. "Watch out for broken glass." "Don't run so fast." "Watch out for the jellyfish." "Don't get dirty."

At low tide, I would run around and stomp on the wet sands to see the clams squirt and then sit in the surf and build a sand castle until the rising tide pulled it apart. The dirty ocean water was always cold, and I had to keep from being stung by those icky, slimy jellyfish. Sometimes when the tide was coming in and the wind was right I watched dark turds from the raw sewage plant on Moon Island float nearby. And whenever a friend standing in the water close to me began to smile, the reason became clear after the water got warm.

One afternoon as Mum and I prepared to go back home, I asked her a question. "What's all that barbed wire doing over there?"

"Oh, that was a prisoner of war camp for Italian soldiers during the war."

"Were they better off here than in Italy?"

"Maybe so. ...Maybe so."

At home Mum hung the wet bathing suits on the clotheslines that straddled the piazza after a day at the beach. At snack time my mother whistled for me from the piazza. A distinctive sound, one high note and one low one, repeated quickly several times. It was her special coded signal and I could hear it far away.

"Come home, time for your Ovaltine," spoke silently to me.

Just Call Me Moose!

The makers of Ovaltine, a sweet chocolate milk drink, sponsored *Captain Midnight*, a favorite radio program of mine. At night after supper in the softly lit parlor, spread out on the carpet with my head on a pillow, I unscrambled secret messages with my decoder shield. Most of them said "Drink more Ovaltine." Surely the tactic increased sales of the beverage.

One bright, summer day on my piazza, it dawned on me that women possessed the power to stir male juices. Josephine Macchi, a neighbor's tall, shapely, and much older daughter, looked down at me from her piazza. Her hair was dark brown and long and her dark eyes teased mine.

"How do ya like these?"

She quickly hiked her skirt to mid-thigh and through the railings I could see her pretty legs. Legs that Josephine had painted a rich, cocoa brown to look like she wore silk stockings. My eyes locked onto hers, then slid down to the dimpled knees.

"Yeah! They, ahh...look nice. Um...gotta go in. My Mum's lookin' for me."

As I backed slowly away, I thought, *Wow, did you see that? No one at school's gonna believe it.*

My mother and Josephine's mother, Caroline, had been childhood friends. When I was a little boy Caroline delivered Charles, a mid-life, two and a half-pound baby boy after a term of only six and a half months.

"Your mother left her own chores every morning and came to bathe Charlie; my mother was too weak," Josephine told me many years later.

Charlie grew over six feet tall. My mother always spoke with pride about the time. It made her feel like a nurse.

In those days my cousin Nilda, a daughter of Zio Joe's, lived on the second floor across from us. She had a husband, Fred Rice, and two children, Mary Elizabeth, a tomboy, and Freddie Jr., still a little boy. Fred was a quiet guy who had served in the Merchant Marine and spent months at sea during the war so I can't remember him too well. Later, Frank Gandolfo, a dark-skinned Italian-American, wife Lena, and their kids lived in a flat on the first floor.

I must have been seven when Pop took me fishing on Jacobs Pond in Norwell. That trip was the first and last time we ever fished together. He took a picture of his chubby son holding up a few small yellow perch. Pop never could spare the time anymore, so neighbor Frank used to take me along to fish for flounders and eels in the ocean nearby. His short, wiry father used to twirl a thick line baited with sea worms over his head then let it fly far out into the surf. I tried my luck using a short rod and a small Penn reel but had little success. I still have memories of the sun peeking through the overcast, the slippery rocks, and the clean tang of the salt spray. After a morning of fishing, Frank's wife, Lena, a stout, happy woman, invited me in for a taste of homemade, Sicilian pizza pie. I usually ate more than my share of the thick crust coated with delicious oregano-flavored sauce.

WHEN I TURNED EIGHT, without any warning, an impulsive desire to create music overwhelmed me. I was a short, soft pudgy kid overcome with an urge to play the piano. I thought it might bring me attention and also please my father. After badgering my mother for days, she convinced Pop to buy me a piano. Brawny deliverymen from Ferdinand's, a large furniture store, near Dudley Station hauled the expensive, shiny walnut Gulbransen spinet up the front stairs and rolled it into the parlor. My mother already had a teacher in mind. Mum's hairdresser, Mrs. Lundberg, had a daughter who taught piano to aspiring child musicians.

Marie was a tall, married woman who wore glasses and rarely smiled. Maybe she fantasized that her new pupil might become a budding Chopin. It took me several years to prove her wrong. Every Saturday morning I carried my lesson books and the gray practice book next door to Marie's mother's house. A simple scarred piano stood against a wall in the front room.

Just Call Me Moose!

Near the end of my first day, my new teacher outlined the rules to me.

"You need to practice at least one hour every day. You shouldn't be disturbed. Use the metronome the way I showed you. Work on the lesson in your book and write down how long you practiced. And have your mother sign the book before you come here every week. Is that clear?"

"Yes, Marie."

The tinkle, tinkle of the high notes and the throbbing sounds of the bass ones as I slid my short pudgy fingers across the keys had captivated me. At first I diligently practiced using a preparatory booklet that contained pieces with Italian titles like *Vivace*—lively—and *Cantabile*—singable, all foreign to me. One of them, *Andante con moto*—at a walking pace with movement—sounded like a rich dessert. Later Marie assigned a music text with snappy-sounding English titles that I understood, like "Hop-o'-My Thumb" and "Dance of the Gnomes."

On the same day as my first communion, I pounded out "Three and Twenty Pirates," a short number my teacher selected. I managed to pull off my first recital in a hall with an audience, to the thundering applause of my teacher, my parents, and guests.

During the summer heat and winter cold of Boston days, Marie tried hard to kindle in me a love for music and the piano. But images of my friends playing baseball kept looming before me. In my practice book to entice me to work harder, she even wrote, "When you get an honor mark you have a reward waiting." Nothing she did worked; my practice sessions got shorter, and my performances showed it. Toward the end, nothing my piano teacher did could deter me. I'd had enough of piano lessons, but Mum wouldn't let me quit.

"You're not going out to play unless you practice first," she said.

It took four years of shilly-shallying in front of the keyboard to wear down my tenacious, yet discouraged teacher. When she finally had enough, she wished me well then said goodbye. My mother never forgave me for cutting and running and for the rest of her life she told me repeatedly, "I gave up a fur coat for your piano!"

After Marie moved on, Mum tucked away all my music textbooks and practice books in the piano bench, a time capsule only to be discovered after she died. A desire to make my parents proud didn't seem too important any more. Sitting and staring at a sheet of music and trying to make sense of all the notes had lost its appeal. And no more practicing on the piano was required after school. Freedom tasted sweet; I could spend more hours on the baseball diamond with friends. I had won the first big battles of my life. First I got a new piano and then *I* was the one who decided when to quit.

BOSTON HOSTED TWO MAJOR-LEAGUE teams, the American League Red Sox who played in Fenway Park, and the Boston Braves in the National League, who made Braves Field their home. At that time all three of the club owners were general contractors, and two of them, Guido Rugo, who grew up off Norfolk Avenue, and Louis Perini, came to Boston from Italy.

In Game Two of the 1948 World Series, when the Cleveland Indians came to town, I sat in the stands next to Pop. Warren Spahn pitching for the Braves and Bob Lemmon on the mound for the Indians sparred against each other; but the Indians prevailed and went on to win the series. A few times on a hard Fenway Park seat alongside Pop, I watched the Red Sox play. It was a classic era when Birdie Tebbets crouched behind the plate and caught Mel Parnell's pitches. Johnny Pesky and Bobby Doerr covered the infield, and Dom DiMaggio roamed center field. Out in left field, a tall, lanky player with number "9" on his back looked back toward home plate. No one ever said Ted Williams was a great fielder, but when he stood in the batter's box, few others surpassed him. Standing erect, he held the long wooden cylinder straight up and close to the shoulder. Just like me, he batted left and threw right. Keen eyesight, quick reflexes, and perfect timing made Williams the nemesis of American League pitchers for decades. Yet many Boston fans and some sportswriters had a love-hate relationship with the cranky legend who wanted only to keep hitting home runs.

BEFORE POP BROUGHT OUR FIRST TELEVISION, the Zenith console radio in the parlor broadcast programs with names like *Gangbusters*, *Sam Spade*, *Boston Blackie*, and *The Lone Ranger*. The common themes in all these programs stressed right over wrong, justice through strength and courage, concepts that Pop had advocated.

One program, *The Shadow*, began with: "Who knows what evil lurks in the hearts of men? The Shadow knows."

A show about a tough, hard-boiled, private eye, *The Fat Man*, opened, "He's walking into the drugstore. He's stepping onto the scales. Clink! Clink! Weight 237 pounds, Fortune: Danger! Who is it? The Faaat Maaan!"

Today, these programs would be considered corny, but then, a fantasy world greeted listeners; the realistic sound effects gave me goose bumps. Thunder and lightning, machine gunfire, sirens, and galloping horses all sounded real to a little kid lying on the floor in the dark.

In 1948, about the time WBZ-TV came on the air for the first time, my father brought our first television home. After Pop put the ubiquitous rabbit-ears antenna on top of the squat 12-inch Admiral floor model and turned on a program, he wanted his wife to see it. But my mother never left the kitchen; she had greeted this unwanted appliance with disdain. But Pop insisted and as we pulled and pushed, she crossed the parlor threshold.

Holding an arm over her eyes, Mum said, "I don't want it."

We shoved her down onto the sofa, pried her arm loose, but after a few minutes, she headed silently back to the kitchen.

Just Call Me Moose!

It didn't take her long to surrender and accept the new gadget. In our darkened parlor the family sat a few feet away from the flickering silvery black and white image. Live telecasts of *I Remember Mama*, a touching family series; Uncle Miltie's hilarious *Texaco Star Theater*, and the wonderful acts presented on *The Ed Sullivan Show,* seemed to help bring our family together. Tuning in to watch the puppets on *The Howdy Doody Show* became addictive to me. All children of that era remember Mister Bluster and Princess Summer-Fall-Winter-Spring. The time I spent watching the boob tube soon became an excuse for not doing my homework.

There was one show that I hungered to watch. During the 1950s Bishop Fulton Sheen had a weekly 30-minute television program called *Life is Worth Living.* A brilliant, charismatic Catholic priest, Bishop Sheen captivated millions of people of all religions with advice that everybody could understand. Viewers could trust what he had to say. And when the white-haired Bishop glided onto the stage and stared into the camera, his wide eyes almost hypnotized the viewers. The red cape he wore didn't show up in black and white; people didn't need a color picture to digest his profound views on secular and spiritual topics such as love, fear, communism, conscience, holiness, and good versus evil. His short, unambiguous parables kept me coming back for more.

VII

ON ONE OF MY SUMMER VACATIONS from school our family packed up and moved to a house next door. It was a surprise the day my mother broke the news.

"We're moving," she said.

"When?"

"Next month."

"Where?"

"Next door. Your father bought Zia Cecilia's house."

I was ten years old.

Our century-old residence sat on a large tract of land between East Cottage and Elder streets and had been the estate of the Holden family long before Boston swallowed up Dorchester.

During the late 1860s, the old estate covered several acres of farmland and records show that Edward Holden, the Dorchester Historical Society's first librarian, lived there. In 1869 the property was valued at $7,000 and a rear stable at $500, large sums for those days.

Before World War I began, my father's married sisters, Mary and Cecilia, purchased it from the remaining Holden siblings, moved in and divided it accordingly for both families. After Mary and Pop's father died, my father and Grandma Rosa lived there.

Just Call Me Moose!

Author's circa 1850 Dorchester home from 1949 to 1962.

The sprawling 28-room, cross-shaped clapboard house with elements of Greek Revival and Italianate styles first appeared on an 1850 map of Dorchester. Large rectangular slabs of thin, dark gray slate covered the sharply pitched roof. The front entrance faced east; its gable end looked out on the street. Each of the tall windows with shutters was capped with a formal, cornice-headed lintel. The rear of the house looked out on Elder Street, which dates from 1884, a year before Grandpa Romeo came to Boston.

Long before our move, the old Holden house had been converted into three separate living areas. We lived in the main area that faced the Boston Edison property. My parents rented out the two other quarters.

By the time we moved, Donald had already left Boston Technical and had finished his freshman year at Boston University. In a few months, Roger graduated from Public Latin School; he planned to attend Boston College. This brother loved to remind me about an earlier double promotion that wiped out one whole school year for him.

Both brothers had mastered the technique of ignoring the interloper, the baby of the family; I was much younger, so I can't fault them. Donald always appeared to act aloof, preoccupied with deep thoughts, as if the family cramped his style. With little to say around the house or during supper, I can't recall him playing much of a role in my day-to-day life. Whenever my exuberance peaked, Donald had little patience for his kid brother and often said, "You talk too much."

Conversely, Roger seemed to flit in and out of my life similar to a moth hovering at night around an open flame, never coming close enough to catch. Yet Roger never turned down my pleas for help with homework; it was an opportunity for him to prove that being studious, not doing pushups, had resulted in superior intelligence. As he looked over my shoulder with disdain, if I hesitated to grasp the sticky science problem before me, he'd say, "I'm tired of casting pearls before swine." And should I press for a solution to a thorny mathematics problem, Roger would roll his eyes and quip, "I've forgotten more than you'll ever learn."

When my parents bought the large house, Zia Cecilia, a widow, owned it. During the summer she lived in a home in Norwell with her daughter's family. Now it would be their full-time residence.

I can't remember our family ever doing things together inside or outside the home. And my mother slowly lost interest in going out on weekends and socializing with others. Like most women in the neighborhood her age, she didn't drive a car and never had a desire to get behind a wheel.

Mum balked when Pop suggested going to visit relatives, except for spending Easter and Thanksgiving with a sister and her family. Both brothers attended college in Boston and rarely joined in but I didn't have a choice. So whenever my parents visited relatives they dragged me along.

Just Call Me Moose!

On those holidays I can remember driving to Melrose with my parents and Nonno to break bread with Auntie Ines and her family. They had a small, attractive house and the street where they lived seemed deathly quiet in contrast with ours.

"You can hear a pin drop out here," my mother often said.

My high-strung, slender aunt typically dressed as an haute couture fashion model with a kitchen apron on whenever we came for dinner. Years later she shared with me how it felt to grow up in her family.

"I was sensitive, the one always caught in the middle of any argument." A feeling, I thought, she had rarely expressed to others and wanted me to know. She told me that she was a neighborhood gadfly, always on the go and the others in the family tagged her *La Gazzetta* because the latest gossip was on her lips. Auntie Ines never lost her touch for the old stories and came to share many of them with me.

Auntie Ines had pushed past 30 when she married, late in life for those days. Her husband, Louis Filadoro, an Italian-American with roots from the area near Naples, owned a popular pharmacy in Revere for many years with his brother. Uncle Louie reminded me of Errol Flynn and cut a debonair figure with his slim moustache and slow, articulate manner of speaking. Always eloquent, he took a long time to complete a sentence and carefully pronounced every word distinctly.

"Tell me—how—is—school—go—ing?" Are—you—get—ting —good—grades? Any—praw—blems?"

There was no place to run from the Chinese water torture of my uncle's probing interrogation. I had to sit still throughout the inquisition and answer all the questions completely and politely. I dreaded my mother criticizing me on the way home should my replies sound lackadaisical or abrupt.

This whimsical uncle of mine stepped forward after my father died, more so than the others, and spoke to me in a special way to give me strength and help me through those dark days. Other times I wondered if he was serious.

Just Call Me Moose!

One afternoon Uncle Louie told me an old story about *il malocchio*, "the evil eye," and the superstitions surrounding it. Italians from certain regions of the country still believe others can stare at them and they would be cursed. Newborn babies couldn't leave the house until after baptism. To scare away the evil spirits, a ritual using olive oil, water and prayers was used. In Nonno's words, it sounded like a bunch of monkey business.

Auntie Ines and Uncle Louie had only one child, Linda, a well-mannered, prim and proper little girl with dark-brown bangs, much younger than me. We never played together and I had little to say to her; most boys didn't mix with girls then. In the early afternoon, Auntie Ines served us bowls of minestrone soup or risotto. Then came plates filled with polenta, turkey, ham or eye of round roast beef. When dessert time arrived, if I filled my plate with pastries and a piece of pie, my mother chastised me in front of everyone.

"Your eyes are bigga' than your stomach."

At home my mother never found fault when I overindulged at the supper table; she always coaxed me to eat more, but I was a guest, albeit at a relative's house and my good manners trumped all. When the dishes had been cleared away, Mum left me with one final warning.

"Don't ever say 'I'm stuffed.' Say, 'I've had sufficient.'"

Later in the parlor, Uncle Louie and Nonno lit up their long cigars and the room filled with dense smoke. I took the opportunity to duck outside and catch a breath of fresh air.

Sometimes, on a nice Sunday, after a great deal of cajoling Pop managed to get Mum into the family's two-door black Chevy coupe and either head "down the country" to Norwell where his married sisters lived, or West Roxbury to visit his brother's family.

As we drove through Milton, I remember Pop pointing in the direction of a small piece of land.

"It's over there, through the trees," he said, as I craned my neck for a glimpse of the property we never took time to see. No words came from Mum's seat in front. Pop must have fantasized about building a new home using his own design someday. Maybe Pop believed he could eventually convince his wife to move to the suburbs, away from the old neighborhood and all her friends. He couldn't have been more wrong. I don't think my mother could bear the thought and so Pop eventually sold the piece of property and buried the dream.

Pop liked to drive along a hilly stretch of asphalt on old Route 3, the main road to Cape Cod. I remember him speeding along the stretch he called the "bumpy road" and at the crest of the hill lifting his foot off the accelerator. As the car flew over the roller coaster, my stomach seemed to float in the back seat. Then Pop yelled, "Whee," a rare display of joy, and I could see him grin at me in the rear-view mirror.

Norwell was a place unlike Dorchester. It abounded with all sorts of wildlife, such as chicken hawks, crows, foxes, rabbits, and deer. Dense wooded areas, New England stonewalls, lakes, and rivers crisscrossed the town, unlike my neighborhood in the city. In the woods my father showed me how to shoot my BB gun, a .22 rifle, and later shotguns. I learned that gray squirrels are very elusive creatures; they like to put a tree between themselves and any shooter. But when their curiosity overcame fear, sometimes they ended up in a red-wine stew on top of a plate of steaming golden polenta.

The two-story brick home of Zia Maurina and Zio Billie, far back off Main Street, would be our first stop. Before they left Dorchester for good, before their dog, Rex, ever snapped at me, my father had drawn the plans for their Norwell retirement home and helped during its construction. A short, portly woman with breasts the size of watermelons, my aunt always greeted us warmly at the door after the car rolled down the long gravel driveway and came to a stop. Zia Maurina liked to give me a big hug, a show of affection that rarely came from a relative. When we pulled up to visit, my aunt wore a tailored dress, nylon stockings and black laced-up pumps. A rudimentary hearing aid hung on her belt. Long twisted wires stretched to a heavy earpiece in her bad ear. If the volume wasn't set just right, I heard a high-pitched teeth-numbing screech that only stopped after she frantically turned the control knob.

"Listen ta me!...Listen ta me!" made the little ones in Zia Maurina's life pay attention.

Inside the heavy, wooden front door, the thick walls kept the rooms cool on warm summer days; the scent of orange peels smoldering on the kitchen stovetop permeated the air. High, rough stucco walls, dark rustic beams and a fireplace made of cut stone in the parlor gave the house a medieval feel. And the deep throbbing sounds of Westminster chimes coming from the old clock sounded spooky. Much of their furniture had an Old Country look; the parlor showed off several museum-quality leather chairs. Before the war Zia Maurina and Zio Billie often enjoyed taking cruises to Italy, but the stories they told never aroused my mother's desire to do the same.

Years later, I came to learn that my assertive Zia Maurina always got her way. In her youth, she was reputed to be the best-looking and shapeliest daughter in the family, and she knew it. After completing the eighth grade, she worked as a seamstress and made beautiful dresses and sewed sister Cecilia's and her own wedding gowns and the bridesmaid dresses.

Zio Billie, a tall elegant man, came from the Lake Como region of Italy. Before he married Maurina, Billie worked as a waiter at the Hotel Touraine, in Boston, then spent 25 years at the Copley Plaza in Copley Square. When Zio Billie retired in 1937 he held the position of a maitre d' of the hotel, the top dog, and the Oval Room was his domain. After management turned over, Billie couldn't cope with the changes. So, at 51 years old, he literally "threw in the towel." He couldn't compromise nor treat guests any differently, so he left.

Behind the Norwell house, Zio Billie had built a high-fenced chicken coop with a hutch to raise bunnies. He told me that at night, hungry foxes roamed close by looking for a free meal. Fresh eggs, chickens and rabbits, along with vegetables from the garden, made their meals special. A family member, who knew, said Zio Billie did most of the household chores. Zia Maurina sat and read the paper while Billie vacuumed the rugs then cooked the meal and later washed the dishes. Every year, as his wife got older, she got heavier and more rotund.

Zio Billie would say to her, "Now you're just right. Don't put on any more weight."

He repeated the phrase often, but his wife had already added a few more pounds. I must have acquired some of the same genes.

From years in the hospitality trade Zio Billie had acquired impeccable manners and a regal, gentle air. In another life he would resemble an Italian count. Never stuffy, yet reserved, he also had a light-hearted side. Sometimes around the table he'd reminisce about the times spent attending to many notable guests. Among them were Douglas Fairbanks Sr. and Mary Pickford, popular film stars of the time, Diamond Jim Brady, a notorious gambler, Enrico Caruso, the renowned Italian tenor, and Henry Ford, the penny-pinching auto magnate.

Zio Billie not only could cook, he served every meal prepared in his kitchen in a special way. With a white towel draped over one shoulder, he used a serving spoon and fork to deftly dole out ample portions of meat and vegetables to each place-setting. Then Billie filled each glass goblet with a vintage wine. At family dinners, no one said grace before a meal. Only the words *Buon appetito* echoed in the airy room. Guests came away with visions of eating in a five-star hotel dining room.

Before my parents decided to head back home, we often stopped to see Pop's other sister, Cecilia, who lived nearby. As we drove through the open wrought-iron gate that guarded the twisting driveway, an image of a storybook castle came into view. Zia Cecilia's home sat on a clearing, part of a large piece of pine-covered property close to the North River. The walls of the house consisted of round, washed river rocks and a large turret with a conical slate roof that rose from the nearby front door.

Just Call Me Moose!

The scene resembled a Norman castle and brought to mind the words of Pop's old fairy tale, "Rapunzel, Rapunzel, let down your golden hair."

Zia Cecilia's daughter Virginia, son-in-law Bill Gemelli, and granddaughter, Gail, a delicate, sensitive child, lived with her. Mother and daughter were two peas from the same pod, but Gail liked to stay on the sidelines. If the weather was nice and time allowed, I swam in the river at high tide after diving off the rocky bank into the frigid water or went boating in Bill's mahogany Chris-Craft speedboat. As we tore up the river through the choppy water toward the ocean, the wind picked up the sour odor of the marshes and slapped my face with the salty spray. But deep, dark waters made me fearful; a career at sea held little appeal for a boy fascinated with airplanes.

Zia Cecilia, a slender, stately woman, always dressed and acted quite formally around me. She stood and walked tall as if the bones in her spine had been welded together. Unlike Maurina, her earthy sister, Cecilia held tightly to her emotions; when something amused her, I sometimes saw a twinkle in her eyes as she held back a smile.

Her husband, Virginio, Virgini for short, a handsome self-made talented businessman, died when I was a baby. A native of Samarate, the birthplace of my father's parents, Virgini came to America when he was 19 years old and worked for a cement company. Later, he founded the Cambridge Cement Stone Company with his brother-in-law Paul who came from the same town in Italy. Zio Paul, a stocky man with a round face, had helped finance my father's MIT education. The company made stone and concrete building components and both Virgini and Paul accrued a small fortune over the years.

Late in the afternoon it was time to return to Dorchester. As daylight faded into night, I stretched out on the back seat and fell asleep as the car gently rolled along. The bright light from neighborhood streetlights and Pop's words, "We're home," pulled me awake.

94

Just Call Me Moose!

In the early 1920s, Grandpa Romeo built a large house for his son, Gene, and Gene's wife, Flora, on a hill in West Roxbury. It had two flats, one upstairs and one downstairs. I assume my grandparents planned to move there in their golden years. Zio Gene may have been the favorite son. Pop rarely mentioned his father's name and displayed only a photo of his mother in our house. Whenever we visited Zio Gene, Zia Flora and daughter, cousin Barbara, they always made us feel at home. My brothers and I always felt at ease with our lively, fun-loving uncle. A gregarious sort, his personality seemed a lot more upbeat than that of my introspective father.

Zio Gene and his wife, Zia Flora, shared the same last name; their fathers were brothers. Cousins often married in those days. Over the years their only daughter, cousin Barbara, passed on anecdotes about our Italian grandparents; some are described in this book. But Barbara never heard the Old Country stories that her parents told her; she was born deaf and had learned how to read lips, understand sign language and vocalize English words at a special school. An accomplished artist, blessed with a near-flawless memory, she absorbed many rich details of the early days of our family.

Of medium build and a tad taller than my father, Zio Gene, a gregarious and affable member of the family, never lacked for words. Unlike my father, Zio Gene swam freely in a sea of strangers; he liked to be around people, and loved to tell old stories and jokes—some racy even by today's standards. My uncle loved to hunt and fish; for many years he was very active in the Sharon Rod and Gun Club and held elective offices. Once at the club, he showed me how to fly cast. It looked so easy, but it had no lasting appeal for me and I never tried it again.

Zia Flora wore her brown hair in braids, carefully wrapped in a graceful crown. Her demeanor was even more enthusiastic than her spouse; she used to sing along with him as she played the piano in the parlor, something my parents never tried. Zia Flora's homemade, needlework sampler on the wall above the piano and its neatly sewn proverb, "*Music Is The Food Of Love. Play On,*" told me a lot.

In the kitchen, Zia Flora excelled as a baker. I'll always remember eating her hot banana bread smothered with butter just after it came out of the oven. My aunt was a tall woman with a large frame and very assertive for her day. One night in our parlor Pop had a few too many highballs and he started horsing around. All of a sudden something said at the table provoked him into lifting Zia Flora. He tried to carry her around but she was too heavy and they crashed to the floor. The liquor both had consumed made them break out laughing. That night Pop pulled a muscle in his back. When Zio Gene and Zia Flora got together, it was fun for me to watch. These relatives enjoyed each other and made others feel at ease.

Whenever cousin Barbara talked to me it was sometimes difficult to understand her speech and I felt uncomfortable. Usually one of her parents stepped-in to explain what Barbara had tried to tell me. I could never appreciate how hard it must be to pronounce words never heard, but Barbara had learned to converse with poise through the help of her loving and caring parents. She worked for many years in an upscale jewelry store in downtown Boston and handled herself with grace and dignity. Barbara helped many customers and made a strong contribution to the company.

To prepare for these visits to my relatives, I tried to craft careful answers in advance to their usual questions about my progress in school and my mundane routine at home so as to appear upbeat and positive about my life. A few common threads seemed to weave through all the obligatory afternoon sojourns with my relatives. I never had anyone my age to talk with; the adults talked about stuff of little interest to me, and the conversations in Italian kept me in the dark.

EXPLORING MY NEW HOME from its bowels to its head, the attic reaches, became a lark. The cellar, off the renovated kitchen, was cavernous compared to the one in our old flat next door. Overhead, a myriad of lead pipes supplied water to the dwellings above. Zia Cecilia had left a pool table in an area that later became my exercise room. Pop set up a workbench, renovated the washroom, and added a tile shower, put in a playroom and a *cantina*, a room for canned goods, liquor and frozen food.

In the attic, a spooky area, I was amazed to see old gas lines used to illuminate the old servants' quarters. Throughout our downstairs living areas, wide, picture-frame molding bordered the high ceilings. Many of the rooms flaunted exquisite parquet wood flooring, and floral or striped wallpaper covered most of the vintage plaster walls. Some of the doors had cut glass knobs—a detail I thought was unusual.

Lacquered knotty pine boards enclosed the small, upgraded kitchen and Pop added a green cushy bench and pedestal table with a top made of bright red Formica. Pop always used to say, "I like red no matter what color it is," a peculiar statement beyond my ability to grasp.

With the move, my mother got a new sink and a KitchenAid dishwasher, a futuristic device that secured my perpetual dispensation for doing the dishes. But as I grew older, Pop assigned me real chores and the huge lawns that circled the house became my responsibility. In the summer I cut them, first with a push mower, later with a gasoline-powered one. And Pop demonstrated, in great detail, how he wanted me to clip the long, thick hedge on the path to the front door. The property covered an entire block, so its sidewalks sprawled along two streets. In the winter when it snowed, I shoveled and sanded the pavement or scattered rock salt to melt the pervasive ice.

Long ago, the ornate gas chandelier in the spacious parlor had been converted to electricity. We used this great room for watching television and eating Sunday dinners. The white marble fireplace, sealed now, had delicate carvings of oak leaves on its face. One small full bathroom upstairs and a tiny powder room downstairs with a sink and toilet served the family.

Just Call Me Moose!

Inside the front door a magnificent mahogany staircase ascended to my bedroom. On the wall leading up the stairs, my father had mounted his school diplomas, framed behind glass. Pop had mounted a tiny brass knocker on my door engraved with my name. My new room was smaller than my old bedroom, but it was all mine; my brothers still shared one. One window faced the street and the other looked out on our old flat. When I left a light burning in my room, I'd hear Mum yell, "Do you own shares in the Edison Company?" After we moved, my parents bought a new bedroom set and gave me theirs, including the full-size bed. And Mum had Pop hang a large colored picture of the sacred bloody heart of Jesus over the headboard—a measure of insurance, I guess, to keep her baby safe.

In time, Pop strung a long bare wire, an antenna, from my bedroom window to the big garage complex that Grandpa built. When Pop was my age, a crystal set, just a primitive radio, allowed him to listen to programs. Now my turn had come. He bought me a tiny and rudimentary one so I could experience something different. At night, to tune in a radio broadcast I had to touch the slim cat whisker to the right spot on the tiny piece of crystal. In a few days I became impatient while straining to hear sounds in the heavens with a set of primitive brown Bakelite earphones.

With the old war movies still fresh in my mind, everything about military airplanes still fascinated me. After school and on weekends, I found time to build model planes in the cellar. Pop had shown me how to make these foot-long, balsa-wood-and-paper planes. A silver P-51, a yellow B-24, a blue F-4U, a silver F-80, and an olive drab P-40 with bared tiger-shark teeth, hung on a wire strung between my window frames. Lying on my bed I imagined these war birds on combat missions.

At the front gate next to the hulking granite posts stood a tall and broad horse chestnut tree too wide to reach around. For nearly one hundred years, the tree had guarded the entrance. The tree had witnessed an old neighborhood and new arrivals that came from foreign lands. If only this sentinel that never left its post could talk. In the fall when chestnuts started to burst from their prickly, green shells, neighborhood kids threw sticks to knock them to the ground. Only the biggest, hardest chestnuts passed the test. We punched a hole through the center, and stuffed a heavy piece of twine through it. Each kid took a turn whacking another kid's chestnut. It took several solid raps to damage another chestnut and a lucky hit to break it. When that happened, someone yelled, "That was wicked."

Another game involved throwing the baseball cards that came with a sheet of bubble gum against a wall, a version of pitching pennies. After taping our card for extra weight, the closest card won.

With the Red Ryder BB gun Pop bought for me, I'd take pot shots at the pigeons in the yard and those sitting on the eaves of our roof. I'd stalk the dirty birds and pelt them with a BB, then watch them scatter. One lazy summer afternoon I broke a gaslight on Elder Street. After poking the barrel of my BB gun, by then a pump action with more power, out the cellar door, I took aim at the large glass streetlight. My imagination made it appear to be a buffalo on the Great Plains. The splat sounds of two or three shots hitting the globe broke the stillness of the street. Looking closer, I made out quarter-size dimples in the glass. In a few days two men pulled up in a city truck; I strained to hear what they said. As they replaced the globe, one muttered, pointing my way, "Looks like the shots came from this house." Fortunately, my dumb deed went unpunished; I never dared to shoot at another streetlight in the guise of a buffalo.

To go off alone to fish, just as Huck Finn used to do, is every boy's dream. After getting permission, I decided to show my mother that her baby could do something besides eat and sleep. I enjoyed riding an old Schwinn bike that my brothers had passed on to me. After tying my rod on the bike and putting tackle and bait in the basket, I pedaled the few miles to the mouth of the Neponset River in the shadow of the old Drive-In

Just Call Me Moose!

Theater. About the only thing I ever caught at high tide was freshwater eels, *anguille*. Long, black and very slippery, they lived in the brackish river and usually swallowed my sea-worm-baited hook. Pickled eels, an Old Country delicacy, were sold from small wooden barrels in neighborhood Italian grocery stores or *cooperativas*. But I was determined to catch my own.

Three feet or more of squirming eels can put up a good fight for a boy out to please his mother. And they always wrapped themselves around an ankle when I tried to retrieve my hook. At home after Mum chopped off the head, I'd hold it with a rag so she could peel off the skin in one piece. After cleaning and cutting them into chunks, she floured and fried the eels, then pickled them in vinegar. Her sons passed when offered a morsel of the snake-like, bony fish. But the smile on Mum's face as she ate my catch made it all worthwhile.

VIII

ON A WEEKEND DAY IN JUNE, North Korean soldiers blasted their way through the south in a vicious attack that took the world by surprise. Downstairs across from Mutrie's Trucking yard, the headlines of all the Boston newspapers stacked neatly in Julia's Variety Store screamed war. *Oh, boy,* I thought, *this looks bad.* Many people didn't even know where Korea lay on the map. But, President Truman understood the consequences and didn't hesitate to act. I had already witnessed one horrible war unfold in the Saturday matinee newsreels and it taught me that blatant aggression must be met head-on.

Julia and her stressed-out spouse, Werther, Walter to everyone, once a prizefighter in Italy, owned the old store and lived in a small flat behind it, just as Zia Maurina and Zio Billie once had. Julia's sister, Angie, also ran a business in the North End called the Café Roma. Angie lived in a flat up the street. Everyone raved about her delicious rum cakes and sweet *cannoli* pastries, filled with sweetened ricotta cheese. One day after school I started a fire in her yard using my clothespin match gun, but luckily it didn't spread. Fire fascinated me, so being comfortable around bombs and bullets as an adult must have started at an early age.

A petite, bespectacled, feisty woman of Italian descent, Julia (Marmai) Arcelli ran the store with an iron hand. Julie insisted that neighborhood kids not hang out in the tiny, venerable landmark with its high, metal-clad ceilings and well-worn terrazzo floor. But when kids played the flashing pinball machine she made an exception to the rule.

For decades, Julia's store had been a convenient place to buy eggs, milk, cold cuts, newspapers, ice cream, and carbonated sodas that we called tonic. Sold only in bottles, drinks like Coca-Cola, Royal Crown Cola, Seven-Up and Moxie, an odd-flavored, New England soft drink were available. Anyone who ever tasted Moxie never forgot its medicinal taste. Eating a Hoodsie, a small cup of ice cream that came with a flat wooden spoon, was a special treat for kids. After ripping off the lid to see a picture of someone famous, I virtually inhaled the ice cream swirls of creamy chocolate and vanilla.

Behind the counter, little Julia stood tall in a soiled white apron, with her legs apart and her hands on her hips. The spunky, gray-haired owner had a favorite expression.

"Just because there's snow on the roof doesn't mean there's no fire in the basement!" *Had Julia begun to feel the onslaught of old age?*

While she helped customers, her volatile, wiry husband made "spuckies" with fresh, crusty French bread. Walter slid from the cold cuts cooler to the counter top in a worn, stretched sleeveless T-shirt and brown, baggy pants.

"Mannaggia l'America! Mannaggia l'America!" chanted Walter as he sliced the salami.

In simple terms, the expression reflected his deep sense of frustration with the American way of life. Around home, Walter liked to sprinkle the phrase over every spuckie he made.

When things got slow, this guy with thinning hair, eyebrow facial scars and a flattened nose shadowboxed behind the counter while he lamented the injury that ruined his welterweight boxing career. Walter made wonderful sandwiches for 25 cents each and he turned out many of them for me.

"Hey, Walter, make me a spuckie with provolone cheese. Genoa salami or mortadella, I don't care."

Just Call Me Moose!

"*Mostardo*–mustard–, *Karlin*?"

"Yes, please, and a pickle. I don't need a drink."

IN THE EARLY 1950's, MY FATHER'S COMPANY had the lowest bid and was selected to build a wholesale food terminal, a meatpacking plant, on filled-in land in the South End. After school one day, he took me along. After parking the car next to the shack that housed the office, we got out and started to walk around.

As we paused near some men working, I looked at my father and said, "Why are there so many holes?"

Looking across the bustling job site, Pop put his hand on my shoulder.

"I'll keep it simple. So the building won't sink, we have to drill holes and fill them with concrete."

Concrete shafts, laced with reinforced steel cages, had to penetrate far into the peat sub base; these pilings were designed to keep the structure from sinking. We wandered toward the ongoing activity and as I peered into one dank, dark hole my nostrils stung from the foul smell of rotten eggs. It almost made me sick. The "muckers," black men who were the only ones who would work in these narrow fetid holes, lowered themselves into the steel-shelled shafts. Other immigrants like the Irish, then the Italians, had once worked in holes like these. A mucker's job involved enlarging the bottom of the shaft, then scooping up the muck into a bucket. When it was full he tugged on the rope and his partner hoisted the slimy smelly contents to the surface and emptied it.

My brief tour of the site came to an end. As we walked away and got back in the car, Pop smiled and said, "Better study *hahd* in school, son. Or do you want to be a *muckah*?"

After watching those workers in the shafts, to further encourage academic diligence, Pop often chided, "If you don't succeed in life you may end up selling fruit from a pushcart."

Other than veiled threats, I guess Pop didn't have the necessary verbal skills to encourage excellence in me.

As the president and treasurer of his company, and later treasurer of the Associated General Contractors of Boston, my father became totally wrapped up in the construction business. Whenever Pop helped me with my homework, especially math and science, it looked easy.

"Remember. I told your brothers the same thing. Math is the key."

We all took his advice and majored in math in college, but our careers took different paths.

Construction jobs are dangerous places, I discovered early on. While on summer vacation from grammar school, Pop brought me to a high school project in the suburbs. It was a cool day and I wore a long-sleeve football jersey, dungarees, and a pair of flimsy tennis shoes.

As the water boy, my job couldn't be simpler. Fill several stainless steel containers with water, add a little ice and place them around the site. Dispensers holding salt tablets hung on each water jug and I kept them full. Pop paid me twenty-five cents an hour and soon I began to get a feel for my father's business. Amidst the stacks of lumber and metal scaffolds, the workers eyed me with caution. Word had circulated quickly that the new kid was the boss's son. Some of these rough-looking denizens of the building trade, all union men, had mastered how to work just hard enough to stay employed. One of them told me, "Don't kill yourself. Work smart, kid."

In spite of Pop's admonition, "To watch where I walked," I stepped on a large rusty nail and drove it deeply into my arch. It didn't hurt when I pulled it out, but someone drove me to a nearby hospital for a tetanus shot. After that blunder, I always wore a pair of thick-soled, leather boots and observed where I put my feet.

While on my rounds, I heard someone say, "Here comes the General!" The first time a nearby laborer repeated the phrase I wondered what it meant. Vito, a gentle burly brute with Italian roots, a man with biceps the size of my neck and a physique I wanted to match, had stopped shoveling then alerted those around him.

"Who's that?" I asked.

"Your father's comin'."

Whenever Romey appeared on a job site to check on its progress, the men who recognized him warned the others. Knowing my father never served in the military, I mentioned it later to him.

"Oh yeah, I don't know who started it. I'm no general, but it's good to keep them guessing."

"JUST A DAUB," MY MOTHER'S FAVORITE suppertime phrase, helped keep the local belt stores in business as my waistline continued to ratchet up. When Pop took me along on a short Sunday drive to Neponset to let me smell the Puritan Doughnuts and watch them meander along the conveyor, my addiction to sweets swelled. It wasn't unusual for me to wash down half a dozen hot jelly-filled doughnuts with a big glass of milk. Mum never restrained my gluttony at the table.

The summer that Pop took me to New Hampshire to Benson's Wild Animal Farm I looked like a small blimp. In the gift shop, a brightly painted, spiked Indian war club made from the root of a small tree caught my eye. Pop got it for me and the club hung on my bedroom wall for years. A new 36-inch bright beaded belt for my pants came home, too.

After seeing Pop's pictures shot during our first and last vacation together I made up my mind to go on a diet. The onslaught of puberty added to the negative feelings I felt about my paunchy persona. I didn't like being a fatso or called one so I decided to emulate Charles Atlas, the muscle man in my comic books. The simple drawings of Atlas, once a skinny weakling on a beach blanket reminded me of my bony brother, Roger. Bullies loved to torment the kid in the comics and kick sand in his face. So, I began a routine of physical conditioning and soon the chubby kid became a muscular boy.

So that summer, through a self-paced program of diet and exercise, twenty-five pounds of adolescent blubber melted away. No more desserts or doughnuts for me; doing pushups and sit-ups burned off the excess calories. At suppertime, as I kept getting thinner, my mother tried to convince me I was starving to death in a concentration camp. Although she kept ranting about my dwindling waistline, it just emboldened me. Mum's words, "Just a daub," had lost the charm it once had. My mother's chunky son had no intention of staying chubby. And Pop just winked at me across the table; I felt, for once, that he understood.

ON A SUMMER VACATION, MY MOTHER took her lean son to New York City to pickup Nonno who was returning from a vacation in Europe. I heard that before Nonno left on his trip, he bought a cheap wedding ring at Woolworth's. When my mother asked him about the ring, he replied, "I don't *wanna* no woman *ta botha* me on the boat."

My mother and I stayed at the Hotel Commodore on East 42nd Street next to Grand Central Station. The 26-floor hotel had been around since 1913. It was Nonno's first trip to Switzerland in more than 40 years. Before the ship arrived, Mum wanted to see the Empire State Building and we rode the elevator to the observation platform. As I walked around looking out over the city, with the wind blowing through my hair, I imagined girders sliding into place and steelworkers slinging hot rivets to hold them together. I could appreciate the tremendous effort required to build it. Designed during the boom of the Twenties, it opened to little fanfare in the bust of the Thirties.

"Mum, I'd like to build a skyscraper like this."

"Why not? Your Pop could."

Just Call Me Moose!

It would be the only trip Nonno ever took to the Old Country. Letizia, his oldest sister was still alive, and Nonno stayed with her. After a day or so, Nonno noticed that his sibling used low-wattage bulbs in all the lamps. So, he bought a brighter bulb to read the paper and also replaced the others. At night when he left his chair to go to bed, his sister replaced the new bulbs with hers. I'll bet she was glad to see Nonno go back to America.

In New York, Nonno embarked from the S.S. *America*, a luxury liner built in 1939: a sea-going behemoth that carried troops to Europe during the war. I imagine that Nonno was proud of his accomplishments in America and to sail on a ship with that name had to make him feel special.

As Nonno moved down the gangplank he spotted us and waived. He had a big smile on his face. He told us later that he had tipped the porter for helping him on the long voyage. Nonno had a reputation for watching his money so I wasn't surprised when he said, "I gave-a-him a dollar."

Nonno brought back a present for me, a Swiss army knife. Red with a Swiss flag on the side, a corkscrew, and several sharp blades inside, my friends at school had never seen a knife like that one.

Most times when I walked over to Nonno's house a squat glass of wine and a few hard crescent-shaped *biscotti*—twice baked anisette-flavored cookies—sat next to him.

He used to say, "You wanna musty?" Only Nonno spoke the phrase—a name he had coined for a little red wine and ginger ale. After great-grandchildren came into his life, he changed it to "juice."

After cataract surgery, Nonno wore glasses with thick, Coke-bottle-lenses. They made his eyes look eerie and magnified. His idea of dental hygiene consisted of a swig of homemade grappa, swishing it around, and then using a toothpick to dislodge food stuck between the teeth. No dentist for this man, problem teeth were pulled using pliers. The Italian version of "white lightning," grappa is distilled from the leftover skins and pulp of grapes used in making wine. To test a new batch, Nonno took a spoonful and lit it with a match. If it burned with a blue flame it contained more alcohol so he'd smile and say, "*questo è buono.*"—"this is good."

At home Nonno spread the Boston Herald out on the kitchen table and scanned it for local and national news, muttering to himself when he took exception to the issues. Should some political tidbit catch his eye, he said, "It's a bunch of monkey business! Big *shocks*, they're all *crooketed*!

When Nonno crossed one muscular forearm with the other, I knew that those politicians in print had just received a "Swiss-Italian salute." The distinct gesture was usually accompanied with a word I never understood.

"*Vigliaccos!*" I came to learn that the term described the lowest of scoundrels. Nonno's tirades, his attacks on our "hallowed" institutions, came frequently. It took me many years to relate to his cynicism about the dirty tricks people play in business and politics.

A few times I remember Nonno asking me to stay for supper and having to call home for permission. In his dimly lit, stuffy kitchen, a thin steak and fries, chunky slices of potatoes in olive oil and garlic cloves, simmered on the stove. As I held the smooth wooden handles of the cutlery, I could imagine his family eating around the scarred table.

After breaking off a piece of Italian bread and sopping up the meat juices on the plate, Nonno sipped some wine. Olive oil and wine vinegar drenched a salad made with bitter dandelion greens—*cicoria*—picked in a local field and homegrown tomatoes. Later, he shared some Swiss cheese and a piece of apple carefully peeled with a small sharp knife. It was a special treat to share a meal alone with Nonno even though few words were ever spoken.

Sports and exercise began to take on a special meaning as adolescence approached. For two summers before high school began, my parents decided to send me to camp in New Hampshire. I didn't know what an adventure it would be.

Just Call Me Moose!

Thinking about going away made me anxious; *I didn't know a soul; what would it be like? Would I be accepted? Make friends? Like the food? What about snakes and bugs? Would I be homesick? Was I tough enough to succeed?* I had never been away from home; sleepovers with friends never took place. Besides, even if they had, I'm convinced that my mother would never have approved.

On the sandy shores of Kingston Lake, hidden away in the tall, dark green pines, is the magical kingdom known to me as Camp Lincoln. Just for boys, only an hour or so drive from home, the sponsor was the Young Men's Christian Association or YMCA. Kids could spend the summer there and learn all about the outdoors, swimming, boating, and above all, themselves. The devoted staff organized a full range of sports and crafts activities for the pre-teen campers. When my parents first sent me there for a large part of two summers, I was twelve.

One Saturday in July, with Pop driving, Mum in the front seat, and me in the back, we headed north on Route 1 to the New Hampshire border, then on to Kingston, down a dirt road to the turn-off to the camp. The tall pine trees filtered the sunlight that splashed over the cleared areas of the camp. The campgrounds were covered with layers of pine needles shed over many seasons. The strong smell of pine permeated the air as we stepped from the car. The director appeared and introduced himself and we met some of the staff who happened to be walking by. After registration, an escort pointed out the dining hall, the nurse's office, our tiny wooden cabins, and the ball field and horseshoe courts.

"What's that long building over there," I inquired. "Oh, that's the Palace," our escort replied with a chuckle.

"The Palace?"

"Yeah. That's what we call our bathroom. You know, where all the campers get to sit on the thrones." My parents glanced at each other; Mum shrugged her shoulders, and Pop grinned sheepishly at her.

Just Call Me Moose!

We ambled along to the sandy shoreline where the canoes, sailboats, and a raft with a diving board, held up by floating metal drums, were moored.

"Wow!" I told our guide, "That's some lake; looks like the ocean to me. Do you ever get big waves?"

He laughed, "Oh, you'll get used to it in no time. Everybody does."

When it was time for my parents to leave I hugged them and said goodbye. So far, it looked like camp might be fun. I didn't realize it at the time but Camp Lincoln possessed some of the attributes of a military camp. The log flagpole where our flag waved, reveille in the morning, taps at night, and teamwork in between, gave me a sneak preview of the structured life in the Air Force that awaited me.

Each primitive wooden cabin housed about six boys of various sizes and shapes. Every morning after reveille sounded we stood to pay respect to the flag and made our bunks, a task I managed to avoid at home. At night the flag came down and later after I heard the mournful sound of taps I fell asleep. For the first time in my life I imagined being somewhere in the military on foreign soil.

The chow hall served us pretty decent grub, especially the hamburgers, fries and hot dogs, except for the time all the kids got sick. One night after midnight I woke up with stomach cramps. As I stumbled across the cabin floor and fumbled to open the screen door I could tell that I wasn't alone. The round floodlight above the door of the Palace bathed the open clearing in light. It revealed a line of campers arching into the shadows, hopping frantically from one foot to another. Most of us had diarrhea, and not enough thrones were available. A few kids had to scramble into the woods to do their business.

One kid in my cabin demonstrated, to our delight, how to "short-sheet" a fellow camper's bed. By folding the bottom sheet in half and tucking it in, no one could stretch out. And once or twice we soaked the hand of a napping boy in warm water to watch him pee. In spite of the tight smile on their faces, we couldn't tell if it worked. On many nice days, we hiked, played softball, ran track races, went canoeing or sailing.

The counselor who taught us swimming was a tan, fit young man. Johnny Sangermano knew how to handle kids and patiently sharpened our swimming and diving skills. A raft just offshore buoyed up with barrels had a springy diving board attached. Johnny showed us how to do various front and back dives and demonstrated swimming strokes with names like butterfly and scissors, until we got them right. Most of us progressed from Minnow to the more advanced Flying Fish level in the YMCA program and earned patches along the way. He also taught us how to sail so campers could eventually pair-up in the small camp sailboat and cruise safely near the shore.

At night, another counselor brought Indian lore to life and regaled us around the crackling campfire with secret stories of the early Native Americans. In the firelight we kids sang many songs that were new to me.

One began, "If I get to heaven before you do, I'll bore a hole and pull you through."

But, I don't believe that kids nowadays would be encouraged to sing the old minstrel classic that began: "In the evening by the moonlight you could hear those darkies singing."

Our pure soprano voices melded with the sweet incense from the burning pine. The spirited songs we sang drifted off into the cool night air and gently serenaded the wildlife deep in the forest. My favorite camp song included verses like: "Oh, we love to swim and we love to play, and someday I know we'll be back here again. For it's Camp, Camp, Camp Lincoln, Lincoln, Camp, Camp...." It went on and on. The song represented the essence of my camp experiences and I'm sure many of the other boys feel the same.

Camp counselors taught us about crafts and how to punch designs into leather belts and wallets; one time I made an Indian war bonnet that looked authentic. None of the other boys had one like mine. I never told Mum about making my bed in a military manner; my personal maid at home might have gone on strike. Although the names of my campmates have slipped away, Camp Lincoln showed me the importance of self-reliance and what makes an organization work.

WHENEVER THE PEOPLE AROUND ME conversed in Italian, I couldn't participate. No one ever encouraged me to learn the language; my parents used Italian as a secret code for conversations I had no need to know. When relatives were around, a cacophony of Italian and English sentences filled the air. Only Italian was spoken when local gossip or off-color subjects were broached, I suppose to keep me in a suspended state of childhood innocence.

My brothers, Donald and Roger had the luxury of knowing three grandparents who talked to them in Italian. So, they picked-up the gist of the language, but when I could carry on a conversation, only two of my grandparents were living. Grandma Rosa lived in a rest home and Nonno spoke only broken English to me.

Grandma had lived alone after my father married and then moved in with Zio Gene and his family. Later, when I visited my frail grandmother at a Jamaica Plain Rest Home, Grandma's cheeks were shiny and rosy with blue, spider-web-thin veins. She coiled her white hair in a bun on top of her head. Grandma always wore the same shiny, navy dress with white polka dots, silk stockings, and laced-up, black leather shoes. A strong odor of camphor floated in the air when I leaned over to kiss her. Now close to her ninth decade, she'd greet me in a trembling voice.

"Karlin, come sta?" "Little Karl, how are you?"

The day Grandma died I bumped into Pop in the yard on my way to the corner store. Tears showed in his eyes and he patted them with a handkerchief. I had never before seen him cry.

"Grandma's gone," he said, as he walked by.

His words caught me by surprise, the first time for me that anyone in my family had died. Mum explained that a funeral for

Grandma was being planned and I understood why Pop had cried. When my tears flowed publicly for my father, I wasn't ashamed because he had taught me how to grieve.

THAT FALL INSIDE ST. KEVIN'S CHURCH, Archbishop Cushing confirmed a leaner, fitter boy. He anointed my forehead with holy chrism; I received the gift of the Holy Spirit during the sacrament of Confirmation. Michael was the name I chose for my confirmation name, not for any particular reason; I just liked the manly sound it has. St Michael is the special patron saint of Christian soldiers and someday I would be wearing a military uniform. At the end of the ceremony, my lips brushed across Archbishop Cushing's ring. When I was a young Air Force officer, he celebrated Mass at the funeral of my fallen Commander-in-Chief, President John F. Kennedy.

My parents' wedding anniversary coincided with the church event. So, to celebrate me becoming a soldier of Christ and their special day, my parents took me to see my first play, the Broadway musical *Oklahoma* at the Shubert Theater. We thoroughly enjoyed the foot-stomping performance, the only time we ever spent together at a play. The weight of my confirmation and my parents' anniversary had been enough to get Mum out of the house.

As the end of grammar school approached, my insatiable need to be acknowledged, backfired. The problem began after the final bell rang and we kids headed home. With notebook and schoolbooks tucked under my arm, and three other classmates tagging along, I walked close to the curb kicking the rocks in my way. One kid muttered out loud, "Why do we have so many stupid rules?" Just then our stealthy Vice Principal, Mr. McDonnell, drove past. Without thinking, I extended my arm and exposed my middle finger. In the car's rearview mirror his empty eyes stared back at me.

"You're gonna get in trouble," a classmate sang.

"Geeze, I hope he didn't see me," I said.

That night in bed I prayed for God to give Mr. McDonnell a touch of amnesia. But the next morning before the bell, the tall, slender Vice Principal approached the line of kids.

"Did any of you see what happened?"

Every one of my cohorts said, "No," shrugging their shoulders.

Then turning quickly to me he said, "Follow me!" His upstairs office was empty and cold.

"I saw you give me the finger. What do you have to say?"

"I'm sorry, sir. It won't happen again."

As I spoke he took off his suit jacket, loosened his tie then rolled up his sleeves. After opening the closet door, he yanked the brass chain on the hanging bulb and time stood still.

Several bent rattan sticks stood soaking in a cheap glass vase; he selected a stout one and wiped it clean then stood aside to test it. The swishing sound gave me chills.

"Put out your hand. This'll teach you a lesson."

As the stick came down, I held my breath. After three careful whacks, he stopped; my palm stung then throbbed. Squeezing my hand under my arm seemed to help.

"Now go downstairs!"

In class, after wiping away my tears, I proudly displayed the red welts on my hand. My homeroom teacher shook her head up and down.

One boy blurted, "Look, Karl just got the *rat hand*." It was our way of saying, "rattan."

To his credit the Vice Principal never told my parents about my naughty finger. Use of the rod to discipline wayward students, a practice passed down from Puritan times, rarely occurred at my school. But on that day it worked for me.

IX

A HIGH SCHOOL BUDDY OF MINE had a pet saying that some may consider offensive today. But Joe intended no harm.

"If you can't get a date, get a Latin boy."

Just as my brother Roger, many gifted boys from Public Latin School carried their books in a forest green school bag over their shoulder; Joe thought it made them look fruity. Latin boys had a reputation for intellectual superiority and some of them displayed sensitive characteristics. Many of them lacked a mechanical aptitude. Most Tech boys came from an earthier environment and so, a fruity look didn't appeal to them.

Since 1893, thousands of boys had attended classes at the all-boys Boston Technical High. Before my turn came, when Pop went there, it was called Mechanic Arts High School. In Donald's days, it was known as Boston Tech, the school colors, buff and blue, were the same. No other academic institution in the city had a distinctive Florentine tower like mine even though it served as an abode for dozens of pigeons. Years later on a trip to Florence, Italy, the old bell tower in the *Palazzo Vecchio* brought back high school memories, but long before, Boston Tech had been razed to build the Prudential Center.

Just Call Me Moose!

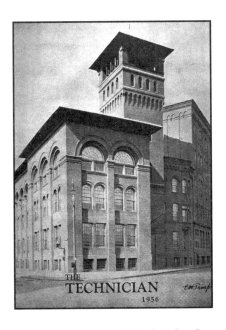

Boston Technical High School
Corner of Dalton and Belvidere Streets.

My father and Donald had told me stories about Boston Tech and their teachers around the supper table so I knew what lay in store for me. When I started classes, everything involving the curriculum, teachers and classmates seemed to be going my way. Getting along with my teachers and classmates came easily and whatever challenges awaited me, I welcomed.

About 60 strong, all our teachers were men. A few had Ph.D. degrees like the thin on top, bespectacled Doc Hasenfus, a connoisseur of the English language, and the bushy eye-browed Doc Moore, a historian with a penchant for getting off the track. Along with regular subjects, such as math and English, we immersed ourselves in the wonders of physics, chemistry, and mechanical drawing. A Tech education was special and the hands-on training in the woodworking, machine, pattern-making, and forge shops broke up the monotony of classroom lectures.

Just Call Me Moose!

As a slim and fit freshman, the result of my self-initiated weight lifting program, I began my new journey. All students had to wear leather shoes, slacks, a shirt and a tie to classes. Sneakers were forbidden. That year, a retired General Eisenhower moved into the White House. Ike's sacred promise to bring peace to the Korean peninsula had resonated with voters. The American people were tired of this professed police action, and wanted to bring the troops home, a theme that would resonate during the Vietnam War.

My parents considered school to be my full-time job; no chores awaited me after classes unlike many of my friends. During summer vacations, Pop lined up a few short-term paying chores for me to show me that "money doesn't grow on trees." I received a small allowance for mowing the huge lawns on weekends and shoveling our extended sidewalks in the winter. Mum's dishwasher did the dirty dishes; she continued to make my bed and do my laundry.

"You take me for granted," my mother had a habit of saying. Funny, during my married life those same words echoed in my ears.

The kids that I chose to hang around were still too young to date and most parents I knew felt a little leery about mixing genders. After school, we put on a comfortable shirt, a pair of "dungies" and a pair of canvas Keds sneakers. I wore a two-inch-wide black leather belt with the buckle facing sideways. Sometimes I wore blue suede loafers, pinstriped pegged pants and a thin rust-colored belt. My V-neck shirt had round shoestrings crossing the opening. With a suit, I liked to wear a Kentucky Colonel string tie like the old gamblers in cowboy movies. All my friends wore their hair short.

WHEN MR. GABLE, our coarse woodworking teacher first stood before us in his long stained smock, we had no doubt who was in charge. His initial lecture to the freshman always began,

Just Call Me Moose!

"I don't think you birds are gonna like it here. Whoever wants to should transfer out now!"

A voice that boomed to the outermost amphitheater seats, along with his prison warden demeanor, intimidated even the most hard-boiled kid amongst us. Inside the large shop the smell of sawdust and hard wood tweaked our nostrils. Every boy had an assigned workbench with a vise and several drawers full of hand tools, including razor sharp chisels and wood clamps that made it possible to complete the assigned projects. The class time flew by as we struggled to precisely measure and cut different wood joints with foreign names like mortise and tenon, rabbet, and end lap. "Good job," Mr. Gable sometimes said while stamping a boy's work with a unique number to discourage cheating.

At Tech, the basics of shaping hard wood and cold steel, including how to work safely around power tools took part of each day. The humming leather belts arcing from floor to ceiling drove the lathes in the metal and pattern-making shops. Our ties had to be tucked into our shirts before class to keep them out of harm's way. The micrometers we handled could measure the metal turned on our lathes down to a gnat's ass. For the fun of it, in our yearbook, my class left the pattern-making instructor, a year's supply of Bazooka gum to keep his belts sticky.

And when I first descended into the bowels of the school for the Forge Shop class, it seemed like ancient blacksmiths once worked there. It took a few minutes for my eyes to adjust to this soot-filled, acrid-smelling expanse where small coke fires and blacksmith anvils dotted the wooden floor. The forearms of Mr. Mower, our silver-haired instructor, looked extra large and muscular, like Popeye the Sailor Man in the Saturday movie matinees. It took years of pounding red-hot slabs of wrought iron into size using tongs and a heavy hammer to get that way.

A bed of hot coals fed by compressed air, an anvil, and a selection of special tools graced each boy's assigned workstation. We wore heavy leather aprons when we heated pieces of the wrought iron to a near molten temperature to mold it into hooks, punches, chains and rings. Many times an errant boy intentionally left the metal in the coals until it became white-hot. Then it would burn and sparkle, shooting flaming pieces into the air. We had to duck after a boy pounded on it and sizzling fragments, like an exploding bomb, flew across the dark shop.

In drafting classes, the squat, white-haired Bill Powers taught us the right way to use T-squares and triangles, to draw in perspective and carefully scribe text or numbers on the heavy paper. These classes prepared us well for college-level mechanical drawing classes. Mr. McMahon, a short, gaunt, ramrod-straight man with thick glasses and watery eyes, tried to teach us French. Any boy who mispronounced his language suffered a banshee-like scream with decibels high enough to puncture eardrums. Messrs. Powers and McMahon couldn't disguise a taste for Irish whiskey or the telltale characteristics of a hangover; the semi-sweet odor of booze clung to their clothes.

In Boston's public schools since the days of the Civil War, military drill had been compulsory for boys. Every freshman cadet could advance through the ranks from buck private to colonel. Brigadier General Breen, a burly, tough World War I army veteran, ran all our military drill classes.

We usually wore khaki pants and a shirt with a school patch on the right shoulder and tucked our matching tie into our shirt between the second and third buttons. An overseas cap at a rakish angle sat on our head. Cadet officers got to wear black epaulets with silver colored buttons.

In a large hall across the street from Tech, we practiced drill movements and the Manual of Arms with plugged 1903 Springfield rifles, their bolts welded shut. The Manual of Arms involves a series of commands involving precise maneuvers such as *present arms* and *right shoulder arms*, to teach proficiency with a rifle. As a first lieutenant I earned the right to lead the group through the commands.

Just Call Me Moose!

In his frayed army uniform with faded ribbons on his chest and a short swagger stick in hand, the gray-haired general cut through the ranks to correct minor infractions in our posture. A rumor floated amongst the cadets about the old scar in his thick, pitted neck, reputedly a bullet wound from the war.

"Straighten up, keep quiet," barked the general.

Cadets who failed to shape up had to perform a high port arms with the heavy rifle. He made them hold the rifle far from their chest.

Every year in late May, bands and cadets from all over Boston competed in the School Boy Cadets Parade. Marching to the drums and bugles of the martial music always swelled my chest with pride. With rifles on our shoulders, each group of cadets approached the reviewing stand until the words, "Eyes, right," reverberated off the pavement. When the guidon, a small pennant on a long pole, was lowered, our heads snapped toward the platform holding the mayor and other dignitaries.

Near the end of the march in Copley Square, hordes of screaming teenage girls rushed forward to snatch a patch from the arm of an unsuspecting boy. These wild-eyed hellions in long skirts and bobby socks cut through our ranks risking a rifle butt to the stomach. I always felt proud to march near the Boston Common in front of hundreds of spectators. Local officials ended this unique program about the time I began to wear a blue military uniform to work.

Everyone in the family knew that Mum feared furry felines.

"It started when that cat jumped on my head in the stairwell," she began whenever cats entered the conversation.

Whenever a cat nuzzled against a leg, my mother panicked and she barely could tolerate dogs in her presence. But, after Patti Page's popular song, "How Much is that Doggie in the Window," flooded the airwaves, I asked my parents to buy me a puppy; it was an opportunity to demonstrate responsibility. They relented and I decided to name the gangly, male Irish Setter after Pop's beagle that disappeared in the woods. I called my new puppy, Vic.

Just Call Me Moose!

Moose in his yard with Vic, a wild Irish Setter puppy.

My cousin Richard, the veterinarian, sold him to us for fifty bucks. Vic's bright coat matched the color of the chestnuts that fell from our big tree and his soft brown eyes talked to me. He had to sleep in the cellar and every morning when I went down to feed him, he looked an inch or two bigger. Whenever I left Vic alone he to be tied to a steel pin jutting out of the lawn. He didn't like being restrained and the high-strung pooch kept digging foxholes. One day after I let him run free, he chewed up Mum's lingerie hanging on the clothesline. After a few months, I grew weary of picking up his poop and trying to make him behave. So, my incorrigible pup headed back to Norwell; he had to leave. And I had to admit to my parents that Vic was more than I could handle.

MY MOTHER KEPT HASSLING ME about my weight loss and in spite of her overt efforts to force-feed me, I managed to keep any new pounds off. Frequent trips to the nearby Bird Street gym and exercising in a room in my cellar made the difference. Boston Tech never had a gymnasium, but all the local high schools offered a myriad of sports programs. A kid into sports with basic talent could compete in baseball, basketball, crew, cross-country, football, golf, hockey, soccer, tennis or weightlifting. In my freshman year when Joe Carey, the lanky track coach, sought to recruit fresh meat for the team, I decided to try out. After watching me run, he said, "I can tell you're a *sprinta*, so you'll run the dashes." Donald ran track at Tech and lettered in the sport. But, Roger, like Pop, never strayed from academics at Latin to join a school sports team. I wanted them to know that their little brother had potential.

Short distances suited me; my stamina only allowed for running no more than 220 yards and hurdles were not an option. And in spite of my small frame, Coach Carey assigned me to throw the eight-lb. shot put. Having been a fat kid for all those years, I felt validated when he accepted me for the team. Under Carey's stern leadership during the track and field competition about 50 boys of all ages, sizes, and shapes practiced hard to excel.

"Develop your mind not your body." Roger taunted me with those words, but my brothers had played baseball and hockey on neighborhood teams and I inherited their old equipment.

Track seemed to be a sport that I could handle; my mother never approved of football. Track rewarded my individual effort and teamwork mattered little. And I liked not having the stigma of losing a game due to a personal error.

During the miserable Boston winters, we trained after school in the fortress-like 101st Infantry Armory on East Newton Street in the South End. When the weather improved, the track team trained and competed on the rough cinder track of White Schoolboy Stadium in Franklin Park. Everyone on the team received a pair of white shorts and a black track shirt. Across the front of each shirt, "Technical" was stitched in large white letters. Coach Carey drilled us hard and he instilled a burning desire in the team to win. Wind sprints around the 176-yard wooden track, endless practice starts, and learning to pitch the leather covered shot put soon made my untrained muscles rebel. In the locker room after practice, a blend of foul odors rolled over me and I wondered, *Did these kids ever take a bath or wash their uniforms? Surely one afternoon of track practice couldn't make us smell worse than low tide at Carson Beach?*

One afternoon, I noticed an upperclassman sitting on a bench rubbing a liquid into his calf.

"Hey, Lou, what's that stuff? It smells like mint."

Lou Sheedy, an upperclassman and our best sprinter, looked up and smiled, "It's oil of wintergreen. Sure helps sore muscles"

Soon after this endorsement from a super star of my team, I kept a tiny bottle of the burning elixir inside my track bag. Although it burned when applied, its soothing warmth helped ease my pain.

For a pubescent boy into sports, the most important item in my track bag had to be my jockstrap. Before the age of automobiles, male bicyclists on the streets of Boston had complained about the uneven, cobblestone streets and the effects upon their crotches. So the bicycle jockey strap, now jockstrap, this ostensible Japanese Slingshot, the protector of the family jewels came about.

When I ran track, a cotton jock strap kept my budding manhood in place. And before hitting the ice for a hockey game at the Arena or Brighton Skating Club, I always slipped on a metal hockey cup to protect my private parts from the hard rubber pucks that whistled through the air.

By my sophomore year, I had earned sufficient points running the 50- and 220- yard dashes and throwing the shot put to get my letter. All the tough training made sense to me whenever I wore my buff and blue reversible jacket with satin fabric on one side. The big T on the left side and the winged foot on my sleeve with two white stripes validated my success in the sport. But the greatest test for us all, the Boston Regimental

Track Meet, still loomed. The coach pressed us onward that winter; losing this final indoor meet was not acceptable. The March meet was held in the old armory. On that cold Saturday afternoon, Pop drove Mum and me there along with two of my neighborhood friends, "Shack" and "Deetch."

Only a handful of parents showed up; Pop carried his Kodak Super 8-millimeter movie camera and shot a roll of film, but poor lighting inside the armory later made viewing difficult.

Mum had pinned a piece of cardboard with a black number 114 to my jersey. After a few semi-final heats of the 50-yard dash, I was excited to be in the final dash. With knots in my stomach, I took my place alongside five other boys from English, Latin, South Boston, and Tech. I leaned over to spit on the dirty, hard wood floor; with no blocks to mount, a little saliva gave extra traction to our rubber soles. My mouth felt dry as I crouched in the ready position. A loud bang erupted from the starter's gun and the line of boys charged toward the finish line. Only the fastest four could place for points. I finished fifth. A runner from Tech had won. Only 14 years old, Gene Thomas, a slender, black classmate, outpaced all the contenders from around the city in the record time of 5.7 seconds.

At the end of the meet, to my delight, the loudspeakers announced that Tech had won. In the Boston Sunday Globe, Ernest Dalton reported: "Confounding the experts by showing quality as well as quantity, Technical High ran off with the 47th annual Boston Regimental indoor track and field championships yesterday at the 101st Infantry Armory, its first crown in fourteen years."

My plan to earn a letter in track had come together and I had helped to win kudos for my school, so I hung up my track spikes for good. The time had come to move on to other challenges.

IT TOOK POP A FEW YEARS TO FINISH several outdoor improvements. In the back yard, Nonno built a stone barbecue against the garage wall. A large flagstone terrace extended from the brick garage wall, a place to put rustic wooden yard furniture. To maintain privacy, a tall cedar fence was added to screen any of our activities from the street. To relax in his spare time, Pop worked on landscaping projects and Mike Fucci, my father's labor foreman, often came over to help out. Pop added a rock garden with flowers and my mother's wish for an herb garden in a plot of ground below the kitchen materialized. Pop planted a pretty magnolia tree in the side lawn; a concrete column stood nearby topped with a volley ball-size, green glass globe as shiny as a mirror.

From the large window in the kitchen, Mum could see the small magnolia tree close to the ivy-covered garage wall. Standing at the sink must have inspired her to memorialize her mother, Marta; I didn't understand since my parents never went to church. One weekend, my father drew the plans for the shrine and made a blueprint. A beautiful white marble statue of the Blessed Mother arrived in a crate from Italy and the project took shape. The impressive life-size figurine stood on a bluestone pedestal inside a robin-egg-blue stucco alcove. Layers of different sized flagstone surrounded the alcove.

That fall, a local priest led a ceremony; many friends and relatives filled the yard. In spite of a shrine dedicated to his wife, Nonno elected to stay home. For personal reasons, my grandfather never attended church. And whenever I asked why, I got the same answer. "It'll collapse on me if I ever go inside."

After Pop died whenever I looked out my bedroom window and saw the statue of the Virgin Mary, I felt at peace. Praying the rosary to her helped me through those dark days of grief, so there was a reason, after all, for Pop to build a shrine.

Just Call Me Moose!

1953—Backyard memorial to my grandmother, Marta.

Every Sunday, Nonno put on a three-piece suit, starched shirt and tie, polished high black boots and a dark fedora. When he spoke to me, in between sentences, he'd gasp air from the corner of his mouth. Years of smoking and chewing tobacco took a heavy toll.

Although the Norfolk Tap sat across from his house, Nonno stayed away; his son Willie drank there. Instead, for years before and after he retired, Nonno liked to stroll up to Walsh's Tavern on Columbia Road where the local working stiffs enjoyed a brew and a shot of Irish whiskey after work. The fumes that rolled out of the murky space were a blend of stale tobacco smoke and sour-smelling booze. The old watering hole provided a place to share troubles and vent hostilities with friends and strangers.

And whenever I'd ask, "Where are you going, Nonno?" It was always the same reply, "I'm goin' *ta* church."

In his youth Uncle Willie often took the subway to Scollay Square, a seamy part of Boston with strip places and seedy bars off Beacon Hill, to have some fun. It was a gas lit square with cobblestone streets, still rowdy in my day. During World War II and the Korea conflict, soldiers and sailors used to get wasted on cheap booze in its seedy bars and taverns before shipping out. After a night on the town with his buddies, Willie sat down in a tattoo parlor and selected an eagle with outstretched wings for one slender forearm. For his other upper arm, a red rose tattooed with the word *Mom*, the special person in his life. No other uncle of mine even came close to Willie. None ever flaunted tattoos. Maybe that's why my mother never let Uncle Willie take me anywhere?

Uncle Willie's build was similar to his six other male cousins, none were tall and all were slim. Uncle Willie carried a gaunt, tired look in his dark eyes; he spent his workdays as a route driver for Eastern Overall on Norfolk Avenue. Helen, his wife, a firebrand with southern-Italian roots, pressed clothes during the day at the nearby National Overall Company. Before they married, Helen had a gig singing in Boston nightclubs and I imagine that's how they met. Auntie Helen's voice was throaty from all those nights singing in smoky rooms; later, her three daughters also sang on stage. When performing, their last name was Berné, the same name our Auntie Marie had used in California.

Even though Uncle Willie and his family lived next door, Nonno never spoke to them. Just as Nonno had cut the ties to his brother Joe, the same followed for Willie, Helen and his three granddaughters.

"I'm the black sheep of the family," Uncle Willie often lamented.

Uncle Willie often came over to our house on Sunday mornings and headed for the cellar after making sure Nonno was nowhere in sight. A lit cigarette dangled precariously from the corner of Uncle Willie's mouth and a cold can of beer stayed clenched in his thin fist. With slicked-down hair, eyes half closed, he spoke with a rasping voice from inhaling the smoke of Lucky Strikes, his favorite brand. Whenever he'd pull hard on a cigarette short butt, his cheeks caved in and I could swear his head got smaller. We exchanged few words, never anything of any substance; my protective mother kept the two of us apart. He never took me to a ballgame and we never went to see the zoo or a movie together. I liked Uncle Willie but never thought to question my mother's rule.

Uncle Willie moved in a much different world than his siblings. His was filled with seedy, smelly bars and some unsavory lowbrow characters who bet on the horses, dogs, and anything else that moved. When this self-styled "black sheep" showed up at my house one afternoon, he looked dejected.

So, I said, "What's the matter, Uncle Willie?"

"Hell, I thought yesterday was my lucky day. Only one number off from hitting the Nigger Pool." For years African-Americans ran this popular illegal numbers game, hence the origin of the derogatory name. And when the Mob muscled in on this lucrative, working-class pastime, the name stuck. This long-shot game of chance derived from the last three numbers of the daily pari-mutuel racing results. Mostly blue-collar guys, like Uncle Willie, spent a few cents each day trying to win a few hundred dollars. Times haven't changed.

X

MY NEIGHBORHOOD PACK had hung around together, like wolves in the wild, since grammar school days. Fortunately, the oldest, Eddie, owned a boxy-looking blue Nash Rambler and so he could drive us around. An outgoing fellow and a respected athlete, Eddie studied electronics at Charlestown High. In a joking manner, we called him "Frog" because of his French-Canadian heritage. Another friend, Johnny, a skinny Scotch-Irish Boston Tech classmate, sometimes slurred his speech. At home, he was known as Jack, but it sounded more like shack, when he said it. So, we called him "Shack" and our pack became known as the Shack Club.

Shack's hardworking Irish mother, Mary, had seven kids in nine years and always looked exhausted. But, unlike my mother, Shack's mother had a nice blend of boys and girls. Whenever she spoke to me she'd often say, "What a nice lad," in a thick brogue that sounded so sweet to my ears.

Bobby "Deetch," a lean kid with eyes close together who lived near Frog, was a better than average baseball player. Deetch attended Boston English High usually stayed in the background. Another Tech classmate, Johnny "Raff" lived on the same neighborhood street as Frog and Deetch. Introspective like Deetch, Raff looked like a short stout refrigerator and sported calves the size of small hams, traits well suited to play tackle on the Tech football team. My friends called me Moose, the same nickname as an older neighborhood kid, an Italian-American friend of Donald. The older Moose excelled in local sports, on the baseball diamond and in the hockey rink. The cool name I chose set me apart from the others.

The temperaments of my Shack Club pals blended well together. The de-facto club had no official leader; every kid spoke his mind and the strongest argument won out. At first none of us smoked tobacco, but alcohol facilitated many of the social activities of the club.

Sometimes we'd head to the Holy Name Church in West Roxbury for Saturday night record hops and maybe a chance to dance with a strange, pretty girl.

And when Frog said, "Let's go 'scoopin' this weekend," we knew what it meant: "prowling for girls."

The large church hall provided a gathering place for kids from all around and the chaperones made sure kids didn't get too wild. We'd circled the perimeter of the dimly lit expanse, like hungry wolves on the edge of a campfire, trying to look detached and nonchalant. If a girl looked tasty and if she glanced our way, the moment merited another slow pass to verify her intent. Getting turned down for a dance made me feel bad, so I tried not to be rejected whenever I asked a girl to the floor.

My pack existed to have fun, in the here and now, rarely expressing our dreams and aspirations to one another. Someone might laugh and make fun of the idea. In spite of the changeable, sticky Boston weather, our summers during high school had a carefree quality, so there were many things to do. On most Saturdays, to play baseball or football, the loyal comrades of the Shack Club used to meander down Norfolk Avenue to the Prairie. For decades, neighborhood kids had called the barren William T. Eustis Playground the Prairie, since it lacked even a hint of green vegetation.

To get to the Prairie, we had to walk by the Marconi Club, a place off-limits to us. I would peek through the old wooden fence to catch a glimpse of Nonno among the raucous members milling outside the club. If we were carrying baseball bats and gloves and bumped into Nonno, he'd smile and say, "One ball, one strike," the only words he ever used when referring to the All-American Game.

My mother always cautioned me to stay away from the Marconi Club and I followed her advice. Those rowdy men behind the fence often came together to play the ancient Roman pastimes of *Morra* or when weather permitted, *Bocce*.

The game of Morra, first played by Roman Legionnaires, often inflamed the emotions of club members, especially after a few glasses of spirits. Typically, two fired-up club members sat at a table facing each other. With sleeves rolled up and fingers extended, each player slammed his fist onto the surface shouting a number, *uno*—one, *due*—two, and so on. Spectators standing close-by heard the sounds of raw knuckles slamming hard on wood, and as the liquor flowed, a cloud of smoke and profanities filled the air. The winner is the player who shouts the number equal to the number of fingers showing. Many times Nonno showed me his technique on the kitchen table but I wasn't interested.

Club members played Bocce outside on a long, narrow hard-packed court. Players formed into teams threw a hard, smooth, grapefruit-size ball as close as possible to the target ball, the ping-pong-sized *pallino*, sitting by itself down court. The team closest won the round.

Auntie Ines told me that on special days and religious holidays prior to Lent, the likes of *Sabato Grasso*—Fat Saturday—, members and their families gathered there. Someone would hop up on a table to play an accordion. While the young people danced under the watchful eyes of their mothers, the men drifted off to the cellar to play cards away from the eyes of their wives and lady friends.

On Sundays and holidays, Nonno enjoyed strolling down the street to meet with friends and neighbors at the Marconi Club, once a large home on Norfolk Avenue. The club's namesake, Guglielmo Marconi, an inventor from Bologna was the first person to transmit radio signals across the Atlantic Ocean from a transmitter on Cape Cod. Blue-collar, Italian-speaking workingmen from northern Italy and Switzerland founded the social club for people like them. Dues that members paid granted them permission to smoke cigars and drink glasses of homemade red wine and grappa alongside neighbors. They played card games brought from the Old Country while the dialect of their homelands rolled off their tongues, at ease with one another in a special place, able to share their fears and hopes with friends.

The playground, located in Roxbury, still sprawls over several acres. It seemed so huge to us. We didn't know that Eustis had been a surgeon and hero of the Battle of Bunker Hill. In 1819, he bought the nearby Royal Governor Shirley Estate before serving as the first Democratic-Republican governor of the Commonwealth. George Washington and Benjamin Franklin once dined there. And while governor in 1824, the year before he died, Eustis hosted the returning Marquis de Lafayette, the famous French general who helped us win the American Revolution. It was a trip to see the nation he helped establish. The renovated mansion still sits on Shirley Street not far from the old playground. But in those days, to venture into Roxbury wasn't a good idea because bands of Irish gangs might attack. So, the rundown mansion remains a faded memory.

One day while I was on school vacation, my mind raced for something to do. Anything different. None of my friends were around; I was bored.

"Mum, can I go down to the Prairie?"

"What for?"

"Nothing. Just to take a walk."

"Okay, you can go, but don't be long."

She didn't see me grab a can opener and a tarnished tablespoon from the kitchen drawer nor a tin of baked beans from the pantry. After hiding everything in a paper bag, along with my Boy Scout cook kit and some wooden matches, I strode toward the Prairie. The landscape was empty; I didn't spot any strange kids as I started a fire with some dry sticks and scrap paper. Open fires always fascinated me; it was fun to lose myself in the dancing flames, a primeval calling from my Neanderthal roots. At Camp Lincoln, wearing an Indian outfit, I had often lost myself in a reverie sitting alongside the roaring log fires. So, it felt natural for me when the Air Force put me in charge of weapons that did more than light up the sky. After dumping the beans in my aluminum pot, I watched them bubble. All alone, squatting on my haunches, I wolfed down the warm beans. The ennui that had held me that day slipped away, as I imagined being on some barren tundra in the Yukon prospecting for gold.

THE NEARBY FRANKLIN PARK ZOO had been an amusement magnet for Bostonians since 1911 and by streetcar it was a short trip from home. Kids could go horseback riding there and in the winter, after a heavy snowfall, we could toboggan on the golf course. The stable horses with their English saddles were quite savvy about handling novice riders. With no saddle horn to grab, staying astride my make-believe stallion was difficult for a kid trying to emulate Roy Rogers chasing villains on the plains. After my brown steed broke into an uncontrollable gallop, the dirt trail took a sharp turn. My swayback charger veered to the left, and I took flight, ending up in the underbrush. After I crawled to my feet and checked myself for damage, everything felt fine. I looked up to see my rented nag hightailing it to the barn. I had to walk back. And Mum's old saying, "Hold your hosses," started to make sense.

The zoo gave kids, young and old, a peek inside a fantasy world of hundreds of different species. Lions, tigers, elephants, polar bears, gorillas, snakes, and tropical birds made up the collection; I marveled over the glories of the animal kingdom. But, some of the odors wafting from the cages made me want to walk faster. I'll always remember the day I tried to pet a wildebeest through the fence. I poked a hand through bars to scratch his scruffy head, but as I made contact with his rough hairy muzzle, the animal pushed back, bending my wrist against the fence. It took a hard slap on his head with my free hand to break loose. My experience with the sinewy creature made me reluctant to get close to any wild beasts again, even some of the girls I dated later in life.

ON HOT SUMMER DAYS, MY FRIENDS AND I used to walk down to Carson Beach, lay out on an old blanket, check out girls, and swim in the dirty Atlantic water. When someone said, "Let's hit the quarries," we'd thumb a ride to the Quincy Quarries and swim "ballakey" away from the prying eyes of girls. It was a rite of passage for boys to swim bare-ass in the deep waters, a few miles south of our neighborhood. Since colonial times, granite from the Quincy Quarries was used to build Boston and other cities. I didn't know it then, but the Bunker Hill monument is also made of Quincy stone.

To reach our old swimming hole we had to climb up a steep hill strewn with rock tailings. At the top, the slick, moss-covered granite walls rose sharply up around the abandoned excavation. Underwater springs and rain kept it full of cold frigid water and each of us knew that kids had died there jumping off the cliffs and hitting rocks or had drowned in the dark waters. The lurid tales didn't deter us. Others had told us about the high ledge called "Suicide" from which only the craziest kids dared jump. Sometimes a kid did.

"Watch this," a crazy stranger yelled to the onlookers, hurling his body as far as possible from the jagged rocks.

Tempting fate wasn't our thing. My friends and I never tried Suicide; it looked too scary to us; we preferred to perform the safer "cannonball" from outcroppings close to the water. Yet, the deeper into the frigid depths that we dove, the more numb we became. The water was cold enough to make a boy start speaking an octave higher; swimming sans bathing suits in those old quarries is an experience I'll never forget.

During the winter, the Prairie was a good place to play hockey; when the weather turned cold, city workers opened a hydrant to flood the large expanse with water. As soon as the water froze, we usually headed for the Prairie to play hockey. All my equipment, except the skates, had been handed down from my brothers. They played on a neighborhood team called the Rangers.

My bulky duffel bag held all my gear; shin guards, elbow pads, padded pants, thick leather gloves, long underwear, protective cup, jersey, and skates had to be lugged around to every game. I shot the puck from the left side, so I used a stick specially made for left-handed players. And I realized that being a left defenseman worked best for me since my lack of stamina ruled out being a forward—either a wing or a center. Only the fastest players with staying power filled those slots. Playing defense made sense to me.

The year before my father died, I talked him into sponsoring a hockey team. The members of the team wore a white, heavy cotton hockey jersey with Pop's company name in bold, red script across the front. I asked Mum to sew a large number "3" on mine. The next day it was done.

Teams in our Class C league played every weekend around two in the morning at the Brighton Skating Club. Getting up so early to play hockey was never a problem for me because I loved the game. Sometimes, my friends and I skated there on a Saturday afternoon to the heavy sounds of organ music and had our skates sharpened.

When we played hockey, it cost $30 to rent the ice for an hour; each player put a few bucks into the pot. In the stale-smelling locker room, to get ready for the game, it took some time to gird ourselves with our gear; kids who wore glasses, like me, spread Glass Wax on the lenses to reduce the chance of them fogging up on the ice

Just Call Me Moose!

Waiting to get on the ice, I often dallied at rink side to watch world-class figure skater Tenley Albright practice. In 1956, she won a gold medal at the Winter Olympics; the perseverance of the local skater made me proud of her achievement.

After the Zamboni ice machine resurfaced the skating surface, it took only a few minutes for me to warm up after hitting the ice. It felt so free gliding across the crisp, fresh ice, firing hard practice shots at our goalie. During a real game, a teammate backhanded the hard rubber puck and all I heard was a loud "splat." The edge of the puck hit a boy in the head and blood spurted onto the ice from an ugly gash. It sounded like someone slamming a watermelon with a baseball bat. No players on the teams I competed against wore a helmet; NHL pros didn't, goalies never used facemasks, and I didn't want to look unmanly. Playing defense meant covering an offensive player closely and protecting one's own goal, so I never got too many chances to take a shot at the goal. And I got "pooped" whenever I exerted myself on the ice so I can't imagine ever scoring very often. Hockey was my favorite sport to play but I don't believe that my father ever showed up to watch me play or the team that wore his name.

After each session at the rink, I was drenched in sweat and the heavy smell of the ammonia refrigerant used in making the ice clung to me. At home, my mother never missed a beat.

"Mum, here's my hockey stuff to wash."

"Leave it downstairs by the washer," she replied, "I'll put it through the laundry."

MANY PARENTS GAVE THEIR CHILDREN A LOT of leeway but I wonder if they really trusted us. Parents tried to make their kids understand the difference between right and wrong and when we erred, they punished us. These benevolent dictators guided us through the minefields of temptations in our paths. In the background, the Church used fear and intimidation to keep one and all on the moral track.

Just Call Me Moose!

Like most mothers, mine often snooped around in my room. To protect my privacy, I built a compact wooden box and locked the lid with a small padlock. I painted it Chinese red and added simple yellow letters that screamed, "KARL'S CHEST KEEP OUT." It became a special place to keep my personal treasures: my comic books, a knife, and a magazine or two with shiny color pictures of Bettie Paige smiling out at me.

Pop had refurbished a room at the bottom of the cellar stairs. The playroom became a place to have my friends over to socialize and drink tonic. But, we looked forward to the day when we could have a beer. Green linoleum made the floor easy to clean. Wooden built-in closets and the old refrigerator with a bullet hole in the door, covered with a piece of white tape, lined one wall. There's a story about the bullet hole. One afternoon after target shooting down in the country, I mistakenly left a bullet in Pop's new .22-caliber rifle, a Winchester. My grandfather was sitting in the kitchen drinking a glass of wine and talking to my mother when I came home.

"Look Nonno, how do you like it," I said, as I handed him the rifle.

I started to tell him about my day in Norwell and was in the middle of a sentence when the gun discharged. He must have playfully pulled the trigger. The barrel had been facing the refrigerator and the round went through the door. Time stood still and I thought, *Oh, shit!* Nonno blanched at the sound. When I opened the door to the fridge, I found the bullet in a piece of cheese. I didn't heed Pop's stern warning to treat every gun as if it was loaded; it was a lesson I never forgot.

In the cellar, a little table held a small phonograph; most of the 45-records stacked nearby belonged to me. My taste in music covered the gamut from "Shake, Rattle and Roll" to "Folsom Prison Blues." The title of the song "Why Do Fools Fall in Love," seemed like something a boy like me should ponder. The sounds of Little Richard's piano made my mother cringe. Whenever I cranked up the volume to get the full effect of "Wa bop a lu bop ...," Mum yelled down the stairs.

Just Call Me Moose!

"For the love of Mary, turn it down!"

On weekends I'd invite my friends over to play stud poker for nickels and dimes. As long as everyone stayed quiet and kept the music low, Mum let us be. All the kids liked her; she usually brought snacks down to us. But, Pop kept his distance and didn't have a lot to say around them.

A door with glass separated the playroom from the *cantina*. My parents stored meats and frozen vegetables in a small chest freezer and also canned goods in the cantina. One wall held a custom cabinet where bottles of hard liquor and wine rested on their sides. The temperature in the cellar stayed fairly constant from being below ground level.

I knew that Pop had studied classical art in college and like most red-blooded men he appreciated the female form. My mother kept her best dishes in the china cabinet off the kitchen. One shelf held Pop's small collection of novelty highball glasses. Rarely used, each glass posed a well-dressed young woman on one side, but when the glass was turned around, her clothes disappeared.

My father subscribed to several popular magazines including *Life*, *Esquire*, and *National Geographic*. Once, while looking for a pen in his big oak desk in the den, I found a stack of Varga Girl playing cards. Pinup artist Alberto Vargas had sketched these cheesecake images, and in the 1940s, *Esquire* magazine dropped the "s" in his name and made the Varga Girls famous. At my age, any picture of a scantily clad pretty woman got me excited. The classic *Life* cover photo of Rita Hayworth kneeling on a satin bed in a silk negligee is a stunning image for all time. And when I scanned the heavy color pages of *National Geographic* and came upon the glistening bare breasts of young African girls, my hormones began to rage. Today, these photos are tame but not for a young male in my time. At night, after I fell asleep, when those sexy pages surfaced in my dreams, sometimes a warm sensation in my pajama bottoms would awaken me. Yet, Mum never questioned me about the "starched" sheets when she came to change my bed.

Just Call Me Moose!

The era of modest pinups began to slip away in the 1950s, as I came of age. The sexual revolution exploded after *Playboy* magazine published a nude Marilyn Monroe on a red velvet background. The image blew the lid off puritanical constraints. But, in the glossy, cheesecake magazines of the day, one girl in particular stood out. On a trash day, I came across several magazines on the sidewalk that featured Bettie Page. Posed in skimpy bikinis on the beach or in sexy black lingerie, Bettie Page, a size 36-24-35 gal, could make young guys' heads spin. With creamy white skin, a charming smile, big blue eyes, full breasts, voluptuous hips and slender legs, Bettie raised my blood pressure and her long, shiny black hair turned me on. An all-American girl, she broke new ground in the sexual rebellion of the times, when sexual taboos began to erode. And with Bettie's body on my mind, my doodles showing the pointed breasts of wasp-waisted nudes improved.

One day a friend said flippantly, "Moose, I heard that jerking off makes hair grow on the back of your hand?"

"Yeah, right. Why don't *you* go beat your meat under the sheet to keep the heat around your feet?"

That retort usually worked; it made the wise guy shut up. And so, the sexual feelings that my Church made a habit of suppressing continued to surge. The only remedy for me was to pray a lot. So, on Saturdays, I knelt inside a gloomy old confessional at St. Margaret's and whispered, "Bless me Father for I have sinned." I'd confess my impure thoughts and impure actions to a visiting priest who couldn't recognize my voice. And my penance of 10 "Hail Mary's" absolved my adolescent sins until next time.

One lazy day as my friends and I were standing around, a lean, older kid who lived up the street began carrying on about Scollay Square. We had heard about this legend of a place, but none of us had ever explored it. Only a few people and military veterans from the neighborhood knew about the tattoo parlors and burlesque houses, a place where drifters, panhandlers, and whores roamed, looking to make a buck. After a few minutes of shooting the bull, Jack, the neighborhood ne'er-do-well, got to the point.

"Any of you guys wanna go see a strip show?"

"Why not," I said. "I look old enough to get in."

No one else spoke up. That afternoon, only Jack and I ended up on the train to the Scollay Square Station: the same station in the song where Charlie's wife used to hand him a sandwich through the open window.

The man with the cigar in his mouth inside the cage at the Casino Theater hardly glanced up when I bought my ticket. At the entrance, a photo of a flaming-red-haired Tempest Storm, showing a lot of skin, adorned the billboard. Jack had a lecherous grin on his face as he pulled a final drag from a cigarette. As we moved down the aisle, I caught a whiff of stale tobacco smoke and the sweet smell of urine. We found two seats toward the front and sat down. Two old guys dressed like bums and a young woman on the stage warmed up the audience with a slapstick comedy routine.

The thin woman with a raspy voice yelled at one of the bums, "I wish I had a camera to take a picture of your dick."

"Why?"

"So, I could have it enlarged!"

I'd never heard a lady talk like that. The barrage of off-color jokes kept everyone in the dark theater laughing, but inside my skull, thoughts of naked women were in full swing.

When Tempest Storm came onstage and began to dance, a crescendo of drums and brassy horns filled the antiquated theater. The spotlight lit the main attraction, a tall slender woman in a tight-fitting evening gown. Still in her twenties, she slowly sashayed to the beat across the stage. Making eye contact to flirt with guys in the audience, Tempest slowly undressed. The audience roared and clapped as zippers opened and shoulder straps came loose; soon she stepped daintily out of the dress. The tiny G-string and sexy black fishnet stockings stood out in contrast against her pearl-white skin. The fantasy girl onstage enjoyed teasing us as she danced on tall black stiletto heels.

The bright white spotlight dimmed to a hazy blue and washed over her. By now, only sequined pasties shielded the nipples jutting from her all-natural 40-DD's. I grabbed my seat tightly and stared as Tempest's huge, firm breasts undulated to the music. All the way home my loins throbbed from the long afternoon of forbidden sexual arousal. After climbing the stairs to my room and resting a while in bed, I remembered my friend's taunt. Later that night, I turned on my lamp and stared closely at the back of my hand.

XI

WHEN I BECAME EXPOSED to the mysteries of chemistry, a topic both weird and wonderful to me, Pop passed on an old expression that a science teacher had once told him.

"There was a boy who is no more; for what he thought was H_2O was H_2SO_4."

It was an old rhyme about a kid who mistook sulfuric acid for water, and it made me cautious handling chemicals in class. Conducting experiments with exotic, often dangerous, chemicals, we used timeworn Bunsen burners. Students drew detailed color pictures in lab books to describe the results.

When the teacher wasn't looking, some capricious class member liked to fill a small glass vial with hydrogen sulfide and exposed the school body in the auditorium to the sickening smell of rotten eggs. And I remembered the same odor floating in the air from those holes in the South End where muckers had labored. Studying about salts, bases and acids may have thrilled some kids, not me. But, years later, when explosive compounds came into my life, I paid attention.

Anyone who has ever had a truly eccentric teacher can appreciate the antics of Doc Moore, our stern history instructor. In graduate school, Moore wrote a doctoral thesis on the Battle of Jutland, an infamous World War I clash of early steel warships. Hundreds of British and German ships, manned by thousand of seamen, had faced off in the North Sea. When the smoke cleared, fourteen British ships and eleven German ships had sunk; thousand of sailors died.

Doc, a history aficionado, lectured us in an animated manner whenever a subject especially interested him. As he paced around the classroom perimeter, he liked to twirl a short piece of dark stained wood between his palms. It had been square once, but now the edges were rounded from all the spinning by nervous hands. Doc seemed to be in a trance-like state as old dates and long-ago events filled the air. Kids with glazed eyes would put their heads on their desks to escape the tedious facts filling their brains.

"Mr. Moore, I have a...question," a boy interjected.

"Later, not now," Doc replied, as his soliloquy mounted to a crescendo. When Doc was on a roll, kids had better not disturb him.

The best way to sidetrack Doc for a reprieve from the deluge of new, testable material was to ask him about the Battle of Jutland. Most times Doc would stop in mid-sentence and the gleam in his dark eyes would grow brighter. Now his brain shifted to the old thesis; he wanted to begin in the right place. All it took was the right question.

"Sir, how many ships got sunk?"

Another kid yelled, "Is this gonna be on the final?"

For the remainder of the period, Doc related once more all the details of the horrific wartime confrontation, oblivious to the boys winking and smirking at one another.

But one spring afternoon, Ken "Boo Boo" Benjamin, an athletic, good-looking black kid across the aisle, pulled a memorable stunt. As Doc lectured us at the blackboard, Ken, a member of the crew team, started throwing a new silver dollar into the air. When it landed in the palm of his palm, Ken smiled; he liked showing off to his classmates. About then, Doc yelled, "Knock it off, Benjamin," and turned away. Joe made a slashing movement across his throat toward Ben and whispered, "Don't do it." Ken grinned and did it again, then once more. When Doc threw the blackboard eraser at the coin floating in mid-air and missed, Ken laughed hard and tossed the coin toward the dusty ceiling.

But Doc had already left the starting blocks. As he tore down the narrow aisle, I ducked as he lunged for the silver dollar, made the catch, and then ran to one of our tall, third-floor windows. Straining to open it wide enough, he stood back and then quickly pitched the coin into the sunny expanse below. All the while, Ken was yelling, "Hey, that's my *silva dolla,*" then he bolted from the room to retrieve it. By now bedlam reigned throughout the room, and as the bell rang, we poured into the hall doubled over in laughter.

Kids can recognize when a teacher goes weird, a man on the edge. And they circle like vultures overhead waiting to strike. I wasn't alone in thinking that our Ph.D. history teacher seemed a few cards shy of a full deck. Even Pop had to laugh when I told him the story.

Although my high school never took on the aura of a Blackboard Jungle, I'll never forget the day that Doc came apart at the seams and threw Ken's silver dollar out the window.

Our teachers piled on a heavy load of homework to make sure we mastered the material presented. Most of my assignments were hand written. At Tech, boys never learned how to use a typewriter, so anything I typed was a tedious two-fingered process. The Royal manual typewriter from my father's college days got a lot of use whenever my assignment had to be typed.

After Mr. Rosengard, my zealous math teacher, first broached how to use a new calculating tool, my father tutored me on an old K&E slide rule. For any budding technician, a slide rule helped unlock the secrets of trigonometry, logarithms, and square roots. In spite of trying to show Pop that these subjects were easy for me, in my heart there was doubt.

Just Call Me Moose!

ONE NIGHT POP CAME HOME FROM WORK with two ringside tickets to a championship boxing match. One of his sub-contractors had passed them on to him. Pop gave the tickets to Roger and said, "Be sure to take your brother along." Seems to me, the tickets for the front row seats at the Boston Garden cost about $50 dollars each. Jimmy Carter, the lightweight champion from New York, and Tommy Collins of Boston planned to square off on fight night. Spectators at sporting events dressed up; men wore a suit and tie and a soft felt hat with a brim. And the few women I saw, wearing hats or bright kerchiefs, appeared to be going to church.

That Friday night in April 1953, Roger and I took the train to the North Station and walked over to the Garden. After the fight started, it took only one round before Collins began to come apart. Carter's punches came from every angle; when a blow landed the sickening thud sounded like an ax handle striking a slab of beef. With no three-knockdown rule in place, again and again Collins hit the canvas in front of us. He kept crawling to his feet. *Stay down*, I thought. *Don't get up.* Collins dropped to the canvas seven times in round 3 and three more times in round 4 before a towel appeared in the ring. Then his handlers rushed into the ring to stop the torture session. Collins's face looked shredded and bloody; clearly boxing was a sport I should only watch on television.

As we broke out of the crowd on the way to the subway station, Roger acted like *he* had been in the ring. His adrenaline must have been pumping, when he said, "Someday, I'll hit you with so many lefts you'll be beggin' for a right."

"In your dreams, Rog," I said. "You couldn't fight your way out of a paper bag!"

From 1936 to 1956, Italian fighters, sons of immigrant working-class people, dominated all weight classes of professional boxing. Men like Carmine Basilio, Willie Pep, Tony DeMarco from the North End, Jake LaMotta, and my hero, Rocky Marciano, the "Brockton Blockbuster," made this boxing era special.

Just Call Me Moose!

Going to an event at the Boston Garden was always fun for me. Looking down from on high, I loved the exciting spectacles of the Ringling Circus and the Ice Follies. And going to watch the Boston Bruins play other NHL teams inspired me to be a better player on the ice. Basketball never gave me a thrill, so I can't remember attending a Celtics game.

Televised professional boxing matches, broadcast on the Gillette Cavalcade of Sports, were very popular with fight fans like me; they encouraged me to learn how to defend myself. After some cajoling, Pop mounted a speed bag in my workout room for me to tattoo. An old mirror let me watch myself whacking the pear-shaped bag around. In no time, my speedy, gloved fists could pummel it without missing a beat.

Everything seemed to be going well at school, but one of my classmates started harassing me. My nemesis was a fellow about my size from East Boston, a kid with a case of diarrhea of the mouth. He liked to wear black chino or baggy pegged pants, pointed black spade shoes, and combed his greasy hair in a ducktail. The only thing we shared was an Italian-American heritage. Many of my classmates, including some of the teachers, thought this greaser acted like a punk.

My passive demeanor must have encouraged him. I absorbed the trash talk for a while, but finally took it upon myself to challenge the class bully. One afternoon, we traded verbal and non-verbal insults; I can imagine him throwing a few spitballs my way and me "flipping the bird" back to him.

After the lunch period, Joe sidled up to me in the hallway and said, "I just heard your 'buddy' call you a fag in the cafeteria."

"Are you serious? "

"Yeah. No joke. I heard him."

"Okay, Joe...That's it. I've had it. Wait ... till ... the bell rings."

At the final bell, everyone headed for the rows of lockers in the basement. After opening mine, I placed my glasses carefully on the top shelf, rolled up my sleeves, removed my tie, and slowly turned toward my smart-ass classmate, only yards away. Surging past a few other kids eager to go home, I came face to face with the big mouth. I didn't expect him to charge, but friends told me later that my pupils dilated during the unprovoked attack. He stepped forward and started swinging wildly, but my training on the light bag made the difference. Again and again my fists dug into the boy's face and mouth and blood started to flow. When he shook his head my shirt caught the droplets. In less than a minute the one-sided brawl came to an end. None of his roundhouse punches ever connected.

At school the next day in the hallway, Mr. Wall, a tall English teacher approached me.

"Good job, kiddo. He deserved it."

Several days later when he came back to school, I walked past him in the basement, near the stained stone urinals. My former antagonist looked depressed and acted strangely meek. One eye sported a purplish, puffy mouse.

"I didn't think you could do it," he said. "I'm switchin' to East Boston High."

"Good! Good riddance," I replied.

My first and my last high school fight had come and gone and I had met the challenge. Pop's cellar gym had helped me prevail. *I'm no wimp,* I thought.

Our Spanish teacher, Mr. Morrill was a flamboyant girlie man with a sparse, blonde head of hair. Long ago, some Tech boys had dubbed him, "Piggy." A turned-up nose that sat on a smooth oval chubby pink face brought to mind the barnyard animal. In class, Morrill, an accomplished pianist, loved to say, *"A un alumno nunca le gusto ser el ultimo de su clase."* He always said it meant, "No pupil wants to be last in his class." Kids often shook their heads and rolled their eyes when Piggy glided around the classroom, one hand under the other elbow, spouting off in Spanish. In spite of his prissy antics, Piggy pushed us hard to learn a language I never planned to use. But the words he wrote on the blackboard came back to me when I was on duty in Spain.

As graduation approached, Doc Hasenfus called me in to his office and said, "I'm assigning you to be the editor of the class yearbook. Any problem with that?"

"No, sir."

The yearbook team worked hard to do a good job—a document to tell the real story of the Class of 1956, one worthy of posterity. For prowess as a pianist and his brazen effeminate behavior, the "Class Will" bequeathed a candelabrum to Mr. Morrill, a veiled reference to Liberace, a celebrated gay showman of the time.

Donald had felt the wrath of Piggy. Close to graduating, Donald and Mr. Morrill had an altercation and Donald lost the right to the coveted Franklin Medal, a medal named after Benjamin Franklin. Only a few top seniors received the award for academic achievement. Our father earned the medal in 1924. Donald never got over it. Whenever I mentioned his infamous Spanish teacher, Donald blurted out, "That son of a bitch!"

Since high school began, I had never shied away from making speeches to classmates and teachers during Forums in the auditorium. And my short stint as a Junior Rotarian at the Rotary Club of Boston gave me additional experience in speaking before large crowds.

In my senior year, although I had little interest in politics, several classmates prodded me to campaign for class president. It must have made my father proud of me since I was the first son to run for an elective office at school. When all the ballots were counted, 60 votes made the difference. A popular hockey player on the Tech team was elected class president.

In retrospect, to be rejected this time was a relief. Juggling extra-curricular activities kept my plate full enough. But unlike others in my class whose good grades came easily, I had to work hard to stay ahead. So, as the end of my buff and blue years at Boston Tech neared, I felt confident about my achievements and looked forward to the future.

At graduation, I was astounded when the principal called me to the stage and placed the heavy round silver medal hanging on a blue ribbon around my neck. Pop never knew; he was dead and whatever Donald said later is lost in time.

MY BROTHERS COMPLETED COLLEGE long before I finished high school. What little influence they had over me slipped away as other events in their lives played out and they moved out of the house. With a degree in math from Boston University, Donald married Betty Beytes, an energetic, strong-willed neighborhood girl. Betty and Donald had been close for years so the wedding was no surprise. With a direct commission in the Air Force, Donald trained many months to become an airborne electronic countermeasures officer, an ECM officer, in the Strategic Air Command. Officers with this specialty were called Ravens in those days.

Roger graduated with honors from Boston College, another math major. Preferring to take orders, rather than give them, he enlisted in the Air Force. Roger chose to stay single for many years; Mum always wanted him to be a priest. But because of his aptitude for languages, the military selected him for an intensive six-month language program. At Yale University, Roger studied Chinese for six hours a day, five days a week. On weekends home from New Haven, Roger broke into Chinese at the supper table. With a deadpan expression, Roger enjoyed calling me names in Mandarin; I came to learn that one name means *stupid*. After Yale, the Air Force sent my airman brother to the Far East. Roger spent a few years eavesdropping on the Red Chinese from a barren hill on the island of Formosa. I recall how Mum made it a point to dash any potential marriage plans after Roger got involved with a Chinese girl. Our mother exerted her influence in many situations; only those of us who stood up to her won out. I was one who never lost.

Before Roger left to go overseas, I'd try to engage my mostly taciturn brother in conversation or ask him a question. Invariably, the reply was, "Are you writing a book?"

I never took his wisecracks too seriously and just shrugged them off since I needed him more than he needed me. Something deep in my brother's makeup received immense pleasure in taunting me. Whenever the desire struck, Roger met the challenge with an outrageous expression.

"You're a gleek of the week."

"Stay away from me. Don't be a leech!"

Other times jibes came out of the blue when our paths crossed. "You've been takin' too many ugly pills."

And when I said, "Goodbye," he usually said, "Don't take any wooden nickels."

But Roger always liked this one best. "I wish you were on TV, so I could turn you off."

Both brothers demonstrated superior intelligence, with a meticulous and obstinate bent, a lot like our father. A stubborn streak in all of us may have been the only quality we held in common.

It's clear to me that I grew up as a de-facto only child trying hard to please a disengaged father in the shadow of two quirky brothers. Yet, after Pop died, I managed to slip the bonds of my doting, yet domineering mother and embark on an exciting journey in the military.

ALTHOUGH MY SCHOOL OFFERED pre-driving education, I never took the class. Since most mothers had never learned to drive, kids got their fathers to show them how to use the clutch, shift gears, and park. Pop spent a few hours at the task, but he lacked the patience to make me proficient. When I tried to get my license at the testing facility in Upham's Corner, I failed. The weary examiner stated, "First, you couldn't parallel park very well, and second, you drove too close to a ragman. His horse bolted. Get some more practice and come back again."

Pop paid for formal driving lessons for me at a local driving school and I finally got my license. With driving privileges, a new world could open up for me.

My father preferred cars made by General Motors. From Chevrolet models, Pop went to Pontiac, then Oldsmobile during my early years. I like the looks of the Pontiac Chieftain sedan with the plastic Indian hood ornament. In 1953, he bought a blue Chevy station wagon for the business. Mum always pinned a St. Christopher medal to the rearview mirror on all the cars for good luck. It must have worked; Pop never had an accident.

In the rock and roll times of the 1950s, pop music hit a new height. The earthy lyrics of the new tunes transcended the old black rhythm and blues numbers. The words articulated teenage problems and horny young love, issues that adolescent white kids from all social backgrounds understood. Simple, easily-understood phrases backed-up with saxophones, electric guitars, pianos, and drums captured our hearts and souls. The music drove us to grab a strange girl in the dark and dance even if we didn't know how.

When the Penguin's sang "Earth Angel...Will You Be Mine," or I heard the strains of "Tutti Frutti" and "Good Golly Miss Molly" reverberating in the hall, all my cares about school and chores vanished.

"Someday, I'll find a special girl for me," I thought, as Elvis Presley crooned the words of "Love Me Tender." Songs like "The Great Pretender," "Standing on the Corner" and Fats Domino's "Blueberry Hill" sounded great to me. We didn't have to take drugs to get high; the heavy throbbing beat of scores of popular rock and roll tunes made us feel good enough.

One night at the Holy Name record hop, I met Mary Ann, a raven-haired Portuguese-American girl with pale skin. Mary Ann lived in the Orient Heights section of East Boston; her good manners and decent Catholic upbringing appealed to me. But when I told my mother about Mary Ann, she said, "You're too young to start dating." Pop didn't have a problem with me going out with a girl and he gave me permission to use the car.

I'll always remember the night I first met her parents. We had a date to go to the movies, and my father let me borrow his 1954 Oldsmobile 98 Holiday coupe. Emerald-green and cream-colored with 16-inch wheels, it sported a 185 hp V8 engine. The car had power windows, power steering and even a button on the floorboard to change radio stations, a feature I often used to baffle my dates. After driving through the Sumner Tunnel, I found the address. In the parlor, Mary Ann introduced me to her mom who suggested I sit down. Mary Ann had mentioned previously that her father was stationed at the Boston Army Base. That sounded interesting to me; I hoped someday that he might share a few war stories and tell me about life in the military.

As I sipped on a glass of tonic, I noticed movement in the corner of my eye. An enormous shadow darkened the doorway as her uniformed father, a sergeant, slipped quietly into the parlor. High on the left sleeve he wore a wide black brassard with "MP" in white letters. A military policeman, he looked as if he didn't take crap from anyone. As I slowly stood up, the sergeant reached to shake my hand, "Hi Karl. I'm Herculano, Mary Ann's father."

"Nice to meet you, sir. She'll be home early tonight."

Any boy dating the Jolly Green Giant's daughter had better treat her extra special, I thought, as we headed for the front door.

MY FATHER HAD DIFFICULTY dealing with criticism and expressing feelings other than anger, traits his sons inherited. Now and then I'd see my parents have minor squabbles during supper, and rather than react to a searing jibe from Mum, Pop usually just bit his tongue. But one night Mum kept needling him, and without a word, Pop rose slowly from the table, moved to the sink and drove his fist into a stack of dirty dinner plates.

My mother hardly blinked and said, "I must have stepped on your toes."

After wiping off his fist with a dishtowel Pop left the room. Mum turned to me and whispered, "Did you see him blow his stack?"

After my father died, I told my mother about the day he got angry with me. Now it's clear to me that Pop wasn't right for a long time. He went nuts over a simple question; it didn't seem like a big deal at the time.

I had gone over to see my neighborhood friend, Shack. We started talking about things to do and within a few minutes Shack said, "Moose, why don't you borrow your father's *cah*? We can take a ride down the beach?"

"Good idea, I think he's home. Let's go."

We walked down the street, opened the back gate, and headed for the kitchen door. Pop lay softly snoring on the green fabric recliner in the parlor. It seemed odd to see him napping so early in the day. My father's head of dark, wavy hair had begun to thin and turn gray in spots. He kept his hair slicked-back and shiny with splashes of his favorite hair tonic, an odd-smelling brew made with more oil than alcohol. To protect our parlor sofa, my mother used to drape a small towel on the spot where his head rested.

"Pop," I whispered, gently shaking a shoulder.

He coughed several times, turned, and opened sleep-filled, watery eyes.

"What?"

"Pop...Can I borrow the *cah* to take a ride?" From the look on his face I knew the answer.

"No!"

The veins in his neck bulged and his face turned red. Rolling over, he pulled his legs up and slammed his eyelids shut to regain the peace I had shattered. The shocked look on my friend's face mirrored mine and I motioned to him to leave.

Outside Johnny shifted from one leg to the other, shook his head and said, "Jeekers, was he *frickin'* mad."

After I told the story to my mother all she could say was, "Well, he must have been exhausted and didn't appreciate being disturbed."

Over the years my father often broke into a soliloquy at odd times, using words I thought were very strange. Foreign-sounding, they struck no chord inside me.

"Ich weiss nicht, was soll es bedeuten, dass ich so traurig bin."

I can't remember the first time Pop deciphered it for me. He seemed to be telling me: "I don't know why I'm so sad."

When I began to write about those days, I discovered the genesis of the expression. It derived from the classic German romantic poem, *The Lorelei,* which speaks about a mythical, medieval siren on the Rhine River and sailors she lured to their death. My father related to its melancholy message and reciting the poem revealed the sadness locked deep inside his soul.

IN MARCH 1956, THE BLUE HILL OBSERVATORY recorded over 50 inches of snow, the snowiest March in history. On a miserable Saturday that month, Pop drove me over to the Boston Public Latin School so I could take my College Board exams. Preparing for these tests seemed to be counter-productive, so I just showed up and hoped for the best.

As the blizzard continued to escalate, when I opened the car door to run to take the test, I didn't know it would be the last ride Popp ever gave me.

"Good luck. If you don't know the answer, just guess."

When my test results arrived, I knew right away that there was a problem. The scores were low in a few critical areas. So, the applications I had carefully prepared and sent to MIT and Yale fell on deaf ears. Only letters of regret came back to me. In spite of my solid academic record at Boston Tech and my long list of extra-curricular achievements, these schools had a different student profile in mind than mine. And having a father who was an MIT graduate didn't help me in the least.

XII

IT WAS AN OVERCAST APRIL DAY, a day that only years keep at bay. It was spring break and I was sitting alone after lunch in the den upstairs. On the lamp table beside me, a radio blared Elvis Presley's first big hit, "Heartbreak Hotel." Not yet a man, no longer a child, I thought about the high school Senior Prom, a few days away, and dancing with my date.

My peaceful reverie came unwound as I heard my mother howling in the distance like a rabid wolf in the final throes of agony, a hysterical plea that tore at my soul and shook it. Peering over the balcony I saw her motion for me to follow. As we ran outside to the garage, she mumbled, "Something happened," then beat me to the side door and pushed it open.

When my father left the house for the last time, he wore a light-brown, salt-and-pepper woolen overcoat and a dark brown fedora; a brimmed, soft hat like other businessmen wore. Later, a rumor circulated that he had dropped a letter in the mailbox addressed to his wife. Mum emphatically denied ever getting a note. Most people who commit suicide never leave a message behind nor express a death wish.

After loading the shotgun, I assume Pop concealed it under his overcoat and quickly strode the few paces to the old garage. He unlocked the door, turned the doorknob, moved inside and reached for the light switch. Inside, a 1954 Oldsmobile sedan and a 1953 Chevy station wagon sat side-by-side. Pop must have removed his hat, sat down on the concrete slab and placed the cold, steel muzzle of the shotgun barrel behind his left ear, next to the lobe, where the flesh is soft. One long, slim red .410-gauge shell full of tiny birdshot sat silently in the chamber. *What final thoughts flashed before his eyes as he pulled the trigger? No one will ever know.* The firing pin plunged into the shell's brass primer, but the loud report that broke the stillness never reached his brain. Most likely Nonno, prowling the property, heard the gunshot and discovered him. A man his age must have operated on pure instinct; moving quickly to the kitchen, he spoke to his daughter in Italian.

Inside the dank garage lay a scene beyond my comprehension; my heart beat wildly in my chest. On the cold, concrete floor my father was stretched out on his back with his eyes closed; his shoulders faced the massive, sliding wooden doors. The smell of cordite hung in the air. Nonno appeared to be in shock, standing off to the side, silently holding the gun.

A creeping circle of dark red blood, with another puddle of light-yellow fluid on top, lay beside my father's head. With both eyes closed, he looked asleep; nothing marred the peaceful face. The yellowish color of cerebrospinal fluid flowing from his skull seemed odd to me. My nostrils picked up the metallic odor of blood and the picture compressed into a backlit tunnel. But I had to kneel and press my ear against Pop's chest, straining to catch a beat. Only the sound of my own heart broke the silence; I felt his wrist for a faint pulse, but Pop was gone.

My father, an invincible man in my mind, the president of what I thought to be a successful construction company, had turned 49 a few months ago. But now Pop was gone and he didn't say goodbye. Mum's mournful screams broke my trance. "Why?...Why?" over and over. Trembling now, a wave of anger rolled over me as I embraced my mother. A cold and empty feeling rolled over me, and later I had to retreat to the inner sanctum of my room.

Just Call Me Moose!

Police Station Nine at Dudley Street and Blue Hill Avenue dispatched homicide detectives to the house. A cursory investigation began, photos were taken and questions were asked. The corpse was delivered to the Boston Medical Examiner; the coroner, Dr. Curtis, performed a complete autopsy. The death certificate recorded "A self-inflicted gunshot while in a state of acute depression" as the cause of death.

My mother concealed her devastation very well and didn't display the anger she must have felt. Nonno hardly spoke to me; I don't believe he was able to comprehend the sight of his dead son-in-law. The early deaths of young Aurelia, then his wife, had desensitized him and repressed any outward display of emotion. A numbing sadness engulfed me during the hours and days that followed; transient thoughts of joining Pop in death came to me. *How could my father do this to us? Did I say something wrong?* Although other relatives tried to help me, their efforts fell short; I felt abandoned and rejected. At a critical crossroad in my life, my mentor was gone; I desperately needed a father now more than ever. Mum never sought out any professional help because she didn't know where to turn. Every day, we tried to cope and comfort one another.

After Pop shot himself, the sedative prescribed by our family doctor left me groggy; I didn't want to talk or eat and went upstairs to grieve in my bedroom. People close to me told me later I seemed to be in a trance. Thoughts of taking my girlfriend to the senior class prom at the Longwood Towers in Brookline didn't even cross my mind. I'm not sure if I ever picked up the rented tuxedo or the flowers. The entire event melted from my mind in a flash. I did my best to cope with the tragedy on my own and prayed to the Virgin Mary for understanding and strength.

I was the only son home at the time. On B-52 missions from a base in California, Donald, a first lieutenant, donned a high altitude pressure suit to fly on top secret missions into Russian airspace where he recorded the electronic signatures of various Russian radar systems. Roger, an airman first class, served on the island of Formosa. Fluent in Chinese, this taciturn brother had a job collecting intelligence information while eavesdropping on Red Chinese radio traffic.

Donald and Betty, his gregarious wife, flew home for the wake and the solemn Catholic funeral Mass. Only a tightly clenched jaw revealed how Donald felt about Pop's death; he turned his grief inward. But Betty didn't conceal her anguish. She sobbed openly and tried hard to cope with the unexpected death of a father-in-law held in high esteem. Too far away to return, Roger had unwittingly said goodbye to Pop over a year before. The terse telegram from the Red Cross announcing Pop's death came as a terrible blow to this young man on the other side of the world.

At the wake inside the Morrissey Brothers Funeral Home, many of Pop's workers, our friends, relatives, and some of my teachers had come to pay respect. Near the casket, many of them wiped tears away and expressed disbelief about 'The General's' death.

Most of my father's key people came from the same roots. Some of them wanted to be pallbearers; Louie Bidorini, a quiet, wiry fellow, ran the carpentry operations and Mike Fucci, led the pool of laborers. The hard-boiled superintendents, Pop's "Supers," Paul Barra and Joe Gillis, ran day-to-day field operations.

A high school student when he first came on board, a young engineering student from the neighborhood, George worked in the office and in the field. My father became his mentor, a role now he would never be able to fulfill for me. George graduated from Northeastern University and had a successful career in construction in the years to come.

Everyone said the same thing at the funeral home, "I'm sorry for your trouble." A trust and mutual respect had existed between Pop and his men; their livelihoods depended upon him winning major jobs. The stakes were high; only the low bidder won. Now they could only ponder who would provide the next pay envelope. On the night before payday, I could visualize my parents around the supper table counting stacks of money and filling the small manila envelopes. And I realized there would be no more paydays scheduled from Pop's business.

Among those who came to pay respect was John Volpe, a Boston self-made construction magnate, an early associate of my father. John A. Volpe would later serve as a Republican governor of Massachusetts for three terms. Later Nixon chose him to be the Secretary of Transportation, and the American ambassador to Italy, significant achievements for a son whose immigrant father was a plasterer.

When Volpe's name came up at the supper table, Pop often said, "John Volpe would make a good president."

For years after my father died, Volpe sent Mum a Christmas card and she always seemed pleased to get it.

During the wake Pop lay in the open casket with a rosary entwined around his fingers, rosary beads that he had never clasped in life. There was no hint of gunshot trauma; his face looked serene and at peace. Many people knelt to say a short prayer and view his body for the final goodbye. As I stood alongside the mourners, my thoughts flashed back to the supper table where Pop often grinned and said, "After I die and I'm lying in my casket, have some naked women dance around me. If I don't get up, you'll know I'm really dead."

No secret to me, Pop always had an eye for a pretty face and a well-turned ankle. And he'd grin slyly after repeating a tired, bad joke that didn't make much sense to a kid. *Why did I remember this one now?*

"One day a man named Wood and a man named Stone were walking down the street. They both saw a pretty girl. Wood turned to Stone and Stone turned to Wood, and they both turned to rub her." It took years for me to get the play on the last word.

Most of my friends hardly spoke at the wake, but it helped that the closest came to give me support. Joe, Eddie, Deetch, Raff, and Shack each gripped my hand.

"Sorry about what happened, Moose."

Just Call Me Moose!

Pop never had much time for them when they came over. Even the girl I'd planned to take to the prom and her parents stopped in to console me. When everyone left the funeral parlor, I felt alone and scared; my eyes stayed wet and red for days.

In spite of my father's suicide, the Church allowed a Catholic funeral. At the funeral Mass in gloomy Saint Margaret's Church, the parish priest recited the words of St. Ambrose, the patron saint of Milan, "We have loved him during life; let us not abandon him, but let us conduct him into the house of the Lord. May he rest in peace and may his soul and the souls of the faithfully departed rest in peace. Amen." Splashing holy water from the aspergillum onto the casket, the priest consecrated my father's remains for all time. The gray, aromatic holy incense wafted slowly upward from a censer the priest had waved over the casket. Pop never went to church; it would be the last opportunity for him. As we dropped onto the hard wooden kneelers, my mother sobbed quietly; I said a silent prayer. A prayer for each smooth black bead of my rosary asking the Virgin Mary, the Mother of God, for strength. And in the gloomy months that followed, I relied upon Mary to keep from being swept into a whirlpool of despair. And she held me up and gave me the courage to survive. Yet anger and resentment hovered over me for months as I struggled to understand why my father had abandoned us.

The black funeral hearse with its bronze casket moved slowly down Columbia Road, Blue Hill Avenue and Franklin Park to the American Legion Highway. No one spoke on the way to the cemetery. My father was buried next to his immigrant parents, below the imposing granite monument in the family cemetery. As the casket was lowered into the damp grave, I picked up some wet dirt and scattered it on the lid. My mother leaned over and dropped a rose into the hole. A deep sadness overwhelmed me, and a knot formed in my stomach. As I turned away from the grave, I thought, *Why did you do it?*

160

Just Call Me Moose!

AS A CHILD I REMEMBER MY FATHER showing little patience for a hyperactive son after a trying day at the office. Children weren't encouraged to express themselves or offer an opinion to their parents. Should I begin to blab, Pop often said, "Children are seen and not heard!" A common expression for adults to say to kids and one guaranteed to keep me quiet. So the attention I craved at home had to be acted out on the streets or in school. And the rules I broke gave someone a reason to finally notice me.

Several months before Pop died, I gave a talk at the weekly luncheon meeting of the prestigious Boston Rotary Club. Boston Technical High and other local public schools each selected a boy to attend the luncheons for three months. As a member of the National Honor Society, I represented Boston Tech. From the lectern in the large, ornate Georgian Room of the Hotel Statler, I looked out on nearly 300 members and their guests. These were professional men and women from all over the area; the first time I ever addressed a group of this size and an audience other than kids my age. It made me a little uneasy, yet I was confident since I'd practiced my speech and felt ready. Bright lights bathed the room and the murmuring in the crowd grew louder as my time to speak approached. I remember getting the premise of my talk, "The Over-Emphasis of College Athletics," from a recent national magazine article.

Pop had been invited to attend the luncheon by the president of a roofing company, one of his subcontractors. As the moderator introduced me, I scanned the room for Pop. When I saw him enter in the rear, look my way then quickly wave at me, I felt 10 feet tall.

After my father died, my mother told me about a letter she found in his private office file; a letter typed on the stationery of the roofing company. She read it to me. The personal note ended with the words, "You ought to be rightfully proud of that boy; I'm sure that he'll make his mark in this world." It made me feel good at the time but sad that Pop never took the time to let me see it. In spite of what Pop often said to me, "Children are seen and not heard," I took comfort in knowing that Pop must have been proud of me.

MY OBJECTIVE TO ATTEND COLLEGE never wavered after Pop died. No other option ever entered my mind since I could never disappoint my mother or my deceased father. The few remaining months left at Boston Tech quickly slipped away; in spite of my deep grief, I managed to stay focused on school activities and my remaining courses. At the end, I graduated close to the top of my class. Many in my class of 333 boys went on to college and subsequent engineering and science careers.

After my father died, all the company assets had to be sold, but Pop had set aside funds for my education. Northeastern University agreed to admit me to the Engineering School that fall. Although my father and the construction business he founded were gone, I remained committed to confronting the difficult challenge of a civil engineering curriculum. Boston University and Boston College, my brothers' schools, catered more to the study of liberal arts. Northeastern provided the technical environment that suited me. Grieving and feeling adrift, I pulled myself together and pressed forward and when college studies took more of my free time, the weekend trips through the Summer Tunnel to see my girlfriend ended, so Mary Ann and I parted company. When I told Mum the news, I thought I heard a sigh of relief.

Donald left the Air Force and returned to Boston to help our mother handle financial matters involving Pop's defunct business. With Betty, and two extra mouths, Pam and Mark, to feed, Donald secured a position in computer sales with IBM. They moved into the back apartment on Elder Street. Not long after, a better career opportunity surfaced and IBM transferred Donald and his family to Rhode Island. Nonno finally sold the old family house and moved into Pop's old office in the upstairs apartment. Nonno, who enjoyed the role of watchman for the property, often took the bus to Melrose to stay with Auntie Ines and her family.

From the start of college, in spite of long hours studying, I had difficulty absorbing all the new, complex material. It felt like treading water at the quarries. Courses in chemistry, engineering drawing, English, physics, and math pulled me in different directions. My freshman grades were mostly C's and D's; the only B that I received was in military science. Classes relating to civil engineering and on-the-job training didn't begin until my sophomore year. In the co-operative program or what we called co-op, I could swap 10-week periods of school with 10-weeks of work.

The university was as old as Boston Technical and located in the same general vicinity. My mother paid $750 for my annual tuition. Most freshman boys were required to enroll for two years in the Army Reserve Officers' Training Corps or ROT-SEE. Cadets drilled on a nearby field in warm weather wearing an itchy, brown-wool uniform and toting a heavy M-1 rifle. Combat-seasoned senior sergeants taught classes in military science. Their tales of real-life battles with people dying of horrible wounds in the mud dampened any yearning for army life, so after completing the mandatory requirement, I resigned.

As the Christmas holidays approached, my father's loss hit me especially hard. What better way to stifle my feelings of despair than to get drunk with my friends? We, the pliable sons of our fathers, had stood in the shadows watching them get tight after drinking highballs or bottles of beer with whiskey chasers. Pop always opened up and talked freely after a few Canadian Club highballs. It seemed that booze allowed people to open up to others and share feelings. I had observed my father consume liquor at home or at a relative's house, never in a bar. A friend told me that his Scotch-Irish father practically lived in local taverns after work to uphold a long tradition of Irish heavy-drinkers who loved to mingle with their peers. Another father I knew, a wiry, gregarious French-Canadian, no teetotaler himself, could drink with the best.

Just Call Me Moose!

Always out to impress my friends, I promised to donate a fifth of Canadian Club from Pop's "stash" in the cantina to celebrate New Year's Eve. That night after supper, Mum gave me permission to go out with my friends. In the cellar, I slipped a bottle of booze under my coat and met the guys on the corner.

The night was cold and we couldn't wait to start celebrating. It was our time to get a big taste of booze, albeit on a frigid night on the neighborhood streets. As we walked into the dark toward the Prairie, a frigid wind whipped across our faces. Bending forward, I tugged at the zipper of my jacket and yanked down hard on my knit scully cap. Frog pulled his stocking cap over his ears and Shack held the brim of his pork-pie hat to keep it from flying off. The bottle of whiskey changed hands frequently and each of us took a quick swig. The bitter brew warmed our bellies and felt good; in no time, only a small amount of the whiskey hugged the bottom of the bottle. Now our slurred voices began to cut through the stillness of the night with an off-key Christmas carol.

"*Jing-al berals, jing-al berals,*
Jing-al all da way,
Oh...what...fun...it...is...to ride
In a one hoss open sleigh..."

As the three of us stumbled deeper into the pitch-black night there was no way to escape from the dissonance.

"How does everyone feel," I asked.

"I'm shitfaced....A cup o' coffee would taste good," another chimed-in.

It was difficult for me to understand the words, since the potent spirits had impaired my hearing. Close to midnight, we lurched toward the distant lights of the Victoria Diner. Although the place wasn't too far from home, there had never been a reason to stop there. But tonight, hot black coffee might sober us up. That's what grownups did after getting smashed. The rounded, well-lit building and its shiny polished metal exterior resembled an Airstream travel trailer or, in our state of mind, a glowing UFO spaceship. The few patrons ignored us as we filed in, sat at the counter, burped loudly, and waived frantically for the waitress.

Outside, sounds of midnight—the sirens in the distance—broke the quiet. Revelers in cars whipped past us on Massachusetts Avenue, blinking their headlights and beeping their horns in an orchestrated cacophony. Laughing hysterically, someone tried to sing Auld Lang Syne and massacred the words. It was the worst rendition of the classic song I had ever heard. The lyrics had never sounded this bad. We held each other up, trying to stand straight without crashing like dominoes to the sidewalk.

And then I remember yelling, "We did it guys....We're wasted."

I hid the bottle with its dregs in a vacant lot across the street and a few weeks later it was still there.

On the way home, Frog kept mumbling, "I'm in trouble. I can't go through the front door." His parents might be waiting up for him and he'd catch hell. Outside his house, after giving him a ten-finger boost with our hands locked together, Frog slipped quietly through his bedroom window. Frog and Shack told me later that they made it home safely. With a ringing in my ears, I walked unsteadily down Elder Street to my house and after opening the front door and peeking inside the parlor, I was surprised to see my mother sitting there bathed in the eerie glow of the television's test pattern.

"Hap...pee...New Yeeah, Ma."

"Don't call me, Ma!"

Her eyes narrowed and she followed me into the foyer as I dove headlong up the steep staircase to bed, clutching the banister tightly and dropping to my knees a few times on the way.

When I came down to breakfast late that morning, Mum chose not to hassle me about my drunken antics. As the following weeks slipped away, she must have accepted the erosion of her control and power over me. My mother most likely understood that it would be counterproductive to alienate "the last of the Mohicans" in her midst.

Early in my freshman year, a few of us members of the Shack Club decided to join the local Knights of Columbus in Dorchester. On most Sundays, we attended Catholic Mass together; the call to join the Knights coming from the pulpit seemed reasonable. The K of C remains dedicated to the ideals of Charity, Unity, Fraternity and Patriotism: the same ideals that Dorchester boys like us held close to our hearts. The Knights allowed young men to join when they reached 18, and we tuned in on the fact that members as young as us could drink liquor.

Soon, Frog, Raff, Shack and me, Moose, had filled out applications to become members of Columbus Council 116 that operated from a building once the headquarters of the old Dorchester Club. Many of the Knights, who came to the old house near Edward Everett Square, just sat around and played cards and threw down a few beers. Most of the guys were a lot older than us, so I felt a little out of place. On a frigid winter night, the council initiated us as Third Degree Knights. Forever sworn to secrecy, I will never divulge any details about the initiation ceremony. All I can say is that the Knights in charge of the ceremony managed to scare the be-Jesus out of us.

Shortly after my friends and I joined the council, the Knights of Boston promoted a train trip to Montreal on Washington's Birthday, a winter holiday weekend. Frog, Raff, Shack and I had never been there and since the price was right, we signed up. About 13 day coach cars crammed with Knights and their ladies left Boston for Canada; the long trip north was one big party. The only memorable part of the train trip to Canada revolved around all the booze we consumed. I remember little about downtown Montreal and the hotel where we stayed, but memories of my hangover, the ice, the snow and the cold, remain. My dark-blue jacket with the K of C patch over my left breast showed me that I could drink as much booze as those Irish guys sitting around playing cards.

Just Call Me Moose!

At Northeastern, I took courses in modern democracy and another that delved deeply into the theories behind socialism, fascism, communism and democracy. The lectures and readings gave me an insight into how governments operate. And when the populace is vulnerable, how easily dictatorships can arise. As a child who grew up during World War II, I witnessed the horrifying deeds of tyrannical states. As an adult I looked into the abyss that the ensuing Cold War brought about. Communism has a fatal flaw. It never worked because humankind seeks self-determination—the freedom to reap the benefits of their labor.

All engineering students in the five-year co-op program were assigned to either the A- or B-Division. With one surveying class under my belt, my co-op experience could begin. My A-Division work started in January at a small Brookline engineering company, H. F. Bryant and Son, and after 10-weeks, a student in the B-Division replaced me. Most of my tasks took place outside and involved participating in land or topographical surveys. Many jobs only lasted a day or two; I liked the idea of going to different places in areas around Boston. Some of my tasks seemed menial; for one, making blue line prints in the attic on an archaic Ozalid machine that spewed nasty ammonia fumes.

Our immediate boss, Ralph Jones, Jr., a short, jittery fellow, assigned the jobs each day. Since I was the new guy, I started as a rod man on the company's only survey party, the person who holds the dumb end of a steel tape measure and carries the long graduated wooden rod for the transit man. Our crew chief, Doug, a man of few words, took his job very seriously. By the time my co-op days were over, I operated a black, vintage K&E Paragon transit. My co-op experience taught me the field practicalities of land surveying during my short stint in the field. But the business of crunching numbers left me cold.

XIII

IN LATE 1957, THE SOVIET UNION LAUNCHED a satellite they called Sputnik into earth orbit. The whole nation stood in shock, and people squinted into the night air to see the small silvery ball pass overhead. Listening to the rebroadcast of its telltale beeps on the radio made me feel sad to know that Russia had pulled ahead of us in space. Our Cold War archrival had done the unthinkable, but their experiment rallied the country to action. Soon issues involving science and technology took on a much higher priority; the race to conquer space had captured the attention of Americans.

In the classrooms, my courses grew more complex as new subjects kept coming and they took the place of the old ones. And I began to lose a sense of accomplishment when my grades didn't improve. My teachers had little time to tutor a kid after hours. So, I plodded along as best I could.

An incident occurred around this period that stays with me. Applied Mechanics, a foundation course in any civil engineering program, covers internal forces in trusses and beams, centers of gravity and the related calculations. The professor who taught the course was a short, bald Jewish man who understood everything about the subject.

Everything seemed to be going well, until I took the first few tests; my grades on the quizzes looked shaky. The overall grade for the course seemed uncertain, so I met with the professor after the final exam. I needed to assess his feelings about my progress in class.

"Sir, I need to speak with you," I said.

He greeted me cordially in his office and I explained how I felt about my grade. As I stammered to justify my academic standing, he listened patiently to me and smiled broadly and tried to allay my fears.

"Don't get *noivus*," he said.

"Thank you for listening, sir."

As I turned to leave, the professor's three-piece suit appeared to morph into the robe of a Rabbi and I felt like a lamb being led to sacrificial slaughter. But when the sound of his words, "Don't get *noivus*," began to echo in the room, I felt a lot better.

That night in bed, I replayed the brief meeting in my mind and concluded I had no worries. A week later, my mother said, "Oh, before I forget to tell you, I think your grades came today." The stack of mail sat on the credenza in the foyer. After ripping open the envelope and quickly scanning the form, in the column next to Applied Mechanics, an F stared back at me. It felt like someone had kicked me in the stomach; I'd have to take the course over. Worse for me, it seemed, my classmates who had passed the course would be moving on. Flunking mechanics deflated any of my aspirations for a degree in engineering. No matter how hard I tried, it seemed to be an unattainable goal.

IN THE PAST, AT CHRISTMAS, Pop had always arranged to give brightly packaged treats, including cheeses and dried fruits, to his key employees and subcontractors for their hard work. One holiday season, I mounted a small speaker inside an S.S. Pierce wooden pail after removing all the goodies. The ancestors of Samuel Pierce were original settlers of Dorchester and had built a chain of upscale grocery stores that carried unique products.

Sometimes I placed a classical album on the turntable and turned the volume down when I was studying in the den. The small wooden pail with the speaker inside rested on the carpet beside my easy chair. For a few hours after supper I used to sit at Pop's oak desk in the same room where I had heard Mum scream for me. Now she kept her distance; she wanted me to finish school like her other sons. As I struggled by myself to understand a complicated problem in math or logic, I felt frustrated. And sometimes tears welled up in my eyes. *Pop I wish you were here; I need you*, I thought. But, I was on my own now; there wasn't any time to feel sorry for myself.

At my co-op job where I worked as a surveyor, an interesting project began to take shape. In 1958, the engineering company was awarded a contract to survey the West End. This proud Boston community consisted of Italian, Polish, Jewish, Irish, black, and Hispanic families. In the name of progress the city had earmarked the 48-acre tract for a so-called "Urban Renewal" project. All the structures would be razed; today, many would be considered architectural treasures. About 8,000 people had to be relocated to other neighborhoods throughout Boston. They didn't have a choice. The contract required a complete survey of the perimeter, elevations of all sewer lines, and preliminary measurements of individual structures.

A few kids I knew in high school still lived there. Now I could appreciate how they felt about their unique neighborhood. Local newspapers broke the news of the impending demolition on the very day we showed-up to begin work. As the three of us strolled along the narrow winding streets, next to rows of old four-story brownstone homes, carrying a survey transit on a tripod, a rod, and long steel measuring tapes, there was no place to hide. Everyone knew why we were there. Young and old alike screamed at us from their parlor windows, "You'll never tear the West End down!" In spite of the hostile reception, in the weeks that followed we were able to complete all our tasks. But dodging cars in traffic, while opening sewers with a pick to measure the depth of the pipes, proved dicey. And when the weather warmed up, the smell made me dizzy.

Soon bulldozers and wrecking balls began to wreak havoc on the vacated dwellings. Generations of poor immigrants once lived and died there; in a few years, only the affluent could afford the spacious new apartments inside the upscale towers overlooking Charles River Park. Years later, I visited Zia Cecilia who lived alone in one of the high-rise apartments. In the living room, I looked out from on high toward Beacon Hill and reflected on the survey we had done. As far as I know, Zia Cecilia never met anyone who had lived in the neighborhood.

HAVING A CADRE OF OLD FRIENDS to telephone and go places with helped buoy my morose mood. After completing high school, Frog landed an outside job at the telephone company; he didn't go directly to college. All of us were too young to drink lawfully, but Frog came up with a solution. Why wait a few more years if we could authorize ourselves to buy booze? One day he brought home a stack of blank, official company identification cards.

"Check these out," he said. "You have a typewriter that works, right?"

"Yeah."

"Good. How about you making up a few ID cards for the boys?"

With two fingers I was able type our real names, and a fictitious job title, birth date, and supervisor's name. With a black pen, I signed as the supervisor then laminated the ID cards in plastic so they looked official. Now all of us could buy alcohol in bars or clubs and never have to sweat it. Since I looked older than the others, I always volunteered to buy the booze. No package store ever refused my request for a six-pack of beer.

One night in a bar, we flashed the fake IDs for the first time; the same job title and supervisor appeared on each green card. The waitress used a flashlight to verify our birth dates then paused to hear our order.

"How's life as telephone linemen?"

I leaned back in the booth and laughed when Frog replied, "It's real dangerous around all those hot wires."

I looked forward to the weekends to relax and put aside my textbooks for a few hours. One Friday night, I attended a party with Frog and a few other friends in a Boston suburb. In the cluster of partygoers, an attractive, animated young girl with hair the color of a dark plum caught my eye. Something about pretty girls with big brown eyes intrigued me. And I liked the look of her full painted lips. After getting a beer, I mustered the courage to move through the crowd of young people, made a silly comment then introduced myself.

"My name's Judith," she said, "but my friends call me Judy." During conversation in the kitchen, Judy said she attended Somerville High. Afterwards in the light of the kitchen, the sparkle in her eyes and her effervescent personality added to my first impression of her. And I felt she was struck by the fact I was a sophomore in college. In the background, I could hear a record playing. Frank Sinatra was singing "Laura," and our eyes met. A slow number like that made me feel comfortable, especially in a room with low light.

"Judy, would you like to dance?"

I followed her into the small parlor packed with partygoers and she found a spot on the wooden floor where someone had rolled back the rug. As I closed my eyes and held Judy close, her forehead touched my cheek. I thought how nicely we fit together. She was just the right height. As we danced, I kept playing "Laura" over and over, until someone hid the record. I made it a point to get Judy's telephone number but had no rush to get involved with a pretty high school girl. I had enough of a job just handling my own emotions. In the car on the way home a friend couldn't resist making a comment.

"Did you see Moose dancing with that Portugee girl from Somerville? She had pillows for lips."

"Knock it off. I like girls with puffy lips," I said. "They feel so soft when I get to kiss them.

WHEN I LEFT THE HOUSE EACH MORNING to go to classes, I carried a slide rule, drafting board, T-square, textbooks and notebooks under my arm. By now my grade point average had sunk to a new low and several classes had to be repeated. The second time around, I picked up a C in Applied Mechanics. And a few B's appeared alongside math and calculus courses. Every morning, Mum yelled up the stairs for me to get up, and although I went through the motions at school, I felt burned out. Becoming a civil engineer seemed to be beyond my grasp. The time had come to cut my losses and redirect my efforts.

Frog had recently enlisted in the Air Force Reserve and spent six months on active duty as a cook. He signed up at Hanscom Air Force Base which is located about 20 miles outside Boston and was assigned to the 94th Troop Carrier Wing, a unit that flew C-119 Flying Boxcars. After talking to Frog and getting first-hand information, I began to formulate a plan. *If civil engineering won't work for me, I'll take a year off and join the Air Force.* When I confronted Mum with my idea, she looked aghast.

"You'll never *finish* college."

Nothing she said deterred me; now the master of my own destiny, I desperately needed some time off from the academic grind to recharge my internal batteries. So I took the qualification tests, got accepted and that summer I was sworn-in and slated to attend air passenger specialist training. An officer told me that after initial basic training at Lackland Air Force Base in Texas, I'd be going to a tech school at Sheppard AFB on the Oklahoma border. That option sounded good to me.

Mum would miss her baby, but it was important to prove myself and be on my own.

That July, when I disembarked from a commercial flight in Texas, the air was thick with humidity. It felt like a wet blanket covered me; a mugginess 10 times worse than Boston. And on the tarmac, the temperature took my breath away. When we pulled up in a bus on the airbase, a few Tactical Instructors—TI's—started screaming at us through the open windows.

"Hey, "rainbows," get outta da bus. Move it! Get da lead outta yur ass. Line up ovah here."

Some of the guys looked shocked, but I was laughing inside at the charade. New recruits arriving on base got tagged as a "rainbow" because of our multi-colored civilian attire. Inside the barbershop, barbers acting like pokerfaced robots moved buzzing clippers around our scalps to remove all our hair. Some of the recruits looked ready to cry as their locks joined the growing pile. Now everyone looked the same, the desired effect, like scared escapees from a concentration camp.

Next stop was the "Green Monster," a large building used to issue equipment and uniforms. It seemed like a rough start, but the mouthy sergeants never intimidated me. Before leaving, Roger cautioned me to follow orders and never talk back. He had been through the same hazing years before and wanted to pass on some rare brotherly advice.

The fast-moving training program of physical training, firing an M-1 rifle on the range, and classroom lectures seemed elementary, compared with my recent college routine. Most of the guys in my Reserve flight had already completed two years of college. They came from many states, so my Boston accent seemed foreign to them. New Yorkers liked to say, "Hey, *Kahl*, let's go play some *cahds*." In turn I was exposed to their accents and heard them say, "I'll have a cup of *cawfey* and a *hamboiga*," when they talked about eating out.

I didn't like being teased about my Boston accent so I made a conscious effort to pronounce the letter R and speak in a more generic manner. It's not easy to disguise a native dialect handed down from the British.

Speaking a little odd, however, wasn't the only way to draw attention. One tall, heavy-set member of my flight, a former airman in the Israeli Air Force, had to put up with a sadistic sergeant who took great pleasure in getting in his face.

"Hey, Jew boy, how da ya like Texas?"

The taunts became more strident. For being Jewish, he had to put up with a lot of crap, but the nasty jibes didn't seem to intimidate him in the least. Our basic training must have been child's play compared with his experiences in Israel. A fellow named Hardick took flak every roll call. Our training sergeant used to yell, "Hard...Dick," while grinning ear-to-ear. The gaunt technical sergeant in charge of my flight was a war veteran; he loved polishing green recruits. In formation, one day, this sergeant told us, "I've been to the east,...the west,...the north...and the south of Texas. If there's *anything* beautiful in this state they must be moving it around."

We bunked in vintage, open-bay, two-story barracks and each recruit only retained a small footlocker for personal things. A little Mexican kid bunked next to me. Growing up, few Hispanics had ever crossed my path and I knew virtually nothing about Mexican food. This kid had difficulty coping with his new environment and the well-ordered schedule. I'll always remember his moans from morning to night.

"Chinga tu madre!...Chinga tu madre!"

Piggy's Spanish class never covered this expression. "Mother" was the only word I could translate.

"Why do you keep saying that?" I asked.

"I'm pissed off about all the chicken shit we have to put up with."

"So what does *chinga* whatever really mean?"

The gesture he made with his hands and hips wasn't difficult to understand. Then he quickly added, "Not *your* mother"

It came to me in a flash. *Some Mexicans like to say, 'Go screw your mother' when they're pissed-off.*

I had to agree with him about the chicken shit: unreasonable tasks and rules piled on us by the people in power. The first time I heard a fellow airman mutter the term "BOHICA," it sounded strange. I came to learn it stood for Bend Over Here It Comes Again.

Every night some of us pulled fire watch. If a fire ever broke out, the tinderbox-dry archaic dwelling would be quickly engulfed in flames. No built-in fire suppression existed. My mother would have been proud to see me doing things I never did at home. I scrubbed floors, cleaned the latrine and washed my own laundry during those long days in basic training. And maybe Mum would have applauded my Kitchen Police duties to see me peeling potatoes at 0400 hours.

Anyone in the group who bathed infrequently received a "blanket party." First, a rough wool GI blanket would envelope the smelly recruit and then others would take turns punching him through the fabric. After a few minutes, the guilty culprit was pitched into the shower area and scrubbed raw with soap and water. Any other recruits who didn't like to bathe got the message quickly after the demonstration. And once, when another recruit wanted to show everyone his pubic area and tried to point out his case of crabs, I passed.

After a month of grunting and sweating under the San Antonio sun while drilling, doing calisthenics, and running the obstacle course, leaping over rows of logs, climbing high walls, and swinging from ropes over pools of water, my next stop was Sheppard AFB. I had to take more basic training and enroll in my air passenger tech school there. On a Saturday morning, I boarded a small Air Force bus with no cooling for the grueling 400-mile trek to Wichita Falls. The rolling, arid, brown terrain had no resemblance to my wooded, green New England landscape. By the time the bus rolled through the main gate, I needed a beer. When we pulled up in front of the Airmen's Club I scrambled for the latrine to take a leak, then headed for the bar. In the background, the strains of country and western music blared from a tired old jukebox.

"I need a pitcher of Lone Star," I yelled to the bartender at the other end of the counter. "We just drove in from San Antonio and I'm dying."

I sloshed-down the full pitcher of low-alcohol 3.2 percent beer and felt rejuvenated. After ordering a second pitcher, the bartender offered me a glass. A new town, a brand new experience, and I thought, *Bring it on.*

Two more months of basic training followed, including classes about every transport aircraft in the Air Force inventory. I learned how to manifest—carefully document passengers and cargo on cargo aircraft and using weight and balance criteria and a big slide rule, I calculated how to load them. Planes crashed if a mistake was made. When I graduated at the top of the class it made me feel good about myself.

One weekend, my flight received a pass to go into Wichita Falls, a flat, bleak, windy city, but we had to wear a uniform. I had heard that the locals didn't appreciate a military presence; the few locals I met weren't too friendly. One guy wouldn't even give me the time of day. Consequently, I felt little desire to leave the base. I turned 21 before returning to Boston. I had to celebrate my birthday in the barracks with little fanfare and no close friends around. In Texas, I hadn't sought opportunities to lose my virginity; I had no desire to get into trouble.

Back at Hanscom AFB, the brass assigned me to the Transportation Squadron. Since there were a few months remaining of active duty, I spent my days in the Personal Equipment Shop, checking parachutes and issuing equipment to the aircrews. After working on base during the week, I returned home on weekends. I could tell that Mum was happy to see me, and I was glad to be home. But each of us had needed a short respite from the other. After my military sojourn away from college, I felt refreshed. Being on my own gave me a feeling of self-sufficiency and maturity.

As a "Weekend Warrior," once a month I drove to Hanscom Field to attend training sessions. Only two of us in the unit had an Air Passenger Specialist job title. There wasn't much for us to do until summer training camp rolled around; then our skills could be better utilized. Grenier AFB in New Hampshire became my home for two weeks during the next few summers. New Hampshire offered a lot of outdoor activities for a young man in the summer. Close to the base, I enjoyed hiking, swimming, and water skiing. And my duties not only fulfilled my Air Force Reserve training obligation, I got paid the same as being on active duty.

A few months before my 22nd birthday, I paid a pretty woman to take something special of mine. At the base in New Hampshire an airman pitched an idea for some weekend fun; it sounded exciting. The Jewish fellow had connections in New York and planned soon to throw a wild time away from the base. He related that for 10 bucks, any invited could drink some cold beer and watch two good-looking babes dance and take off their clothes. "That's for starters," he said. Glancing around, he grinned, made a pumping motion with his forearm, and added, "Getting' a piece of tail can be arranged." So Frog and I looked at each other and grinned.

"Let's go for it."

"Why not," Frog added.

On Saturday night, a caravan of 15 cars and trucks belonging to other airmen began to form. We had lined up early next to the barracks, waiting for the procession to begin. The officers in the unit weren't invited; everyone participating had been sworn to secrecy. Only a few participants knew the location. The event coordinator showed up and collected the money, then pulled up in front and yelled, "Follow me." The convoy snaked slowly through the base and soon reached an unlit, rutted, dirt road that led into the woods. After we pulled up next to a stained wooden building, in the dim light I barely made out the sign above the door. *A rod and gun club?* The place had been rented to us for the night. Inside, after turning on the lights, Frog and I helped set-up a number of folding metal chairs in a big circle in the main room.

The guys told jokes and bantered with one another while waiting for the girls to show up. A few cases of beer on ice lay floating in a galvanized tub off to the side.

"Frog, you bring a church key?"

"Yeah. Here it is."

After using the beer opener to open the can and watching it fizz, I sipped the cold Schlitz and exchanged a few pleasantries with a few of the others.

"Hey," one said, "Did ya hear the one about the new cereal in the grocery stores called Prostitutti?"

Frog leaned forward in his seat.

"Nah. What about it?"

This stuff doesn't snap, crackle, or pop. It just lays there and bangs."

"That's funny. We'll have to tell the guys," I said to Frog.

Surrounded by other airmen waiting for the action to begin, I wondered if we'd been had. Finally, two big guys with grim faces came through the outside door followed by a tall blonde and a shorter brunette. Both young women looked stacked; they had first-class bodies and appeared very attractive. The Jewish guy had been right; these girls weren't dogs. My loins, girded for so long, needed to unveil the mystery. Tonight, maybe I'd get lucky.

I can't remember any music playing in the background as the shorthaired blonde entered the circle of clapping guys, began to move around and peel off her street clothes. Now just in high heels, she undulated close to us; some guys reached out to cop a feel. Not me. The powder she had daubed on her smooth face and soft body smelled sweet. Some of it ended up on the laps of guys when she sat down on their lap. And when she slipped out of her panties, I thought, *where's the hair?* After awhile, the brunette, the girl with the larger boobs, completed her solo routine to a round of applause. Judging from all the whooping and clapping, it had been worth the wait.

Our airman director announced that for the right price, both dancers would do the dirty deed. I looked over at Frog.

"No, not me. You go for it," he said.

The thought of having sex with a woman seemed overwhelming. The Church considered sex outside marriage to be a taboo and sex was a mystery only unlocked for procreation. I suspected that most of the young guys my age in the crowd had never had the opportunity to roll in the hay with a girl. Rumors abounded about the act of sex; we kids were ignorant about a woman's body and terrified by the thought of getting a girl pregnant, then having to marry her. Pop had never taken the time to talk with me about the "birds" and the "bees." Mum used to snicker when a neighborhood girl got pregnant out of wedlock, winking as she spoke.

"She delivered a nine-pound baby, a *preemie*. Right?"

So, when a buddy said to me, "Keep it in your knickers," it made a lot of sense.

Although I tried hard to squelch a rush of impure thoughts, the urge to merge with the hard-bodied brunette won out. After striding to the doorway of the room off the hall, I took my place in line and paid one of the escort goons. We did it on the rough plank floor in the missionary position, on top of a scratchy brown GI blanket. Maybe other guys fantasized about losing their cherry with a princess in a candle-lit canopy bed listening to classical music, but on this night I couldn't wait.

"Here, put this on," she said, as she handed me a safe. I never carried a condom in my wallet; why take up valuable space for nothing? As I knelt, she guided my manhood and we connected. To hold myself back, I ran square root problems in my head, thrusting hard for as long as possible but my partner may as well have been munching on a pear. Friction from the wool blanket made my knees burn, but I kept at it and soon a wave of gentle spasms rolled over me. Everything had worked as designed and when I rolled off her and stood up to slip on my jockey shorts, my nameless partner said, "First time?"

"How'd you know?"

Only a silent gloat came across her face. It said volumes. Not until a few years later on my honeymoon night in Denver, did my heart and soul sing gleefully as I made passionate love to my virgin wife.

During my time in the Air Force Reserve, my Wing participated in a major joint service operation. Our Flying Boxcars flew out of Donaldson AFB in Greenville, South Carolina, to drop hundreds of paratroopers in the 82nd and 101st Airborne Divisions. The operation was Operation Swift Strike, the largest airborne drop since World War II. Being part of it made a huge impression on me; the thought of serving in an organization with noble goals, one with a higher calling, began to capture my attention. When a plan comes together smoothly to complete a mission, it's something to behold. But, sometimes, plans don't work and people get hurt in the fog of operations. Thus far, being a member of the military had been a positive experience, but to serve as a commissioned officer made more sense. But, first I needed to finish college.

XIV

WITH MY SIX MONTHS OF ACTIVE DUTY OVER, a few months before resuming my college classes, I took a job in the Lamont Library at Harvard University. Working in a place full of books soon became tedious, but the pleasant staff and my exposure to world-class literature helped ease the boredom. During that time a recent graduate vanished while on an anthropological outing to the jungles of New Guinea. Michael Rockefeller, heir to the family fortune, had once browsed the same library stacks. No sign of him ever resulted from the extensive search; it was rumored that cannibals ate him. *Life seemed to be such a fragile commodity, even for someone so privileged,* I thought. Destiny spares no man from what is already written.

Back at Northeastern after a year away, with my batteries recharged, I met with the dean of Liberal Arts, Dr. Lake, a quiet, serious man. The meeting concluded that the best option for me was to pursue a degree in mathematics. Pop's words, "Math is the key," started to make sense. All my old engineering classmates had stayed on track to graduate, but now a degree in math seemed to be a viable alternative for me. After completing a required course in French that summer at Boston College, I received my first college-level A and I resumed classes on a full-time basis in the fall. My goal to graduate as soon as possible was in sight, even though it remained unclear how a career would play out.

Joining a fraternity never appealed to me and rarely did I hang out at the Lobster Claw, a popular nearby pub. My social life revolved around the guys of the Shack Club. With a full schedule, taking 16 credit hours most quarters, I needed to race through the next two years. Courses like Differential Equations, Advanced Algebra, Logic, Vector Analysis along with English Literature, Accounting, and Statistics drained my mental faculties.

When the tall, grim Dr. Statknis, a strict math professor, began to explore the depths of abstract algebra, it made my brain hurt. As fast as he wrote lines of equations on the blackboard, with the other hand he'd be erasing the board. All year round, this odd professor wore a thin polyester short-sleeve shirt with a pack of Winston cigarettes visible in the breast pocket. I kept trying to grasp the concepts he threw at us but I never succeeded.

Unfortunately for me, not even Roger could help me now. Still single and living at home, after leaving the Air Force he ended up at the U.S. Army Intelligence School at Fort Holabird in Maryland, a place insiders called "The Bird." My brother never alluded to being a "spook," but the tiny 8mm Minox spy camera on his bureau made me pause. Every movie about spies I ever saw included a camera like his. And I began to imagine that James Bond might be sleeping in the room next to mine. As Roger's graduation day approached, I asked him what he'd be doing as a civilian employee of the Army Security Agency.

"I'm a Research Analyst. That's all I can say."

Fluent in Chinese and with new skills in the field of intelligence, within a few years Roger left for an assignment in the Far East. One day something he said he surprised me.

"I'll be going to Seoul, Korea."

"So, it's back to the Orient for you, Rog?"

"Yep, but I'll have to kill you if I tell you anything more."

"Very funny," I said. "You're still a turkey."

I didn't know it then, but in a few more years we would meet again in Japan.

THE GUYS IN THE SHACK CLUB often joined together to go on day trips in the summer. One bright day, I piled Raff, Frog, and Shack into the Olds and headed for Lake Pearl, a giant of a waterway, in Wrentham. We must have brought a cooler with sandwiches and beer because a day at the beach without a few cold ones wouldn't seem right. Raff spotted an opening on the sand, close to a few decent-looking girls our age lying on a large blanket. They hardly glanced our way, but I watched them sneak peeks at us from behind their sunglasses and heard their whispers about the strangers hovering nearby. Trying to be blasé, we looked around and nonchalantly spread out an old yellow bedspread and put the cooler and our towels down. After dropping our chino pants and removing our T-shirts, we sat down in our bathing suits and scrutinized the landscape.

"Boy, this lake is huge," I said. "Wonder if the water's warm?"

"I'm going down to see," said Shack.

Raff added, "Let's check it out?"

Experience told us that part of any scooping ritual involved looking apathetic. It was important to choose the right moment to make a move. Girls didn't like guys who came on too fast or acted aggressively. After strolling down to the water and swimming for a while, we returned to our things and dried off. Frog, most likely, said something funny to the quarry sitting next to us. Most girls liked guys who had tanned hard bodies and an easy smile; Frog filled the bill and wasn't shy, like me.

After a beer or two, I found the courage to start chatting with a pretty blonde with short hair and blue eyes. Maybe I offered her a beer. She had a great complexion and a cute cleft in her chin and the one-piece bathing suit didn't hide any of her curves. I always found it difficult to talk to strange females:

what to say and how to say it? So, after dropping my name, I asked, "What's yours?"

"Janet."

"That's a nice name."

"Thanks. Where are you guys from?"

"Dorchester," I said.

"Where's that?"

"Next to South Boston."

"Oh."

True to form, alcohol let me open up, like it always had done for Pop, and I started telling her about myself. To impress her, I even brought up Northeastern. She had a job and lived with her parents in the small town of Plainville on the Rhode Island border. Right away, I noticed that her accent seemed a lot different from the local girls I knew and later confirmed that people from her area didn't talk like Bostonians in spite of being only 35-miles away. To my surprise, Janet let me have her home telephone number and I pledged to call her.

On the way home, the guys started razzing me about the babe I liked on the blanket.

"Is she stacked or what?" said Shack.

Raff added, "Did you notice the boobs on that chunky chick?"

"Like a pair of bullets," Frog chimed in.

That's all it took for the name to stick. Thereafter, during idle chatter with my buddies, we called Janet—"Bullets"—in light of her magnum-sized breasts.

On the first date, it was clear to me that Plainville didn't offer much in the way of entertainment, something Janet already knew. The local drive-in had to be the only place young people could go to have fun. For several months of weekend dating, we haunted the drive-in theater, necking and petting our way through many feature films, never ending up in the back seat. Today, kids would chuckle over our innocence and, in their parlance, be dumbfounded that we never chose to reach home base.

One afternoon while visiting Zio Gene, I mentioned my new acquaintance and how we had met.

"Where does she live?"

"Plainville," I replied.

"What's going on down there?"

"Not much. I usually take her to the drive-in."

He looked puzzled, scratched his ear, stared deep into my eyes and leered, as he said, "Isn't that a long way to drive to watch a movie?"

My face turned a dark shade of red.

"Uh...Zio Gene, it's not what you think."

After a few months had passed, the lack of places to go, and time constraints at school deterred me from driving so far to date the nice girl from Plainville and I said goodbye. Being indecisive was never my weak suit.

TO EARN EXTRA MONEY during the summer, I landed a job in heavy construction. Zio Gene arranged for me to work for the Thomas J. O'Connor Construction Company. He knew a foreman, Gene Sullivan, an amiable, husky pipe-smoking Irishman who had a reputation of being effective in the business. On my first job, a hospital addition in Arlington, I dug ditches and carried long, thick planks and 90-lb. bags of cement. I learned to use a jackhammer, and pushed unwieldy carts full of sloshing concrete. It was better than a hard workout in a gym, but every night I drove home exhausted. Wearing an aluminum hard hat and stripped to the waist, my upper torso soon turned red, then bronze. The local labor steward threatened to strike unless I joined the union for the summer. The $50 dollar fee seemed a little steep, but I had no choice. The salary of almost three dollars an hour was excellent and my job, working alongside other hard-working guys, exposed me to different personalities. One laborer, recently released from prison, droned a special mantra all day long.

"Sam's no cat. Sam's a rat!"

Just Call Me Moose!

The young fellow, the target of his persistent taunts, took it well. But if I was Sam, I'm not sure I'd remain so docile.

My last job with the O'Connor Company was in Everett, helping to build a huge power-generating station. By now, I knew the ropes and felt at ease not only with the job, but also felt comfortable amidst the lot of rough construction workers. I cursed just like they did, but one laborer stood out amongst the rest. Up close, this guy's face looked bad; scars encircled both eyes; his dented nose and cauliflower ears resulted from years in the boxing ring, I came to learn. The foreman took care of the tall, blond-haired, muscular guy with the small potbelly. None of the jobs he was assigned seemed to take a lot of energy.

During lunchtime while munching on a salami sandwich that Mum had made, I heard a commotion. The man was shadow boxing, stabbing the humid air with lightning-fast silent punches and moving from side to side, in front of another worker, making fun of him.

"Look, it's the candle kid. One blow and he's out!"

I laughed and said to a worker sitting on the shanty bench, "Who's that guy over there?"

"Oh, that's Irish Bob Murphy, the ex-pug."

A decade before, Murphy fought Joey Maxim for the middleweight championship of the world. That televised fight ended with Murphy losing the 15-round decision. Just a kid in grammar school, I had watched both men duke it out on the tube in New York. Later at work, I learned more details about Murphy's career.

"Irish Bob made over a million bucks in the ring, but handlers took most of it," said someone who knew the sad story.

Now, virtually penniless, he eked out a living doing manual labor, a long step down from his former life. Whenever we met, he always spoke to me. A man who had lost everything, he was once a noble contender but now he was a punch-drunk fighter on the skids. *Pop, too, had lost everything, but he chose to die,* I thought.

One day, I heard the job siren blow at the wrong time. Soon the reason for the untimely sound raced through the throngs of workers. Some of them in the distance started running in my direction. A cloud of dust filled the air.

"What happened?"

"The scaffolding inside the chimney gave way and I think a few guys fell," a stranger said.

There had been an accident at one of the tall concrete chimneys under construction. A few men died after falling about 80 feet. I moved into the shade and quietly said a prayer for those men and their families. Management shut the job down for the day and I left to go home. It was my worse day ever in this business.

The extra spending money from construction jobs came in handy for school expenses. Pop had left a small insurance policy and other cash, but Mum struggled to pay all the household bills. Bankruptcy had taken all the hard assets the business owned. I opened a bank account in my name at the Shawmut Bank in Upham's Corner. My mother closely watched my cash balances and if I spent too much money, she let me know.

"Money goes through your hands like water! You spend money like a drunken sailor."

Her ranting and raving slid off me like water off a duck and led me to squirrel away some of my hard-earned cash to do things without having to ask for an allowance.

DURING MY SENIOR YEAR, I began to date Judy, the girl from the party, the night I played "Laura" over and over again. After receiving a postcard from her, I called. Judy planned to be a nurse after graduating from the Mount Auburn Hospital School of Nursing in Cambridge. Her vivacious personality compensated for my more reserved approach to social demands. Judy loved to sing and dance and with practice our cha-cha routine improved. Sometimes our peers would stop dancing and form a circle to watch us and start clapping. We enjoyed the attention our polished routine got.

After some sweet-talk from her, I agreed to take her to see *The Fantasticks,* in Boston. After sitting there a while, I actually began to enjoy this joyous journey of the heart and began to tap my foot to the sounds of the heartwarming musical. On another occasion, I asked Judy to come with me to see the Dave Brubeck Quartet perform at the MIT Kresge Auditorium. Watching these musicians onstage playing "Blue Rondo a la Turk" and "Take Five," was more to my liking. I loved hearing the pure, sweet, jazz riffs that rolled forth from Brubeck and his group. The near-perfect acoustics of the hall made my heart sing. Many of the quartet's records remained in my collection for years.

My girlfriend, whose parents were born on Madeira Island, lived in Somerville near Porter Square with her neurotic hard-working Portuguese mother, a widow for many years. When Judy was a baby her father died of a heart attack. In the months to come, a falling out with her mother resulted in her leaving home for good.

When the Senior Commencement Ball took place at the Hotel Somerset in Boston, Judy clung to my arm. As our relationship developed, I took a big step by giving her a special birthday present. A gift of a little furry lion with a music box inside might be considered by some to have a Freudian element. Or maybe I identified with the Cowardly Lion in the Wizard of Oz and was trying to look courageous to a special girl in my life?

As graduation day approached, I began to contemplate a lifetime of shuffling papers in some bureaucracy, a career that could never fulfill me. Military service gave me a good excuse to cut the apron strings. Only a profession with a strong element of ongoing action could make me happy. Years of living alone in the big house under my mother's control had to end; I didn't need Mum to wait up late for me anymore. And the thought of becoming a long-term caretaker seemed worrisome. Mum must have understood that it was time for her baby to leave. We both knew that Donald wasn't too far away.

In the Boston Garden on a warm June day, a shiver rolled down my back as I waited to receive my diploma. Six years before I had graduated from high school. My struggle had been worthwhile; I was completing college, albeit not with the degree I set out to get. Governor Volpe spoke to the graduates on that day, but my heart ached for my father. Pop would have been pleased; a Bachelor of Science degree in mathematics is a worthy achievement. When I returned from the stage, Mum gave me a demure Mona Lisa smile and hugged me. I felt great. Through gentle badgering and untiring support, she helped make it all possible.

XV

WHEN I RECEIVED THE OFFICIAL LETTER accepting me to Officer Training School, I knew that my life was about to change. In the place where my new "Specialty" was described, the word "Armament" had been typed. With my math degree, meteorology seemed a more likely choice. One line in my Webster's New World Dictionary defines "armament" as "an arming or being armed for war." That didn't help. Since poor eyesight disqualified me from a flying program, Air Force weapons would be my destiny.

Over the years, I often walked below the large hand-painted signs that greeted visitors to Air Force munitions units. My favorite, "Without Weapons, This Operation is Just Another Unscheduled Airline," made fighter jocks laugh and shake their heads. Fighter pilots are taught during training to be invincible; many of them have large egos and rightfully so.

After a few drinks, some of the more strident ones bristled, "If you ain't a fighter pilot, you ain't shit." No matter what they thought, rubbing elbows with these noble knights of the sky made me feel part of the team. In spite of my non-rated, non-flight status, I held them in high esteem, for they took the good fight directly to the enemy using the weapons in my charge.

It didn't take long to realize that rivalry among the different weapons specialties was widespread and had been pervasive for eons. Bomb dump people often showed disdain for weapons release and gun shop people and they all disliked aircraft weapons loaders. Any munitions squadron with groups of these types needed a solid cadre of top sergeants to keep the entire team focused on the mission. But it made me chuckle when I heard a sergeant from the weapons release shop yell at a storage area troop.

"Hey, you with the size-6 hat and the 20-inch neck. Get ovah here or I'll bury my brogan up your butt."

IN SPITE OF MY LOUSY OVERALL GRADE POINT average, to be an officer in the Air Force, and according to military convention, a gentleman, seemed like a worthwhile objective. To travel the world, learn new skills, and change jobs frequently, along with meeting new friends with similar interests, fascinated me. Mum used to say, "Variety is the spice of life," and I had to agree. And I felt a need to step forward and serve my country. My entire upbringing told me so. Thoughts of danger never entered my mind; the ordered lifestyle suited me and as a member of the Air Force Reserve I had already tasted military life.

Two gold bars on the shoulders of my Air Force uniform would soon replace the three stripes of an Airman First Class stitched to my sleeves. With over two years of Reserve service, my starting pay as a commissioned officer was higher. Although I didn't look forward to 90 days of chicken shit in the San Antonio heat, to become an Air Force officer I had to do it. It was a lot different than a mother telling a son to mow the lawn or put up the storm windows. When I left home Mum could pay someone else to do those chores. Packing my bags in my room, I hummed the Air Force song, "Off we go into the wild blue yonder," and finally understood why my mother always wanted a girl.

After packing the Olds, I kissed Mum goodbye and turned toward the Mass Pike for the long drive to Texas. Driving through the South in the early days of freedom marches and civil strife gave me an anxious feeling. With a Massachusetts license plate on my car, it was prudent not to linger. Stopping in Birmingham, Alabama, for a sandwich, I felt sad to see public water fountains marked for whites and colored people. *Change is coming, but it won't be easy,* I thought. Someone might confuse me with a Freedom Rider, so I kept rolling hard toward San Antonio. The drive to Texas was my longest behind the wheel. Every day on the road the thermometer and humidity readings rose higher as I bored deeper into the alien Southern landscape.

Just before graduation day, a serious international incident occurred that shook the world. That night, days away from becoming a "90-day wonder," I stood with my classmates in our Day Room, glued to the small black and white television tube. President Kennedy solemnly revealed clandestine photographs of missiles with nuclear warheads: ominous weapons that the Russians had secretly installed in Cuba. The mood in the room was tense and the personal implications of the dilemma became clear. At the time no one realized how close the world came to nuclear war.

On graduation day, we stood in formation under the Texas sun; I was anxious to leave town. When the ceremony on the dusty field ended, everyone pitched his hat into the air. Sergeants looked like vultures as they darted through the ranks, throwing a quick first salute our way, then collected the obligatory dollar bill. Whenever second lieutenants received their bars, an old military tradition held that in order to earn every salute a new lieutenant had to buy the first one. Silver dollars are often used, but we handed out paper money.

I felt good about my new life as a military officer. To be part of a formal structure with a clear hierarchy suited me. Wearing a uniform eliminated any wasted time picking out a daily wardrobe. And having to salute one another let me verify in real-time if an airman had an attitude problem. Unlike my entrepreneur father whose life revolved around a business and his money, my risk of personal failure only affected my promotions.

Months before, Judy, my steady girlfriend, had moved to California to live with her sister after a heated argument with her mother, a lonely woman I perceived to have a runaway imagination. In an emotional fit, she accused Judy of being a tramp and implicated me in the discussion. The resulting imbroglio caused festering wounds that never healed. Consequently, Judy ensured that our offspring never got to know this grandmother.

After a brief stop in California to see Judy, the girl I loved, and meet her siblings, my next stop was Lowrey Air Force Base to begin technical training. I began an intensive, six-month, six-hour-a-day Aerospace Weapons Officer training program in the Logistics Career field. Students needed a degree in physics, chemistry or math. My class of a dozen second lieutenants seemed eager to begin in spite of the 0600 hours starting time. Only officers with a secret clearance could enter the inner sanctum of nuclear studies; colorblind guys were rejected. Since red is used to denote an armed weapon, in the name of safety, everyone involved had to discriminate between red and green. The instructors bombarded us with facts about nuclear, conventional, chemical, and biological weapons. Students examined the intricacies of nuclear weapons in the custody of all the U.S. military services. I looked forward to the day of playing a role in field operations.

Every day, dozens of reels of mind-jarring 16mm color movies flickered in the darkened classroom. They depicted nuclear explosions from the dawn of the atomic age to megaton hydrogen bombs exploding in the Pacific. An anthology of film from the primitive Hiroshima and Nagasaki blasts exemplified how destructive atomic weapons could be. Yet, to me, these horrendous weapons ended World War II and continued to preserve our national security. Teddy Roosevelt once said, "Walk softly and carry a big stick." I had to agree with him.

Just Call Me Moose!

Every morning my class had to sign out stacks of nuclear weapons publications. Inscribed on the blue covers of each manual were the words *Secret Restricted Data NOFORN.* NOFORN is a government acronym for "Not Releasable to Foreign Nationals." Many of the technical manuals contained Critical Nuclear Weapon Design Information (CNWDI) and only people with a special clearance had access. Each of us spent hours learning about nuclear physics, the hazards of nuclear radiation, and the sequence of a nuclear reaction. Instructors detailed the intricate maintenance, storage, and handling procedures necessary to keep stockpiles operational and safe. On large rolls of paper, we traced the multi-colored circuits of these so-called special weapons. The ordinary names assigned to a nuclear accident, i.e., "Broken Arrow" and "Bent Spear," or incident, i.e., "Dull Sword," seemed benign when compared with their potential catastrophic consequences.

My college technical studies had prepared me for the training; the material was easy to digest and we learned the Two Man Rule. It came about after some unstable military personnel gained access to nuclear weapons and threatened to damage them. Now, only two authorized persons could be allowed near a weapon. The Air Force Human Reliability Program continually screened the psychological status of those whose duties involved Special Weapons.

Outside, the ground had already frozen solid; temperatures dropped far below zero for one full week that winter. The class took a field trip to the explosives range so we had to wear thick Korean War-vintage parkas. Our instructors set off various military explosives including smoke and white-phosphorous grenades; they detonated a thirty-lb. shape charge, a device designed to penetrate earth and structures. We kept hopping from foot to foot trying to stay warm on the frigid field while observing the proper technique to rig a charge.

Before the blast, everyone took shelter in a distant bunker. A siren sounded and a sergeant yelled, "Fire in the hole." The "whump" sound of the blast made everyone cringe. The explosion caused a deep tear in the frozen field. Then a large can of ammonium nitrate was lowered into the hole; the blast resulted in a gaping, smoking crater that smelled like fireworks on the Prairie at home. A crater in a runway of this size temporarily prevented air operations.

Judy began to hint about marriage during casual conversations. *Didn't everyone my age get married?* Roger had stayed single thus far and people began to wonder. Did he really like girls or was he just taking his time? As for me, I can only speculate that Judy's relatives encouraged her to put the wedding pedal to the metal. A vulnerable, naive fellow is ill-equipped sometimes to resist a woman bent on nuptials. But, I was ready to march to the altar so we set an early date and Judy and her sister made all the plans for the California ceremony. My primary responsibility was to show up at the church.

Mum didn't sound too thrilled when I broke the news on the phone.

"Why so soon?" she exclaimed, when I told her the wedding date.

"Mum," I said, "It's a holiday weekend and I'll be able to take leave."

"Yes, I'll be there," she said, as her voice trailed-off.

While on the phone with my mother that day, she managed to slip in some advice.

"Remember, love makes the world go round, but it takes money to give it a push."

"Yes, Mum, you're right."

And when she said, "You know, it takes money to make money," I feigned a bad connection and signed off.

On our wedding day at St. Mel's Catholic Church in Woodland Hills, I wore my Air Force blue uniform. Mum and Donald's wife, Betty, had flown in from Boston to witness the event. Most of the guests in the church and at the reception were strangers to me, but my Auntie Marie, and her husband, Bill, drove down from Camarillo. At Oxnard AFB, Uncle Bill recently had hung up his uniform for the last time.

Just Call Me Moose!

Any plans for a honeymoon had to be postponed because of my classes, so my bride and I flew back to Denver. The stewardess on the flight tagged us right away as being newlyweds; I guess we couldn't hide the glow in our cheeks. As the end of the nuclear training program approached, I thought about my first assignment as a weapons officer. On my "Dream Sheet," I selected California as my primary choice. From an earlier briefing, everyone in my class expected to spend only 18 months stateside, supposedly enough time in the field to learn the ropes before filling an important overseas billet.

Costs to keep the 1954 Olds Holiday coupe on the road began to mount, so I traded it in for a used, gray Volkswagen Bug. Just before graduation, I received orders for California; a good omen since my wife's family lived there and I felt at ease around them. My new unit, the 456th Fighter Interceptor Squadron, an Air Defense Command (ADC) unit, was located at Castle Air Force Base in the San Joaquin Valley. By coincidence, it was Donald's last base. My squadron was a tenant unit on a large Strategic Air Command (SAC) base and shared the long runways with B-52 bombers and KC-97 aerial tankers. The air defense unit operated 18 fighter interceptors, each capable of carrying four missiles and a nuclear rocket.

When I reported-in, I met a young airman in the orderly room. "Sir," he said, "I believe you'll be replacing Major Chisa. He's leaving soon for a remote base in Canada."

A 30-day overlap had been planned to acclimate me to the job. Major Chisa was slated to head up the nuclear weapons operations at a Bomarc surface-to-air missile squadron in a remote part of Canada, a base operated jointly by Canadians and Americans. On that Friday afternoon when Judy and I rolled into the base, the major greeted us.

"Welcome to the 456th. Dan Chisa here. I'll be showing you around later, but first you and your wife should get settled in guest quarters. But lieutenant, after that, I need to see you at the Officers Club for Happy Hour at 1600 hours."

Just Call Me Moose!

After putting on my uniform, I found the O' Club on base and made my way to a private room. The major introduced me to a group of cocky squadron pilots and several more subdued maintenance officers, including the Chief of Maintenance, Lieutenant Colonel Art Mimler. One of the pilots encouraged me to try beer and tomato juice and I liked the taste. I met a seasoned warrant officer who wore World War II glider pilot wings and another, Oba Hanchey, a good old boy from Brownsville, Texas, who ran the missile maintenance shop.

As I sipped on the cold, red beer, one of the pilots I'd met yelled, "Let's say hello to the new guy. One...two...three.... Hello,...ass...hole." It's the standard fighter jock greeting for a new arrival. Just as the words rang out, the squadron commander, Lieutenant Colonel Jim Price strolled into the room. He scanned the crowd and frowned, trying to comprehend what just happened. Major Chisa grabbed my arm and pushed me forward to meet him.

"Welcome aboard," said the tall, lean commander with a stack of ribbons and command pilot wings on his blue Class-A uniform.

"So you're my new Chief BB Stacker? You've got a big job managing the Nuclear Weapons Storage Area. I'm sure Dan will square you away."

"Yes, sir. I'm glad to be here"

I tried to answer with conviction. A good first impression made a lot of points.

After Colonel Price queried me about getting settled in and being ready to go, the major moved me off to the side.

"Lieutenant, there's a few things you need to know."

He looked over his shoulder, and then turned to face me. His words peppered me like bullets from a machine gun. "Happy hour is mandatory for all squadron officers. It starts at 1600 hours every Friday afternoon and lasts till 1800 hours or until the keg floats. So don't *ever* miss it, 'cause your ass will be grass and the lawnmower's Colonel Price!"

Just Call Me Moose!

I'll always remember this dramatic opening scene, the start of my military journey as an officer. In the days that followed, I began to feel that the older, seasoned weapons officer resented a green lieutenant taking his place. I dutifully played the role of an apprentice and ran everything important by the major for approval. It worked, and soon I was on my own.

Our commander, a veteran of World War II, a rigid "old school" officer who rarely smiled, reminded me of Army Air Corps movie stars I had followed as a kid. After the chief of staff of the Air Force, General Curtis E. LeMay, decreed that officers should learn a second language, our commander acted. Henceforth, every Monday morning at 0700, all squadron officers attended Spanish classes on base. Even pilots coming off several days in the alert barn, the hangar where nuclear-armed aircraft stood primed for war, had to attend.

The pilots in my squadron flew F-106 Delta Dart aircraft, an all-weather interceptor designed by Convair. The mission of this single-engine plane, capable of flying Mach 2, was to shoot down Russian bombers attacking from over the North Pole. Most 106s were single seat A-models, but two B-models with an additional cockpit were assigned. Each aircraft carried four air interceptor missiles—two-radar guided and two heat seeking—inside the bomb bay. In between the missiles rested an AIR-2A Genie, a 10-foot-long unguided rocket with a nuclear warhead that was capable of destroying scores of enemy bombers up to six miles away. The unit's motto, "Exertus Mostus, Fightus Bestus," a phrase in pigeon Latin, inspired us to work hard and fight hard should the time come.

Most of our pilots referred to the unguided snow-white Genie as the "Blivet" and some of them hoped they never had to fire a live one at a formation of enemy bombers. Not only could the blast's shockwave destroy enemy aircraft, but the lethal neutron flux generated during the atomic explosion incapacitated or killed the Russian aircrews. Our pilots may have wondered if the same radiation could affect their days as a stud. The nuclear stockpile that my troops maintained contained more than five times the explosive power of the atomic bombs dropped on Japan. Nuclear weapons troops took their jobs very seriously; but senior sergeants had a propensity to view green lieutenants as irritants, an impediment to their judgment. So life as a new lieutenant, a "butter bar," could sometimes be difficult.

A few months after I arrived, our "hard-ass" commander got orders to attend the National War College and Lieutenant Colonel John "Buck" Rogers, a more laid-back type, replaced him. Years later, on duty in Spain, I read a piece in the Stars and Stripes relating how Major General Price had died after lightning hit his F-106 aircraft during takeoff. Knowing him, a macho, balls-to-the-wall fighter pilot, I'm confident he would have felt that dying in the clouds was a good way to be remembered.

Only through ongoing, realistic exercises can a unit maintain a high level of operational capability. Using live weapons or practice shapes, all loading crews sharpened the skills necessary to turnaround aircraft quickly and safely. A Quick Turnaround amounted to refueling an aircraft, replenishing the pilot's liquid oxygen, and reloading its nuclear and conventional weapons while the pilot stayed in the cockpit. This carefully-choreographed operation, conducted in a 15-minute special sequence, had to be performed flawlessly. And during wartime the unit had 30 minutes to turnaround McDonnell Douglas F-101 Voodoo aircraft flown in from other bases. This bird carried two Genies and two air-to-air missiles on its revolving weapons pallet. Our practice wartime operations paid off since the unit got high scores during an intensive no-notice Operational Readiness Inspection. To fail would have likely resulted in a major shakeup in squadron leadership. Careers of the key players often plummeted should a major inspection turn sour.

One day while maintenance officers critiqued a mass loading exercise in the office of the Chief of Maintenance, someone ran in and told us that the president had been shot.

Not long after, the news reported that John F. Kennedy had been assassinated in Dallas. Pregnant with our first child, Judy cried openly as if a close member of her family had died.

The assassination of a standing president shocked young and old alike; Headquarters 28th Air Division immediately placed my squadron on a higher defense condition alert. Like everyone else, I wanted to know the whole story behind the president's death; it took me a long time to read the Warren Report. The facts presented left me with a lot of questions; questions that would take me years to begin to answer.

When my wife told me the Air Force doctor said she was pregnant, I began to look forward to being a father. Judy often spoke with trepidation about childbirth; she had observed deformed babies in school learning to be a nurse. All the details about babies with heads the size of cantaloupes and other problems made me anxious. I had a pristine picture in my mind about childbirth.

We were living in town in a small, furnished apartment the morning that Judy rolled over to poke an elbow into my ribs. Close to dawn, I helped her into the Bug, drove to the highway, and raced to the base hospital. I checked her into the aging wooden facility and waited. For an hour or so I kept pacing back and forth. Then I heard a baby crying and another tiny voice joined the chorus. Soon a nurse wearing captain's bars approached with a big grin on her face.

"Congratulations, lieutenant, your wife just delivered twins." After a long pause to view my reaction, she added, "I'm kidding. Your new son weighs eight and a half pounds."

My legs felt a little wobbly as she led me back to see my wife. The delivery seemed to go smoothly; but I was only the father and could never relate to her ordeal.

"How do your feel, honey?"

Judy looked a little pale, but managed a faint smile. "I feel okay," she said quietly.

I leaned over and kissed her forehead and whispered, "I love you. I'm so happy we have a healthy baby, my love."

Just Call Me Moose!

I followed the nurse to a narrow hallway and a large window and peered in. She pointed to a dark purple infant wearing only a tiny diaper. A narrow plastic identification band encircled one wrist. When I held Douglas Roger, the baby boy who had my nose, I could hardly wait to call my mother.

The first squadron Dining-In for me took place at the O' Club. I wore my white mess jacket, shoulder boards, black pants with a black stripe along each leg and looked forward to the bachelor night out. The tiny red and yellow National Defense Service Medal over my left breast seemed out of place in comparison to the rows of colorful medals the pilots wore. In those days a Dining-In was a wild, macho, male bonding formal event. While World War II raged, Army Air Corps officers and their British colleagues in the Royal Air Force often blew off steam during the ribald night. Anything could happen after the booze began to flow. As I stood outside the men's room that night, I noticed a veteran squadron pilot, an older major, staggering toward me. A spattering of fresh blood covered his jacket and many of the ribbons showed signs of the stains.

"What happened," I asked, as he weaved past me toward the bar.

"Some headquarters weenie shoved me while I was taking a leak. I damned near pissed my pants so I slugged the asshole."

Over the years all my other Dining-In experiences never matched the night that a major tried to punch-out a colonel.

At Castle, I took my first ride in the back seat of an F-106 after getting certified in the SAC altitude chamber. Major Russ Greeenberg made the flight easy on me, so I didn't throw up. After landing, I watched an airman approaching and waving a piece of paper. Over the flightline noise, he yelled, "Lieutenant, you just got orders to Japan! Some place called the Yamada Ammunition Storage Annex."

During a call to headquarters I was told that my new assignment was on the island of Kyushu and my family could come with me. *Fantastic,* I thought, *we're going to love it.*

XVI

TWENTY YEARS AFTER WORLD WAR II, I left from
Travis Air Force Base in California for Japan, once a country
Americans hated, to begin my first overseas assignment. Judy
held baby Douglas as we boarded a C-121 Super Constellation
on Travis AFB for a lumbering 28-hour Military Airlift
Command flight. On the way, we had to stop to refuel on
Hawaii and Wake Island. After a night in a roach-infested room
at Tachikawa Air Base, we rode a cargo plane laden with lumber
for Itazuke Air Base, near the city of Fukuoka. Planes flying
from Itazuke had played a key role during the Korean War and
now the base provided primary logistic support to the Yamada
Depot. The high-pitched scream from the C-130 turbo-prop
engines made the flight especially noisy and "Dougie," cried
incessantly from the pain of his throbbing ears.

The two-hour drive to Yamada in a bone-jarring Ford
Econoline van would become routine. It was a hazardous drive
through the rice-paddy-dotted countryside over a congested
road filled with motorcycles, trucks, bicycles and passenger
vehicles. And having to smell the exhaust fumes or human
excrement used for fertilizer always made the trip to back and
forth to Kokura unpleasant. Within weeks, after an ocean
voyage, our VW Bug arrived, allowing us to travel freely around
the area.

Just Call Me Moose!

In the early 1920s, the Japanese military began construction of the sprawling ammunition depot, a place the locals called *Yamada Butai*. In 1938, after Japan invaded China, the Japanese Army forced 50 families to vacate their homes and rice fields in order to build earth-covered igloos, other magazines, and facilities for inspection and maintenance of munitions. Korean and Chinese slave laborers were brutally employed during the construction

When World War II ended and American forces arrived in Kokura, it took two more weeks to occupy the base, but only after the Japanese commander came down from the hills to surrender. No one had told the American forces that the military complex existed. The depot, with its own rail line, sat in a lush green valley on the outskirts of the city. In 1945, only a cloud cover saved Kokura, a high-value military target, from the bomb that destroyed Nagasaki. During my tour, I was invited to visit the nearby expansive Yawata Steel Mill, where American POWs had once toiled. Factory management treated me like a visiting dignitary. It became clear to me that the complex facility, one of the largest steel mills in the world, had helped keep the Japanese war machine on track.

Yamada had several miles of winding gravel roads dotted with domed earth-covered concrete igloos and one-story buildings containing hard pine floors. The walls of these buildings were lined with cork for explosive safety reasons. In August 1964, Congress passed the Gulf of Tonkin Resolution and just as Pearl Harbor decades before had been a catalyst for conflict, now the focus turned to Vietnam. My new job took on a sense of urgency as I assumed management responsibility for the inspection, maintenance, storage and safety of a wide variety of conventional munitions, anything at the depot that could go "boom." The inventory of weapons included high explosive general purpose and cluster bombs along with bomb fuzes, small arms, grenades, and air-to-ground missiles—the AGM-12 Bullpup—which contained corrosive, highly volatile chemicals. Only a small cadre of about 50 enlisted personnel monitored the Japanese civilian munitions workers. The "ammo" troops fulfilled a critical overseer function, since the Japanese often cut corners when complying with operating procedures.

When air operations in Vietnam accelerated, our workload increased sharply. In 1966 the depot handled more than 56,000 tons of munitions; weapons unloaded at the Moji port from ships off shore arrived at the Yamada depot in a steady stream of civilian trucks contracted by a U.S. Army Transportation unit. It didn't take long to fill the igloos with 15,000 750-lb. general-purpose bombs, each containing nearly 400 pounds of Tritonol high explosive. Later ships arrived with 100 3000-lb. bombs, each the weight of a Chevy Corvette. Only F-105 Thunderchief fighter-bombers based in Thailand could carry these babies. In the early days of the war the Yamada depot acted as a staging area since Vietnam lacked suitable munitions storage facilities. Due to the large amount of explosives contained in all the weapons arriving, rigid storage safety criteria could not be met and so to continue operations, I had to prepare safety waivers and get Headquarters Pacific Air Forces approval. The depot prepared and shipped weapons by air and by sea to Vietnam and Thailand, to units conducting air operations. They had a voracious appetite for our bombs and bullets.

Early in my tour the commander came to me.

"You see that new flagpole out there?"

"Yes, sir."

"Well, it's for a Jap flag. And you'll be representing the unit at the flag-raising ceremony."

Our commander, a thin, intense major with virtually no sense of humor, had served during World War II and wild horses couldn't drag him to recognize anything Japanese. Later he confided in me that I represented the new generation and he the old. Unnamed bitter memories made him feel that way.

A few days later, I held the flag of Japan, the red meatball on a white standard, and watched it be raised up the pole. *How ironic,* I thought, *for a Japanese band to be playing their national anthem on a U.S. Air Force base and the flag of a former enemy is flying alongside Old Glory.* It only took 20 years.

On a vacation from his job in Seoul, Roger flew over from Korea to visit us and see Douglas Roger, the little boy who bore his name. Dougie had to stay home with a babysitter while the three of us jumped into my Bug and we headed for Nagasaki, the city that Puccini's opera *Madame Butterfly* and then an atomic explosion made famous. Our guide, an elderly Japanese man, who spoke English, had been on the outskirts of the city on the fateful day. Now he related in English what it felt like to be a survivor. Spending time inside the Atomic Bomb Museum allowed me to see the devastation from the Japanese perspective; but I still feel that President Truman's decision to use the horrendous weapon saved many lives on both sides.

After Roger returned to Boston he married a local girl, raised a family, and lived in Hawaii and Germany, working in intelligence until shortly after the Berlin Wall came down in 1989. During a telephone call, I asked my brother why he was planning to retire.

"We *won,*" he replied in his typical dry, laconic manner. "We won the war."

Many of the Air Force bomb dump troops had a proclivity for acting crude, a way of letting off steam. Their everyday speech covered a variety of raw expletives. When something went well, the term of choice, "I don't know whether to shit or go blind," had the same level of acceptance in the ranks as "Good morning, sir." And if events didn't turn out as planned, someone yelled, "Shit, piss, fuck!"

In another attempt to escape from the boredom of a remote assignment, one night a bunch of the troops decided to hold a special event at the combined officer and enlisted club. As I sat at the bar having a drink, I noticed a large number of local girls dancing with a few of the young airmen.

Just Call Me Moose!

"Hey, Sarge. What's going on?" I asked one of the old heads beside me.

"They're havin' a contest tonight, captain. Someone named it the Annual Dinosaur Roundup. The GI who brings the ugliest chick wins fifty bucks."

From the looks of the Japanese girls in the club, it had to be a tough decision. I didn't stay to see who won.

After Judy became pregnant again, I had to move her and Dougie to Hakata Air Station, closer to medical facilities, but a long drive from Yamada. I could only come home to my family on weekends. After Judy gave birth, a Navy nurse telephoned me at home.

"Lieutenant, I have some good news. You're wife just delivered a healthy 8-lb. baby girl."

Two years after the birth of our son, Deborah Lee was born and I was thrilled. "Debbie" Lee "came ashore" in the U.S. Navy Hospital in Sasebo, several hours away since the local Air Force dispensary lacked obstetrics capabilities. My job prevented me from staying at the Navy base a week or so waiting for Debbie to be born.

I called my mother in Boston and she was happy to get the news about her new granddaughter. But Judy didn't appreciate me missing Debbie's arrival; it was another crack in the wall of our impending troubled relationship. Our blond-haired, doll-like daughter stood out amongst the other babies on the streets of Kokura. All the girls in the Japanese department stores used to swarm around her and say, *kawaii*. Everyone she met thought Debbie looked like adorable. At home, Kyoko, our gentle part-time Japanese maid, assisted Judy with the children and cooked native dishes.

My first overseas tour to the Far East allowed my wife and me to explore the ancient culture of Japan; Judy and I traveled throughout the country, stayed in Tokyo, and walked the streets of exotic places like Kyoto and Nagoya. I took many photos of the colorful festivals and beautiful castles.

In my free time, I taught colloquial English to Mitsubishi office workers. They had a strong desire to learn the language and the ways of the foreigners amongst them. The phrases they learned contained a strong Boston flavor and in turn, I wanted to expand my meager Japanese.

After six months of an intensive karate program, I shed many pounds as I punched and kicked my way through the nights of intensive training. Japanese judges awarded me a purple belt after I passed the test in a downtown dojo. Sparring barefoot with young airmen, and carrying them around on my shoulders was a good way to lose weight. In addition to the grueling physical side, my two deadly, black-belted Japanese instructors demonstrated the importance of mental discipline in this martial art.

Of all the cultures in the world, Japan is infamous for ritual suicide: seppuku or the more vulgar term, *hara-kari*. As kids, we called it "hairy carey." *Seppuku*, part of the ancient Bushido honor code, allowed samurai warriors to rid themselves of shame in situations involving disgrace, a form of repentance. In a strange way, I imagine that my father's death was like a seppuku for the disgrace he himself felt.

Overall, the Japanese people treated Americans with respect in spite of the term *gai-jin*—outsiders or foreigners—they used. As my time in Japan slowly evolved, the stereotype of buck-toothed Jap soldiers, once depicted on neighborhood movie screens, gave way to a keen perception of a vibrant culture, perhaps as flawed as ours, but nevertheless noble.

As the end of my tour approached, I felt a measure of satisfaction about the depot's excellent safety record in handling tons of explosives. Working around explosives, if a serious mistake is made, one doesn't get a second chance. I learned that since 1946, when the U.S. Air Force first assumed control of the Yamada depot, there was never a major accident. Many professional weapons people helped make it possible. Among them was a supervisor of mine, Captain Paul Tatum, a "mustang" who came up through the ranks and knew how to work the military system. Paul introduced me to the dangerous world of bomb disposal and could reel off stories that made me curious about the voluntary specialty.

I applied for the school from Japan and was accepted to the 22-week bomb disposal program, a training program that covered the entire spectrum of new and old, U.S. and foreign weapons. Back in the states, after a brief stop to visit my mother and show off both grandchildren, I drove my family to Indian Head, Maryland and signed-in at the U.S. Naval School for Explosive Ordnance Disposal, EOD, for short. An entry for hazardous duty pay appeared on my next pay stub. The extra $110 a month came in handy.

Through field exercises at Stump Neck, an isolated area on base, I learned about the special craft, solving various tricky potential problems involving simulated nuclear weapons and conventional ordnance, self-styled weapons of mass destruction. We'd yell, "Fire in the hole," before driving the handle of the "hellbox" down to set off the explosive shot. Over many years, thousands of students from all the services had completed this intensive program. But the inherently wild Navy EOD guys went a little further than the rest and learned to swim and disarm mines and weapons underwater. An old Air Force EOD joke went like this: "If a dud bomb is lying on the beach, wait till high tide, then call the Navy."

Many of the Navy EOD guys I met in Nam spent their days either swimming and checking ships for mines, getting wasted or sleeping.

At Ft McClellan, army technicians taught us about chemical and biological warfare–horrific weapons that gave me pause, some already used in modern times, others developed for the future should an enemy use them first. My Boy Scout motto—"Be Prepared"—came to mind and made more sense than ever. Some of the deadly devices contained mustard gas, phosgene, nerve agent and anthrax or botulism toxins.

One day an army instructor said, "Class, I have here a little diluted mustard agent. I want you to put a drop on your forearm. You'll be able to see the effect tomorrow."

Everyone followed his orders without question and the next day I had a blister the size of a dime. It took a few days to heal, but the scar on my forearm remains visible today. A demonstration like this can be quite effective as a motivational tool.

As I sat alongside my EOD classmates in an amphitheater with a gas mask on, instructors demonstrated the effects of one dangerous chemical. A white rabbit died in a flurry of short spasms after a few drops of VX nerve agent touched a patch of skin. After pulling a goat onto the field and exposing the animal to the deadly chemical, the instructor administered a shot of atropine. Atropine Sulfate is a counter-measure used in the field to counteract the effects of nerve gas. The terrified creature lived to be a guinea pig another day.

At Indian Head, after a day of intensive training, most EOD guys headed for the Longhorn Bar, just outside the main gate. It was a place with a legend, where every EOD class added ribald stories and raucous times to events played out there. I believe Wednesday was the night the bar catered especially to the local ladies by offering cheap drinks. In another time, some Navy chief had dubbed it "P and E night," and the name stuck. It's shorthand for two four-legged animals. One of the creatures is a barn animal and the other is associated with a circus. After spending time in the bar on P and E nights, I only observed a few of the local visitors that met the criteria.

After graduating, I proudly wore my silver EOD badge, with its wreath, bomb and lightning bolts, but going to a teaching job back in Denver did not please me. A short reprieve occurred, however, when a Teletype message—or TWX—arrived directing me to attend Squadron Officers School in Alabama. The 14-week temporary duty stint, geared to junior officers, taught team-building and leadership skills. Two foreign officers complemented each section; mine had pilots from Bolivia and Turkey.

At the classified intelligence briefing in the SOS auditorium, a place called the Blue Bedroom, I learned about the USS *Pueblo*. The North Koreans had hijacked the secret surveillance ship and its crew on the high seas, obtaining sensitive classified operational data. I was appalled and thought that the Navy crew had been used as bait. The ill-advised mission had been a disaster due to the inability of local forces to react in time and illustrated once again the failure of military services to interact.

Weeks later Colonel Robin Olds spoke to us about integrity and its critical role in the military. Colonel Olds, a seasoned World War II combat veteran, had been a wing commander in Thailand and flew the F-4 Phantom against the North Vietnamese. In the air, Olds prevented four MiG fighters from ever landing again. A proven leader, he epitomized the qualities of many sierra hotel–"shit-hot"–pilots that I knew. "No guts, no glory," was their credo. Many maintenance pukes, like me, agreed with the sentiment. During Olds's inspirational talk, he gave an example that I'll always remember. It involved an Air Force pilot who had strafed a Russian ship sitting in Haiphong Harbor and later tried to cover it up by destroying the gun camera film. It turned into an international incident and ultimately involved President Johnson. When the truth came out, the pilot suffered severe repercussions. I remembered the values of integrity and honesty Pop had taught me as a child. *Would I have acted differently?* I remember thinking.

XVII

AFTER THE 1968 TET OFFENSIVE and the capture of the USS *Pueblo*, I began to think seriously about volunteering for Vietnam. Every time I read a newspaper, an article about a military operation stared me in the face. I wanted to be a part of the action. Recent Squadron Officer School graduates received approval to call the Military Personnel Center in Texas to arrange a new assignment. Choosing a place on my terms made sense since I knew that a long trip to Southeast Asia loomed on the horizon. A base described in the Air Force Times appeared to be a great place to spend a year. It was located at the edge of the seaside city of Nha Trang, a place with a strong French flavor. I called Randolph to inquire about an EOD assignment there. I wanted to lead a bomb disposal team, but my request fell on deaf ears. The sergeant on the line said the only slot was filled and offered me Phan Rang, a base with none of the charm of the city I had read about.

"Sergeant, I'm volunteering *now* and I want Nha Trang."

"Yes, sir, I'll get back to you tomorrow."

The next day, my phone rang; the same sergeant began, "Sir, everything's a go for Nha Trang. You'll be leaving in October to head-up the EOD team."

"Sounds good. What about the other captain?"

"No problem, sir, I'm sending him to Phan Rang."

After putting most of our stuff in long-term storage, then moving my family to California, I rented a furnished apartment for them. A local hospital hired Judy to work on the staff as a nurse. When the sad day arrived to say goodbye, I said a silent prayer. Although fighting in the jungle wasn't on my agenda, anything can happen during wartime and this adventure might turn out badly.

I was dressed in fatigues on an October afternoon, when my black boots touched the hot, sticky tarmac of Nha Trang Air Base. Part of Khanh Hoa province, Nha Trang sits about 200 miles north of Saigon and 40 miles north of Cam Ranh Bay. Many considered this sun-splashed area on the beach to be a choice assignment. That night I went to sleep in a run-down French villa near the beach, on Pham Phu Quoc, a street Americans called Airport Road.

Solid sheets of rain pelted the bent corrugated metal roof. Lying exhausted on a bunk smelling of mildew and draped with mosquito netting, my thoughts turned to my family in the states. Through the deluge, in the distance, outgoing 105mm howitzer rounds chunked into free-fire zones. Before drifting off to sleep, I felt all alone and anxious about my decision to volunteer to go to war.

The four other officers who shared my new abode, called it Passover Villa since many who had lived there had been passed-over for promotion. Soon after arriving, I heard a new arrival say to a fellow officer, "These local women look pretty rough. Are there any pretty ones out there?"

"Hah, just wait a few months. They'll start to look like Miss America." It didn't take me long to realize that he was right.

But our maid never reached that lofty height. Hoa, a swarthy, short woman with deep burn scars on her arms and a mouth full of gold teeth, did our laundry and cleaned our rooms. My fatigues and underwear never smelled clean after Hoa did the wash and hung the clothes on a barbed-wire clothesline to dry. In time, I grew accustomed to the rancid odor as I slipped on the soggy garments. About once a week

Hoa stammered to anyone within earshot, "You buy me case of Coke?" One of us usually satisfied the request. Her wizened mother sported teeth stained black from years of chewing betel nuts, a mild narcotic the GIs termed "beetle" nuts. On most weekends at the villa, as they began to work, their high-pitched, singsong chatter rudely awoke me before dawn.

As the months slipped away, I eventually moved to a room on the ocean side of the villa, one with a ceiling fan and bathroom. One morning while in the shower I smelled something awful; it seemed as if the toilet had backed up. But the source of the putrid odor eluded me. While having a few beers that night in the TV room alongside my villa mates, I asked, "Anyone besides me smell something bad today?"

An old colonel from Alabama took a hefty gulp of beer and shook his head.

"It smelled like shit," he said. "God awful. I climbed up on the roof and checked-out the cistern."

"See anything?"

"You bet your ass, I did. A dead cat just a-floatin' and a-rottin.' I guess it fell in and couldn't get out."

Another in the room exclaimed, "You gotta be shittin' me!"

THE COOL, DARK-BLUE WATERS of the South China Sea caressed the sugar-white, palm-lined beach, bordering the villa and the base. Nearby, rows of petite white, weathered dwellings the French had built years before dotted the main seaside drag. A few miles away in the city, the population frequented a bustling market place with chattering vendors selling the foul-smelling *nuoc mam*, a pungent fish sauce, I never dared try. And I used to drive to a bakery in town to buy bread made from rice flour laden with tiny bugs; a little extra protein never hurt anyone. At night, as I drove along the streets of the city I could see dimly lit bars, with their resident whores. These tired women plied their bodies to anyone in need, including the local GI's and, rumor had it, transient Viet Cong fighters.

Just Call Me Moose!

In 1951, the French military opened an air-training center at Nha Trang. Fifteen years later, as the American military and materiel poured into Vietnam, the 14th Air Commando Wing, later renamed 14th Special Operations Wing, set up shop there. Colonel "Scotty" Allman, a man of few words, and later Colonel Bill Bush, a man with a dandy moustache, commanded the wing. Allman began carrying a pearl-handled 25-caliber automatic pistol after an irate Army GI, bent on a fast trip stateside, threatened him. Neither commander ever came across the street to chat with the EOD team. With the motto "Day and Night, Peace and War," the one-of-a-kind unit achieved a special reputation for supporting troops on the ground. Many GIs in besieged jungle enclaves owed their survival to the unit's gunships.

During the five years the unit operated in SEA, it conducted a variety of unconventional combat missions. Assigned aircrews flew eight different aircraft types from 10 bases throughout Vietnam. A typical day involved 175 missions. Principal operations included close air support, interdiction, airlift, reconnaissance, illumination and psychological warfare.

Over 100 USAF aircraft of all types operated from the Nha Trang flightline, presenting an ongoing maintenance challenge. Aircraft maintenance people launched O-1 Bird Dog and O-2 Skymaster, Forward Air Controller aircraft, Green Hornet choppers that operated deep in enemy territory, Ranch Hand "Agent Orange" defoliators, electronic warfare Blackbirds, and AC-47 Spooky, and AC-119 Shadow gunships. From their side of the base the Vietnamese Air Force flew the tiny Cessna AC-37 Dragonfly armed with shiny napalm bombs and high-explosive iron bombs. The EOD team supported their emergencies also.

Members of the seven-man EOD team, part of the Field Maintenance Squadron, disposed of unexploded or hazardous ordnance on or off base. And with "blanket" travel orders, we could easily travel anywhere in Vietnam and Thailand.

Just Call Me Moose!

Left to right: Doc Springer, Don Devening, Wil Selvage, Pappy Yochem, Kurt Gustafson and Bill Furr at the EOD Bar.

The men I remember best were sergeants Alexander, Yowell, Springer, Devening, Yochem, Gustafson and Selvage. These professionals knew the business; years of experience helped make my job relatively easy. Two EOD technicians, including me, shared a rotating alert schedule. Every day brought a new challenge for the team, the only one of its kind between Cam Ranh Bay and Ninh Hoa that also supported the 5th Special Forces Group and other local army units. Our constant training involved a careful effort to disarm the risks. Best of all we did our job without a USAF Inspector hovering over our shoulder. With a war on, Vietnam was the place to get practical experience in a combat setting, a way to earn my hazardous duty pay.

In town, an emaciated Vietnamese man ran a chrome shop; the EOD team paid him to chrome-plate dozens of "pineapple" grenades after one of the team removed the explosive powder and its detonator. The fins of Viet Cong mortars recovered after an attack were also chromed for souvenirs. The tiny facility was a hazardous waste dump; any stateside environmental agency would have padlocked the doors. Another industrious local used to heat and pound 40mm and 105mm shell casings into shapely brass vases. The scene brought back memories of me molding wrought iron pieces in the Tech forge shop.

Some of my guys lived to "scrounge," the term for acquiring contraband. For a "scrounger," any souvenir became "trading material." When a new head cook arrived on base, one of my guys invited him over to visit. Later, the smiling Hispanic sergeant, dressed in his kitchen-white uniform, walked out of the EOD facility with a chrome-plated 45-caliber submachine gun, a vintage piece known as a Grease Gun. In return for the gift, the Air Force cook swore an oath to send over frozen steaks and chickens to the EOD team for the next 12 months.

The EOD area, about 2,000 square feet, across from Wing Headquarters had a workshop, a training room, bedrooms for the enlisted guys and a large day room with a bar and rudimentary kitchen. I shared a large office with my top sergeant, initially Dave Alexander, then Milo Yowell. A large safe held all our classified manuals, the secrets of our trade. The bathroom had its own washer and dryer and a Vietnamese woman came in to clean and do the laundry.

The team owned two 4x4 crew cab trucks called six-packs, a jeep and a small utility trailer. Behind the building, a small barrel had been converted to a barbecue. The facility offered all the necessary resources to support a USAF EOD team. It was the envy of all visitors, especially the army troops in the field who rarely had access to a shower. Our training room with a blackboard and student chairs was packed with a wide selection of Viet Cong, Chinese and Russian ordnance including enemy B-40 rocket-propelled grenades. All the deadly explosives they contained had been removed.

When the phone rang the team never knew what to expect. One time, Staff Sergeant Don Devening came with me on a call involving an HH-43 Pedro rescue helicopter brought down by small-arms fire on a mission to extract a wounded soldier. We were flown to the jungle location and the chopper crew waited while we cleared the area of potential explosive devices. None were found. After the chopper was repaired, an aircrew flew it back to the base.

Another incident involved our response to the lethal consequences of a firefight in a nearby jungle clearing. The Vietnamese Regional/Popular Forces—"Ruff Puffs"—had ambushed the Viet Cong the night before. During the skirmish, Ruff Puff forces had fired 40mm high explosive grenades and several failed to detonate. When we dismounted from the jeep our U.S. Army guide briefed us on the situation. Several VC soldiers had been killed and a handful of grenades needed to be destroyed. Once fired, grenades of the type used during the ambush should never be picked-up; the hair-trigger fuze is too sensitive. The recommended render-safe procedure—RSP—is BIP—blow-in-place. Using golf-ball size hunks of C-4 plastic explosive, blasting caps and pieces of primer cord and safety fuse, we detonated each grenade in a loud flash of energy.

The raw stench of death filled the air. Several young, bloody bodies stretched out on the grass; one was a slender woman. Crude cardboard placards in Vietnamese lay over each chest. *Must be propaganda*, I thought. These insurgents had died for a cause they considered just, a cause that would ultimately prevail. To deter them from taking over South Vietnam was never in the cards. As I walked back to the jeep, the image of those bodies hung on and I remembered the day Pop died. He, too, lay on his back, but on cold concrete. They lay on warm, damp grass. My father wore a light-brown suit; they were dressed in black pajamas.

XVIII

AFTER NIXON NARROWLY WON the presidency in 1968 and assumed power, the war began to be Vietnamized. Months later my team gave a crash course in explosives recovery and disposal operations to several Vietnamese Air Force EOD sergeants. These men seemed motivated to learn, since soon the Americans would be leaving. But, my father's old adage, "You can lead a horse to water, but can't make him drink," came to mind and I wondered if they could meet the challenge.

All Air Force EOD team leaders kept in touch with their 7th Air Force counterparts at Tan Son Nhut Air Base in Saigon. Every new EOD technician had to complete a mandatory course on Viet Cong explosive devices. A typical day in an EOD unit involved standing alert, responding to calls for support, blowing up unserviceable ammunition, or training. Every week at our seaside disposal range, 25 miles north of the city, we blew up hundreds of pounds of "bad ammo." Headquarters authorized EOD people to wear plain camouflage fatigues with no rank so no one stood out to the enemy. The policy didn't make me feel any safer. We wore bulky flack jackets and heavy steel helmets, and carried an M-16 assault rifle with a 20-round magazine of 5.56mm cartridges. A K-bar knife and a blasting-cap "crimper" dangled from our web belts. Each team member was also issued a Smith and Wesson 38-caliber revolver.

Just Call Me Moose!

Left to right: Vietnamese Air Force Senior Master Sgt. Do Dang Gia and the author examine remnants of an 82mm mortar cartridge after a Viet Cong attack in 1969 on the nearby 5th Special Forces Group.

My loaded 38-revolver in a leather holster always accompanied me when we had a job off base. On range day, a combination of 2.75-inch rockets, high explosive and white phosphorous, "Willy Peter," 81mm mortars, MK-24 illumination flares, 105mm rounds, hand grenades, and small-arms ammunition typically filled the bed of one truck and its trailer. Two Air Policemen in a jeep with a mounted M-60 machine gun drove behind us for security but thoughts of an ambush always crossed my mind.

When the Wing Command Post alerted EOD about a problem on base, the guys on alert jumped into a vehicle and raced to the incident with the siren wailing and a red light flashing. Incidents usually involved suspected booby-traps, aircraft with hung ordnance, or clearing the base after a Viet Cong attack. For other incidents off base, we kept a lower profile and didn't use a siren or a red flashing light to advertise our presence.

At night other American bases were often shelled with 122mm Russian or 107mm Chinese Communist artillery rockets. These deadly weapons made a distinctive loud crack when they exploded. During my year in Vietnam, only ChiCom 82mm mortars and 75mm recoilless rounds landed on Nha Trang. Every one of them detonated; we never found a dud round. No significant damage resulted to personnel or facilities but shortly after I left to come home, rockets struck the base and airmen died.

After a forklift punctured a napalm bomb in a crate on the flightline, EOD was called-in. Damage to the thin metal skin caused the volatile contents to ooze onto the asphalt. I got upset after an errant bystander attempted to light up a cigarette and he realized the careless act could have started a fire. The damaged bomb was transported to a secluded area to burn. In the movie *Apocalypse Now*, when I heard Robert Duvall's character say, "I love the smell of napalm in the morning," I had to laugh.

One morning the Command Post directed us to inspect several C-130 pallets of fruits and vegetables arriving from Dalat, a city in the central highlands. The load was suspected of being booby-trapped. After we checked the pallets and arranged to segregate them, Devening radioed EOD Control to bring paper sacks to the flight line. He needed the sacks to collect a "random sample" of the scarce, fresh fruit and "veggies," there being no sign of an explosive device. And for the next few days the EOD can opener stayed in the drawer.

After every incident or operation, an Explosive Ordnance Disposal Report had to be completed. The ubiquitous AF Form 1058, had to be typed in multiple carbon copies to document what occurred so that anything unusual could be examined more closely at various command levels. EOD is a job similar to that of a fireman. Periods on alert, sometimes hectic, are interspersed with bouts of anticipation waiting for something to happen. But the potential for peril always hung over us.

Just Call Me Moose!

The small, dimly-lit Nha Trang Officers Club became a place to spend idle time while off duty. Some of my friends had formed a group called the Bears and everyone had a name. Dancing Bear, Drinking Bear, Silver Bear, and me, Bushy Bear, because of my thick dark moustache. The Bears put a lot of inexpensive liquor away most nights. One of the them, an Irish fellow and former Marine, from Boston, didn't stop there. Jack Rooney liked to call me "Boom-Boom," I thought, because of my work with explosives. But I think Jack had a different meaning in mind, the one the Vietnamese girls alluded to whenever I got a massage.

The Vietnamese waitresses, as most young women did, wore the delicate *ao dai*, the native costume. With its mandarin collar and very close-fitting bodice, the gossamer skirt is split to the waist. Loose silk pants are worn underneath it. After most duty days, I'd drive my jeep over to the club. With a drink before me on the bar, when I wore camouflage fatigues the waitresses liked to tease me. First they called me captain, then tiger.

"*Dai uy*, how many VC you kill today?"

I'd put up three fingers on one hand and kept drinking.

"Tiger, you *dien cai dao*," another added.

It means "crazy in the head" and for all I knew, some of these servers had VC boyfriends or husbands. Employment on base provided an excellent opportunity for the bad guys and gals to collect good intelligence.

With several military clubs in the area run by the Green Berets and other army units, most nights the Bears made the rounds and got "sloshed" before hitting the sack. A private bar, lit by candlelight, next to the base perimeter and owned by two Vietnamese sisters became a favorite haunt. It was so small fewer than 10 customers could be seated. It stayed open after curfew and I can recall sitting in the dark drinking American beer. Inside the place we called the Quiet Bar I could watch flickering illumination flares eerily float to the ground.

After I left the bar to go back to the base in the EOD jeep, the Air Policeman at the main gate often asked, "Why are you past curfew, Captain?"

My standard reply, "I was on a bomb run," always worked. It wasn't a lie; I *was* "bombed."

An open-air theater for movies and USO shows on base and other Army Officers Clubs in the area provided additional diversion. At the clubs Cambodian or French-Vietnamese girls, now attractive to me, entertained the troops by putting on strip shows. At one of the Army clubs in Nha Trang, I got caught up in the moment and jumped on a chair to keep the white spotlight shining on the dancer and I thought about Scollay Square and Tempest Storm on stage at the Casino Theater.

Sometimes a few of us Bears would go into town for Korean food. A few soldiers from the Republic of Korea White Horse Division, a unit camped outside Nha Trang, had opened the restaurant. They missed their spicy Kimchi and the delicious Bulgogi fire-beef made with garlic and red pepper; foods I still enjoy eating.

A FEW MONTHS AFTER I ARRIVED ON BASE, the AC-47 Spooky gunships with their side-firing guns were replaced by the Fairchild Hiller AC-119G Shadow, a modified "Flying Boxcar." The Shadow carried four miniguns, compared with the AC-47's three, and a great deal more ammunition. As part of Vietnamization, all AC-47 gunships were to be transferred to the Vietnamese Air Force. For the valiant Spooky effort, the 14th Special Operations Wing was awarded the Vietnamese Cross of Gallantry, the first Air Force unit so honored. Thirty-two Shadow gunships were deployed to Nha Trang, Da Nang, Phu Cat, Phan Rang, Bien Hoa, and Binh Thuy. Both the aircraft and personnel came to us from the Air Force Reserve. Their squadron motto, "Deny Him the Night," said it all since no allied outpost was ever overrun while these protectors were overhead.

Just Call Me Moose!

Armed with four six-barreled 7.62mm Gatling guns, Shadow gunships fired thousands of rounds of ball and tracer ammunition a minute. In a matter of seconds an area the size of a football field could be blanketed with bullets. To find possible targets and assist friendlies on the ground, Shadow released illumination flares. A 20,000-watt variable spotlight could also be turned-on to light up the night. Mounted in the front, a Night Observation Sight, or NOS, capable of amplifying available starlight, provided navigation support and also identified targets. Most operations took place after dark to support troops in contact in isolated hamlets or provide air base defense.

The parachute-retarded Mk 24 flare was encased in a yard-long metal tube. After release and at the preset time, an explosive charge ejected the parachute and a two-million candlepower magnesium candle ignited, if everything worked, and lit up the sky for three minutes. When flares didn't light, the enemy could slip away into the jungle. After a sharp spike in the level of dud flares, the Deputy Commander for Operations, Colonel Bill Ginn, sought corrective action. EOD got the call.

Colonel J.B.L. Levesque, the Deputy Commander for Materiel, was a vinegary World War II veteran who headed the logistics effort on base. He directed me to assist aircraft operations in finding a solution. Members of my EOD team made cutaways of the flare's operating mechanism and a few of us traveled throughout Vietnam and in Thailand to brief aircrews about the proper technique for setting the fuzes. Flying over Laos in a Gooney Bird to brief operators in Thailand, I prayed that someone didn't shoot us down. After the flare dud rate improved, everyone on the EOD team involved felt good about helping to fix a serious operational problem.

To get a taste of combat, I requested Colonel Ginn's permission to fly on several night gunship missions. A typical Shadow mission usually lasted five or six hours and occurred sometime between 2000 hours and 0400 hours. My first ops briefing seemed humdrum until the officer began to discuss bailout procedures over hostile territory. From then on he had my full attention. When the time came, I picked-up my parachute and survival radio and patted the loaded 38 caliber revolver on my hip. The crew shuttle transported us to the black, tan, and green aircraft, over bumpy, pierced aluminum planking. The flight crew, consisting of eight men and me, loaded quickly in the still, humid night air. Stacked neatly across from the SUU-11 mini-gun pods were rows of cans containing metal-linked, small arms and tracer ammunition.

As I looked around, a gunner told me, "Captain, there's 35,000 rounds of ammo sitting there. If we lose an engine on takeoff, we're all gonna have a bad day."

The guns peering out through the fuselage reminded me of cannons mounted on ancient galleons. Twenty-four MK-24 flares were already loaded in the pneumatic LAU-74/A Flare Launcher. One at a time, the two 3,500-horsepower engines slowly turned over and then roared to life in a plume of smoke. The tower cleared us for takeoff. When Shadow lumbered into the air, I felt a lot better, and as we climbed, the cool night air, blasting through the forward entryway, evaporated the sweat on my back and gave me a chill. Soon the pilot was directed to assist a platoon of army grunts in contact with the enemy. Shadow circled in a pylon turn at 3,500 feet above the ground, firing two guns in short bursts while ejecting flares.

On one mission, the steel band restraining the barrels of a minigun broke and bullets began to diverge wildly. Quickly, the pilot stopped firing. If the strap had broken on a different gun, an engine could have been destroyed. Had that scenario played-out, you wouldn't be reading this book.

The deafening high-pitched whine of the mini-guns made using the intercom mandatory. In the moonless dark at our altitude it was virtually impossible to follow the stream of red tracers to the ground. The flames spewing from the guns reminded me of the fire-breathing dragons I read about in my youth. Later that night I was told that mortars on the backs of enemy troops on the ground exploded from Shadow's firepower. As each gun was emptied, it was pulled off-line and I helped the gunner reload another 1,500 rounds. My arms felt weary from turning the crank to load the linked rounds. It wasn't long before the torrent of lead discouraged the attackers and they broke-off their assault. The last radio call from one of the friendlies ended with, "Thanks for helping me make my DEROS," the term the military uses for "date of return from overseas." Typically, when Shadow worked its magic, the last radio call of the troops in contact with the enemy was, "Good night, thank you, and God bless you, Shadow." Shadow gunships became a critical component of the special operations effort; their courageous aircrews flew over 3,000 missions, fired 35 million rounds of ammunition and dropped over 20,000 flares. I shall always stand in awe of those men who flew and fought during the war.

Tragically, shortly before he rotated home, Colonel Levesque and six others died in a Huey chopper crash resulting from hostile action on the return leg from Ban Me Thuot in the central highlands. In the club that night, we Bears were unusually quiet. The alcohol flowed freely, with extra rounds of doubles downed, in between the muted conversation. After midnight, I maneuvered my jeep toward Passover Villa, and sprawled on my cot. After staring awhile at the slowly moving blades of the ceiling fan, with a heavy heart, I let go of the day.

As the Explosives Safety Officer, I had to investigate a fatality near Bien Hoa Air Base close to Saigon. A master sergeant, a tested flight engineer, was fatally injured while engaged in C-47 "Moonshine" illumination operations over Long Binh. As he prepared to release a heavy MK-24 flare it inadvertently went off inside the aircraft and the canister caused a fatal head injury. I had to review all the facts and perform a thorough analysis and in the allotted 30 days I completed an extensive final report. Serious deficiencies came to light and after consulting with other experts I listed numerous steps to correct hardware, training and operational anomalies. With my investigation completed, it was the task of others in the chain of command to prevent a recurrence.

On a typical workday, I loved to wake up to the sounds of one crazy character as my radio boomed, "It's Chi...ck...en Maaaan." As I put on my fatigues, the kooky dude kept me in stitches. A detachment of the Armed Forces Vietnam Network broadcast AM and FM radio programs and television programs in our area. The shows, music and news from home were a great morale builder and kept the troops in touch every day with the "world." Radios across the base bombarded us with Billboard hits. "Hey Jude," the biggest single ever by the Beatles and "Crimson and Clover," by Tommy James and the Shondells, were played over and over. And songs like "Leaving on a Jet Plane," and "Someday We'll Be Together," made me ready to come home. In July 1969, after setting my alarm to go off in the dead of night, I turned on my radio and heard Neil Armstrong's words, "The Eagle has landed." Apollo 11 had touched down on the moon.

As I climbed the ramp to board the flight home, my thoughts turned to the lyrics of a favorite tune. "Lonely days are gone, I'm a-goin' home. My baby just-a wrote me a letter." I knew that the lives of many South Vietnamese I had met would never be the same once America pulled-out. I had come to Vietnam with a heart full of optimism to be part of a noble fight for freedom. On the day I left to come home, a wave of sadness overwhelmed me. My government never understood the Vietnamese or the inherent reason the North and the South fought. Many of the South Vietnamese, I believed, lacked sufficient "fire in the belly" to fend off a determined enemy. I could feel that the end was near. After unleashing the dogs of war, Washington never allowed the U.S. military to fight to win. The civilian command authority micro-managed the war, virtually stifling the possibility of victory. Today, when my thoughts turn to Vietnam, only bittersweet memories linger. In hindsight, I'm glad that I chose to go. But I will always be disappointed with what I saw. What a waste!

Just Call Me Moose!

MY FAMILY JOINED ME on most new assignments, but Judy became increasingly irritated by the relentless disruption and began to record all our moves in a meticulous manner.

After Vietnam, I reported to Torrejon Air Base near Madrid, Spain along with my family. Madrid was a choice assignment for everyone in the family. Still a captain, within a few months I had the good fortune of being selected to command a large Munitions Maintenance Squadron in the 401st Tactical Fighter Wing. It was perhaps the highlight of my military career to lead a squadron consisting of 400 men. The wing had three fighter squadrons with 54 McDonnell Douglas F-4E Phantom II fighters assigned. Every month a number of squadron aircraft loaded with nuclear weapons sat on alert at forward operating bases such as Incirlik in Turkey and Aviano in Italy. In Spain, aircrews flew to the Zaragoza training range to conduct air-to-ground gunnery missions. My squadron supplied the practice bombs and my loading troops loaded the bombs into dispensers on the aircraft.

A wing commander is constantly under pressure to perform. And when things go wrong the wing commander becomes the sacrificial lamb for the sins of the unit. Several of them that I knew in Spain had to retire on short notice or were relieved of duty. The best leaders I ever met expected their people to display a "can-do attitude," a "sense of urgency" and to "be flexible." Being flexible made a big difference when it came to a spouse. Military wives without this attribute have difficulty in keeping a family together.

A few of the wing commanders I came in contact with used fear to achieve results. Yet, quiet, strong leaders with empathy for their men like Colonel Wilbur L. "Bill" Creech, an Air Force fighter pilot and manager whom few will ever match, gained respect through personal example. Whenever he asked a question about weaponry in the daily Operations and Maintenance "Standup" briefings, I had to have the answer. Sometimes I failed the quiz and got chewed-out.

Just Call Me Moose!

One former boss, the Chief of Maintenance, always told me, "Don't bring me your problems; bring me your solutions!" And in spite of stressful times at work, the Director of Logistics, Colonel George Hedge, managed to cheer me up. When a wing commander, a colonel who was ultimately fired, told me in a meeting, "Captain, if I go down the river, you'll be lead paddle in my canoe."

Colonel Hedge looked at me across the table, winked and concealed a smirk. Later he told me something I never forgot.

"An army of rabbits, led by a lion, is stronger than an army of lions, led by a rabbit." I'll always remember what he told me.

Sometimes Dougie and Debbie came along when Judy and I set out in the "Blue Goose," our Ford Fairlane Station Wagon, for a day in Toledo, Avila or the Escorial, a monastery and palace where Spanish Monarchs are buried. A short distance away is a 500-foot-tall stone cross sitting atop a gigantic underground church and tomb in a place called *El Valle de los Caidos*—The Valley of the Fallen. Generalissimo Francisco Franco, the longtime Fascist dictator of Spain, built it as a personal memorial using slave labor; thousands who died during the Spanish Civil War rest in the ground. Absolute power manifests itself in excessive and extravagant ways.

At home, Judy started to drone on about the concept of "Open Marriage," where each spouse is free to pursue other romantic relationships. And one day, books like *Jonathan Livingston Seagull,* and *The Prophet,* by Kahlil Gibran mysteriously showed up on the dining-room table. I'm sure that the themes in these books, about a higher purpose in life, resonated with my sensitive wife, but I had a job to do, no time to ponder the esoteric thoughts of a Lebanese poet. When Gibran wrote about marriage, he said:

"And stand together yet not too near together:
For the pillars of the temple stand apart,
And the oak tree and the cypress grow not in each other's shadow."

Just Call Me Moose!

It is a beautiful sentiment to ponder, but at the time, one lost on a husband, a captain determined to manage a critical mission who was one step away from a pissed-off colonel getting ready to mow his lawn.

It's highly likely that close friends already knew that Judy had been thinking about hooking-up the line to her parachute and was waiting for the green light to bail out of the marriage. When our children were older the light started to flash.

After we returned to the States, my wife resumed her nursing career in Florida and we bought our first home using a VA mortgage. Shortly after I arrived, I pinned on my new major leaves. My job on Eglin Air Force Base as a Project Manager at the Tactical Air Warfare Center involved testing newly developed exotic munitions. Inside the unguided munitions branch I was responsible for writing test plans with the help of an operational analyst, conducting realistic field tests, and reporting on the secret results.

One operational test program I managed was called Pave Rock. A Pave Rock rocket pod contained sixteen 2.75-inch rockets. A long high explosive warhead made of high-tensile strength steel was screwed on each rocket. Fighter aircraft fired the rockets and the warheads with their void-sensing fuzes were designed to penetrate earth-covered, reinforced concrete Warsaw Pact hangars and destroy the aircraft inside. Air Force civil engineers had built a replica of an enemy hangar for about $50,000 on one of the Eglin ranges and I arranged for a junked fighter plane to be parked inside to assess weapon effects.

The Pave Rock contractor, Aerojet General, had advertised that a salvo of rockets could damage or destroy sheltered enemy aircraft. The operational testing revealed serious shortfalls in the Pave Rock system. To achieve a likely penetration of the hangar, pilots not only had to approach the target in a steep dive; they had to hit a "sweet spot" on the curved hangar surface. Testing proved that in actual combat, pilot attrition would be high due to the delivery constraints of the rockets. During field tests, the contractor reps kept following me around the weapons test range. After a week of mixed results watching rockets bounce of the hangars or penetrate and do only minor damage to the bird inside, I had gathered sufficient data to make a conclusion.

"Major, what do you think? What are you going to put in your final report?" a contractor, I knew asked.

"Are you kidding? You know just as well as I, this rocket doesn't work," I replied.

Headquarters Tactical Air Command eventually killed the program. The $5,000,000 for a pilot production budget the Air Force Systems Command had requested was never funded. Realistic testing made a major difference in the outcome and it gave me satisfaction that I may have helped save money and lives. Yet, the data collected during the development program allowed the Air Force to field "bunker buster" bombs employed during desert wars decades later.

For any Air Force officer, higher education can facilitate promotions. I enrolled in a Master of Science program in Counseling and Guidance offered by Troy State University at nearby Hurlburt Field. The subject of Psychology had always fascinated me; my courses revealed a lot about human behavior. During a practice group therapy session I divulged details of my father's death to virtual strangers for the first time. Tears welled up in my eyes and I choked on my words.

"My father committed suicide. He shot himself when I was still in high school."

It wasn't easy to confront what had happened decades before. A torrent of suppressed emotions poured forth and I felt relieved that strangers could listen to me and not pass judgment, people, like me, who carried secret demons themselves.

After three years in the Panhandle, the Air Force sent me on a solo assignment to Ankara, Turkey. As an adviser to the Turkish Air Force, I worked closely with a weapons officer, a unique character. *Yarbay*–Lieutenant Colonel–Guneri Yalem taught me how to drink *raki*, a potent, clear anisette-flavored

231

alcoholic drink, that Turks call Lion's Milk. Whenever we drank raki together, Yarbey Yalem loved to amuse me with classic Turkish stories, some of them off-color. And when it came time for me to say goodbye, my legs felt like pieces of soft rubber. A devotion to the Muslim religion appeared to be threads that ran through most of the people I met, but that didn't stop them from drinking alcohol.

In the Turkish language, a major is a *Binbasi*; it sounds like Bin-Ba-She. So anyone in the Turkish military would greet me as Binbasi Bossi, quite a mouthful. During my unaccompanied 15 months assignment in Turkey, I traveled to operational Turkish bases throughout the country with the Director of Logistics, to coordinate U.S. logistic support. Colonel Carl "Chet" Rawie, a former F-100 fighter jock, an even-tempered man turned logistician, taught me a lot and helped make my job a lot of fun. The Turks were modernizing their forces, trying to shake the effects of the U.S. arms embargo implemented after Turkey attacked Cyprus in 1974. New F-4E Phantom II fighters, laser-guided bombs and their target designators, Maverick "tank buster" missiles, cluster bombs and other weapons had already arrived or were on the way to Turkey. Our Turkish-national interpreters traveled with us and translated our discussions with Turkish military officials. And just as I had done in Japan, Vietnam and Spain, I acquired enough of the Turkish language to converse a little with some of the locals.

One day as I prepared to take a Turkish Airline flight, our chief interpreter in the Logistic Section, Doğan, pulled me aside. Doğanbey—Mr. Doğan—had a warped sense of humor and loved to tell Americans unpredictable jokes with a local flavor. Before I left the office, his smile caught my attention.

Binbashi, did you know that Turkish Airlines is actually Turk Hava Yollari, THY?"

"No, I didn't."

Do you know what THY stands for?"

"No."

Doğanbey grinned and underscored each word. "It means Turkey...Hates...You."

"You got me again," I said, as I headed for the door.

On my free time in Ankara I traveled to visit ancient Roman and Byzantine ruins or drove an Air Force utility vehicle with friends to go hunting with the Kurds. After a day of stalking wild boars, quail or snow geese, we returned to the village to eat and drink tea. The wild boars tore up local gardens and the Turks were happy for Americans to help kill them. Later we crawled inside our sleeping bags on top of the rug-covered floor behind the thick walls of a simple home made of mud. The village had no electricity or toilets that flushed, yet the Kurdish people treated us with kindness. And eating baby lamb with pilaf rice and sitting on a thick rug with my back to a large pillow drinking hot *chai* from tulip-shaped glasses made me feel like a character in *Lawrence of Arabia*. My son spent a few months in Turkey with me during his summer break and still talks about it with fondness. No classroom could duplicate the sights, sounds, and smells of this land and the rich diverse Turkish culture. We drove around Turkey in my Ford Pinto, the car I called the "Golden BB." It's a term that fighter pilots use for the piece of metal that might shoot them down.

When my time in Turkey ran out, I moved to New Mexico for a new assignment. Judy elected to stay in Florida, the final straw for me.

"I'm a Pisces," she said, "I need to be near the water."

Okay, I thought, *you can stay in Florida. But you can't stay married to me.*

The nomadic life in the military that I dreamed about in my youth had become a reality. But after 15 years of marriage, in spite of all my accomplishments, I didn't have the stamina to sustain the marathon of a loving relationship. And the roses in our marriage bed slowly withered away as both of us failed to water the garden. To admit failure and dissolve the marriage made me sad as I had grieved when my father died. So, when people told me that a divorce is like a death of a loved one, I had to agree.

I regretted losing my ongoing influence over my children. In the past, whenever I had scolded them for misbehaving, Dougie cried easily, but my daughter bit her tongue. Although Debbie was a happy child, she revealed less and less of her feelings to me as she grew older. One day, I realized that the Air Force had given me tools to manage people, yet not grasp the emotions involved; there was no tech manual available for raising sensitive, creative kids.

I spent my last few years in uniform as a lieutenant colonel in the Land of Enchantment. Albuquerque became a favorite city of mine. Assigned to the Field Command, Defense Nuclear Agency, I immersed myself in the complex technical world of nuclear weapons, managing maintenance and quality assurance matters relating to the nuclear stockpile. Working as an interface between the Department of Energy and the military services in the field, I played a small role in the final act of a play set on stages around the world. The Air Force wanted me to take another assignment but I chose to move on. I felt that I had accomplished everything I set out to do and retired with over twenty years of military service.

A new opportunity in the city arose and I accepted a challenging position as a logistic engineer with a respected aerospace contractor, Sperry Flight Systems, later Honeywell Defense Avionics Systems. It turned out to be a wonderful experience because my military background complemented the company's critical efforts in fielding advanced avionics products. During my 15-year second career, I worked for and alongside talented professionals who recognized the importance of a strong national defense.

I have a feeling my father would have supported my decision to serve my country; the son who never forgot the wisdom of Aesop's Fables he read to me on the couch.

Epilogue

WHEN THE FATEFUL SHOT RANG OUT, the sound never reached my ears, but its echo reverberates within me to this day. Research shows that in the month of April, depression and death by suicide often go hand in hand. The disease of depression, if allowed to progress, is as serious as any brain tumor, diabetes or cancer, and most authorities believe that serious depression, once diagnosed, is not readily treatable. In the 1950s, when my father died, little was known about preventing this crippling malady.

I believe that anyone who takes their own life should never be stigmatized for their lack of character or in death, branded a coward. People who commit suicide are incapable of saving themselves, just as a victim of terminal cancer has no choice. Signs that my father suffered in silence all his life are revealed in the recurrent quotes from the poem, *Lorelei,* and a "nervous breakdown" in his youth. Over 90 percent of people who commit suicide, my father included, lived with a significant psychiatric illness at the time of death. And the scientific link between artistic individuals, like Pop, and suicide is more than just a coincidence. Brooding, creative souls such as the British novelist, Virginia Woolf, and Dutch painter, Vincent Van Gogh, killed themselves during fits of depression.

Along with my father's mounting personal problems, it was the season of corporate and personal income taxes. Earlier, he had vacated a leased office suite on Leon Street, near the

Museum of Fine Arts, most likely due to a cash crunch, and set up an office in the house. On the last day of his life Pop shaved in the upstairs bathroom and slapped Old Spice on his face, then put on a light-brown suit and a conservative tie. Breakfast usually consisted of buttered toast and black coffee, no sugar. On spring break at the time, I slept late that morning. Pop never spoke to me that day.

Shortly after noon, I speculate now, he slipped into the cellar through the outside door and opened the tall, padlocked, gray school locker, where the firearms were secured. It contained a Winchester Model 61, .22-caliber pump rifle; a Winchester, Model 59, 12-gauge automatic, full-choke shotgun, with a 30-inch barrel; a J.C. Higgins 12-gauge shotgun with removable chokes; and the one he used on himself, my .410-gauge, bolt-action shotgun.

Some time before, Pop had invited me to help test the shotguns inside the garage.

"I need to fire the shotguns to see how different shells work," he said.

"Great, tell me when, Pop."

When the day came, my father drew large circles on pieces of heavy, brown paper and stapled one to a piece of plywood.

"Let me fire the Winchester, Pop. I want to watch the shell eject."

We put on shooter's earmuffs to dampen the sound of the blasts. Using different shotgun shells with various size pellets, we fired at a different sheet to compare the shot patterns of the guns. As each shot exploded in the chamber a flame leaped out of the barrel and the smell of gunpowder filled the damp air. My father never forgot the results of the tests. He was a man with a methodical approach to just about everything in life, except for sharing his feelings with others. A marriage counselor confronted me many years later about my inability to do the same.

After ten years at the helm of a thriving business, the company he held dear began to disintegrate. Incapable of sharing news of the impending bankruptcy with my mother, close to the end, Pop must have felt helpless, isolated, and in deep despair; yet at peace for the end was near. It's clear to me now that Pop was a sick, impulsive man; with no inkling of how he felt. Although my father had never embraced religion, I remain convinced that he harbored faith in a supreme being.

The additions and new buildings that Pop erected for federal, state, and private entities, included: New England Telephone buildings in Weymouth, Lexington and Dedham; a nursing home in Waltham; schools in Boston, Newton, Arlington, Hanover, Melrose, and Watertown; an incinerator plant in Brookline; and a wholesale food terminal in the South End. In 1952, Pop completed the Methuen Tenney High School, a million-dollar project. Most of the jobs involved fixed-price contracts; the low bidder typically was awarded the job. People in the know had told me that my father always played by the rules; winning new contracts on the merits of each bid alone.

Tom Marcucelli, Pop's former chief estimator and primary troubleshooter, was a construction engineer and a Sea-Bee during World War II. After he resigned to launch a personal venture in engineering and construction, Tom later told me he had warned my father not to bid on a Watertown school addition. Tom thought it was a risky proposition; he had a feeling that the architect firm involved might cause problems. Pop didn't heed the advice and after winning the contract, it turned out to be his final job.

I learned that in the final stage of the project, my father ran into cash-flow trouble when the school's building committee withheld progress payments. Final approval of certain contract items needing correction, the "punch list" had dragged on for months in spite of the company's best efforts. As a result, Pop lacked sufficient funds to pay the sub-contractors and other creditors, and for reasons unknown to me, he elected not to fight. Years later, Vince Hennessey, my father's Boston attorney, gave me an insight into the predicament my father faced.

"I told Romey bankruptcy was the only option."

Bankruptcy for my father, a way out of the financial debacle confronting the enterprise, was viewed in a much different way then. To face failure and disgrace and live with such a personal defeat overwhelmed this product of the Great Depression. After Pop completed college, my father had been John Volpe's supervisor at Frankini Construction, a company in serious financial trouble at the time. Pop and foreman Volpe worked sixteen-hour days, six days a week and estimated new work on Sundays. A year later Mr. Frankini declared bankruptcy. I have to believe that the turmoil surrounding those days must have troubled Pop, an experience that stayed with him.

As the company he had nurtured began to unravel, his depressed, distraught mind followed suit; he could not face failure or confront *his* twisted reality of a tarnished reputation. To lose the respect of peers, creditors, and potential competitors trumped in his mind any penalty of going broke. And the thought of being marginalized in the construction community caused his shredded psyche to lose the ability to tolerate the pain.

After Pop died, the incorporated business went into receivership; all its assets had to be liquidated to pay creditors. Bankruptcy laws and insurance ensured my mother's financial survival. Fortunately, four years before, my father's attorney had drawn up a will to protect all non-business assets.

After Pop died, when Mum left the house to go shopping, I used to sneak into the master bedroom and open a drawer in the tall washed-oak bureau. Mum saved the last pair of pajamas that her husband wore; she never washed them. All alone in the quiet house, I would hold the folded garment to my tearful face to catch a final scent of Old Spice and Kreml hair tonic. And in the darkened room, my heart ached; I missed my Pop so much. On many nights, only my pillow muffled the sobs before I drifted off to sleep. The ghastly scene stayed with me, and for a long time, anger and shame, like heavy, cold chains, wrapped me tightly. At first, I blamed Pop for the selfish, cowardly act, then myself. *Had I failed him in some way?* It took a long time to turn all guilt aside.

As time passed, it hurt me to know that my father and I had never had a heart-to-heart conversation. Nor can I remember us ever sharing the words, "I love you." There wasn't any time for much advice, comfort or guidance to prepare me for what lay ahead. And I felt horribly cheated. Pop never showed any predisposition to suicide and he had never threatened to kill himself. When my father used to say in an off-hand way, "You know I'm worth more dead than alive," we thought he was trying to be funny.

My mother snapped, "Don't talk like that!"

When people asked me then, "How did your father die," I replied, "A heart attack. Oh yeah, he was pretty young." It was my canned response to avoid replaying the shocking footage of his death and answering their curious questions.

In the months and years that followed, the only solace for me was my mother's words, "My dear, in every life a little rain must fall."

And whenever Pop's death came up, my brothers changed the subject. It was too painful to confront, and they sequestered the happy times they had shared with him. So the memories of our father slowly faded. It took many years for me to finally forgive Pop for killing himself over just a bankruptcy and decades more to confront the tragic death. A brilliant, sensitive, yet flawed private man, he had never learned to love himself nor tried to express his love for me.

My Catholic faith, rosaries and prayers to the Virgin Mary sustained me in my darkest hours. A weekend retreat sponsored by the Knights of Columbus with the Stigmantine priests in Waltham helped console me. Father Nick, a devout Italian-American priest, spoke with authority and persuasion on Catholic dogma and about leading the good life. His inspiring thoughts refilled my drained moral tank and gave me hope. Any one who has suffered a tragedy must find the strength to move on with life and heal; it takes many years. Some never recover.

Just Call Me Moose!

As for my hard-boiled Nonno, who retired after half a century in the bricklayers' union, any lingering anger about Pop's death slowly dissipated. At breakfast, shortly after my father died, Mum casually mentioned, "Yesterday Nonno got rid of the company sign in the garage." I didn't believe my ears. The large metal sign with the seal of the Associated General Contractors of America had hung over the field office on company job sites. When I worked as a water boy during the summer I took quiet pride whenever the sign came into view. Now it represented all that was left of my father's business and the next time I saw Nonno in my yard, I exploded.

"That was my sign. You had no right to throw it away!"

His face looked grim as he turned away without a word.

Neither of us conversed for over a month. But, finally Mum intervened and said, "You need to apologize to your Nonno. He didn't know how attached you were to that old piece of tin." So, I swallowed my pride and apologized. Although we never shared a close relationship, I needed Nonno on *my* side, now and then, to help shield me from my mother.

On a trip to Boston on military leave from my base in Spain just before Nonno died, I drove my mother to the hospital to see him. A cancer had invaded Nonno's tongue. These were his last days and he knew it.

"I'll be in the hole soon," was his way of talking about death.

I could see that death was near as I helped him shave, touched his shoulder, and then kissed him on the forehead. The kiss, something I had never done before, Nonno accepted without protest. He was too weak. My grandfather never showed affection; it was just his way. Nonno never learned to reach deep inside and touch his feelings, a fault I struggle with every day.

As I turned to leave, my eyes filled with tears. I knew this would be our last goodbye.

"Watch outta fer da bull," he said. The words brought a smile to my face.

"Yes, Nonno, I'll be careful."

Just Call Me Moose!

In spite of all his shortcomings as a husband, a father, and a grandfather, Nonno tried hard to provide well for his family. An honest man and a good bricklayer, like many other immigrant blue-collar workers of his generation, he had faced tough economic times and made his mark in America.

Mum managed to stifle deep feelings of grief and never stopped loving her dear Romeo. My mother took no responsibility for the death of her husband. The day Pop died, no one had an answer for my mother's screams, "Why?...Why?" But long after that sad April day in the garage, I can understand why Pop died.

A few months after her 81st birthday, my mother told me during a phone call from New Mexico that a tumor was growing in her throat.

"I don't understand it, I just had a physical not too long ago. I've decided to go in for an operation."

Then she said, "Qué sera, sera," the only phrase in Spanish that she knew.

Donald said he'd call me after the operation but before he did, a cousin called me at the office.

"If you ever want to see your mother alive," Martha said, "you better come home."

Mum had only a few days left. The tennis ball-size lump turned out to be malignant; surgery occurred too late to stop the wild fire that had spread through her body. The Gulf War to free Kuwait loomed in the news when I boarded an airline in Albuquerque and flew back to Boston. A few hours after midnight, I reached the Faulkner Hospital and found my mother's room. Inside the private room the light was dim. Mum sat propped up in bed with her eyes closed. An oxygen mask covered her nose and an IV tube snaked from the back of one hand toward the stand holding the morphine dispenser. Watching her take labored breaths, my eyes turned to the drip, drip of the pain-killing liquid and I cursed out loud for not coming a few days earlier.

Moving closer, I squeezed her hand, the warm skin felt like soft parchment.

I whispered, "Mum, I'm here. It's Karl."

At first there was no response, no hint that she heard me.

"Mum, I love you. I'm here. Don't be afraid."

I leaned over and drew her close. All that remained of my dear mother reminded me of the brittle shell of a cicada. A tear slid slowly down her ashen, unblemished face. From somewhere deep inside, my comatose mother had heard my words and I began to sob. For the anguish she had endured, I felt a deep malaise for the woman known as "The Martyr" to her boys, a woman stoic to the end.

The next day, Donald called me at my mother's apartment to tell me that Mum had passed away. The doctor had phoned him in New Hampshire. Mum hung on for her baby to come and say goodbye so she could let go and be at peace.

At the wake, friends, my brothers, their families and relatives came to pay respect. During the funeral Mass in the Holy Name Church, a woman sang "Ave Maria," a song she wanted at her funeral. On that cold winter day, they buried my mother in the family plot beside her beloved Romey and I tried to imagine Mum and Pop together again.

When I returned to her silent flat, I looked around at all the things Mum had once held dear. We had connected in recent years and shared jokes and other funny conversation on the telephone. As I stood in the kitchen one of our calls came to mind.

"Mum, guess what? Last week, I dated three women with different nationalities: a Japanese, a Mexican and a German. Isn't that something?"

The line went quiet and I thought she had hung up.

"Sounds like the United Nations to me," she quipped.

On her refrigerator, she always kept a simple card with the words of the Serenity Prayer.

Just Call Me Moose!

God grant me Serenity to accept the things I cannot change, Courage to change the things I can, and Wisdom to know the difference.

The simple message helped my mother overcome the emotional pain in her life. I carefully removed the faded piece of paper, took it with me when I flew back to Albuquerque, and taped it on my own fridge.

Donald took care of our mother's paltry estate and sold virtually everything in the flat. Mum had set up individual bank accounts for her sons; she had spelled out everything in her last will and any money left over Donald divided equitably. For personal reasons Donald decided not to let his brothers read Mum's daily journals and view her intimate feelings about daily life. The emotions that she chose *only* to write about. I protested, but to no avail. Roger kept his opinion to himself.

WHILE CLEANING OUT MUM's FLAT, Donald found a faded shoebox tied with a single ribbon on a shelf in her bedroom closet. Sometime later he told me what he found.

"What was in it," I asked.

"Looks like some old letters Pop wrote to Mum."

"Did you read them?

"No. But, a few of them are from Mum."

Donald mailed all of them to me. When I read my parents' letters, written when they were courting in the 1920s, they revealed how they felt about each other. One undated letter written in pencil, that Pop wrote on MIT stationery, begins:

"My own beloved-

There are times when one's own thoughts drift into dreams of love and I am now in a whirlpool of fascinating reflections. Dearest, you cannot surmise how strongly I crave your love. A feeling of monotonous gloom surrounds me, and I am

*inspired by a vision of your face....Do not think me
absurd when I say that I would terminate eating if
I could have your affection, for you are beyond my
doubt what-so-ever divine....*

"From one who loves you everlastingly"

Another letter mailed from Italy in 1926 includes these words:

*"...Well Pia, there may be plenty of Italy that I
haven't seen but I wouldn't trade even East Cottage
Street for all of Italy. I certainly miss Boston
and you....*

"Yours 'til death do us part, Romeo"

Letters from my mother had a more whimsical, less effusive quality. In 1929, before the wedding, she wrote to Romeo from her job in the Upham's Corner Market.

"To my little Freshie,

*Back again on the job and surrounded by
fish on all sides. To tell the truth I do not feel like
working on such a nasty day. Yesterday I was in
all day and my, didn't it pour and the wind was so
strong it blew a sky-light off the roof from the
house across the street....*
"Well dear I guess it's time to sign off, as usual,

Lovingly yours, Pia"

I can imagine my mother opening up the old box and reading the letters from her past, a gentle reminder of her Romeo's eternal love for her. In the course of working on this book, I felt Pop's touch; he spoke to me with greater clarity than he ever had in life.

Just Call Me Moose!

But I often wonder how my lifelong journey would have unfolded if my father had never died on that bleak April day. How would I have faired under his tutelage? Would I have measured up and made him proud?

Unlike my father, a man who left behind buildings made of brick, steel, and stone, my destiny took me on the same path of others who wore a service uniform, loved their country, and chose to help keep the flame of freedom alive. It's clear to me now that the day my father died, an extraordinary journey opened up for me, replete with travel to foreign shores, steeped in exotic cultures and a plethora of new friends. A career filled with unique challenges, achievements and rewards. And so, I believe that the old saying on the picture, "In Youth, We Learn; With Age, We Understand," will always ring true for me.

Acknowledgments

The author is grateful to everyone who made this book possible. It could not have been written without the recollections, support, and encouragement of many of my family, friends, and acquaintances. Among them: Joseph J. Argento, Richard J. and W. Jeanne Bando, James S. Black, Barbara M. Bossi, Donald E. Bossi, Douglas R. Bossi, Deborah L. Bossi, George F. Cavanaugh, Frank E. Colombo, Jr. D.M.D., Janice L. Colombo, Marilyn A. Colombo, Alyce (Joseph) Cugnasca, David A. Cugnasca, Louise (Varnerin) Ditullio, Francis A. and Marie (Mazzuchelli) Facchetti, Louise (Varnerin) Feroli, Ines M. (Bernasconi) Filadoro, John McColgan, Thomas J. Marcucelli, Virginia M. (Bossi) Mazzucchelli, John Carl and Helen Milhouse, Frank and Joan Putaro, Robert Rugo, Martha (Bernasconi) Shine, R. Gary and Jean Sleater, Earl Taylor, Josephine (Macchi) Tillet, Joanne (Bossi) True, and Ida M. Zopatti